Advance Praise for *Leading Against the Grain: Lessons for Creating Just and Equitable Schools*

"A rare and wonderful book about visionary, incredible, inspirational, exemplary, and diverse leaders. Just the tonic needed for today's educational leaders in today's complex, difficult, confronting world."

—Bill Mulford AO, emeritus professor, University of Tasmania

"Leading today's separate and unequal schools requires an expanded view of what it means to lead and to what end. In *Leading Against the Grain*, Brooks and Normore provide an impressive resource for anyone committed to developing leaders or preparing to take on the mantle of leadership themselves. A breath of fresh air for those in search of new conceptualizations of leadership in an increasingly divided and unjust world."

—Sonya Douglass Horsford, Teachers College, Columbia University; author of *Learning in a Burning House: Educational Inequality, Ideology, and (Dis)Integration*

"For those of us who have suffered through the staid, unimaginative prose of most educational leadership texts, this book is a godsend: Gifted authors guide us to study leadership through the eyes and lives of our world's great leaders. The lessons they reveal are eye-opening, pragmatic, and greatly needed!"

—Lisa D. Delpit, Felton G. Clark Distinguished Professor, Southern University School of Education; Southern University Laboratory School Liaison

"This unique and enlightening book is a must-read for anyone interested in school leadership. It provides inspirational profiles of such an incredible range of leaders from across the globe, and the lessons imparted are truly impressive."

—Martha McCarthy, Presidential Professor, Loyola Marymount University; Chancellor's Professor Emeritus, Indiana University

"A fresh and essential perspective on leadership, going beyond the norm, engaging the essence of leadership, which is always, in some respect, about going against the grain. Linking leadership to equitable schooling is an especially important challenge for our times, and this amazing cast of diverse scholars engages in this critical issue."

—James P. Spillane, Spencer T. and Ann W. Olin Professor in Learning and Organizational Change at the School of Education and Social Policy at Northwestern University

"Brooks and Normore provide a unique and powerful voyage into diverse models of leadership from around the world. A brilliant format introduces the reader to new ideas, and the narratives prompt some wonderful reflection. *Leading Against the Grain* is the perfect combination: Great leaders, great authors, and great leadership lessons."

—Joseph Murphy, Frank W. Mayborn Chair of Education and associate dean, Peabody College of Education of Vanderbilt University

"Brooks and Normore have pulled together a distinguished cadre of authors who profile a beautifully diverse group of international leaders. I applaud this thoughtful work to bring lessons and inspiration to school leaders from this bold group of global citizens. It affirms the diversity of our planet and allows school leaders access to people outside of their daily lives whose work can inspire and lift."

—George Theoharis, professor and chair, Teaching and Leadership Department, Syracuse University

"These days leaders are not always leading. *Leading Against the Grain* presents leaders that we often don't think about because their stories are neglected. These stories are inspiring and courageous, and they exemplify what we need in leaders today. Moreover, these leader stories cut across a wide array of cultural perspectives to offer rich and nuanced views of leadership."

—Marybeth Gasman, Judy & Howard Berkowitz Professor of Education, University of Pennsylvania; director, Penn Center for Minority Serving Institutions

Leading Against the Grain

Lessons for Creating Just and Equitable Schools

Jeffrey S. Brooks
Anthony H. Normore
EDITORS

Foreword by William Ayers

TEACHERS COLLEGE PRESS
TEACHERS COLLEGE | COLUMBIA UNIVERSITY
NEW YORK AND LONDON

Published by Teachers College Press, 1234 Amsterdam Avenue, New York, NY 10027

Copyright © 2018 by Teachers College, Columbia University

Cover photo by westend61 / Getty Images.

Chapter 5 contains an abridged version of "From liberation to salvation: Revolutionary critical pedagogy meets liberation theology" by P. McLaren & P. Jandrić, 2017, *Policy Futures in Education*, 15(5), pp. 620–652. Copyright © 2017 SAGE Publications. Reprinted by permission of SAGE Publications and available to view here: journals.sagepub.com/doi/full/10.1177/1478210317695713

All rights reserved. No part of this publication may be reproduced or transmitted in any form or by any means, electronic or mechanical, including photocopy, or any information storage and retrieval system, without permission from the publisher. For reprint permission and other subsidiary rights requests, please contact Teachers College Press, Rights Dept.: tcpressrights@tc.columbia.edu

Library of Congress Cataloging-in-Publication Data is available at loc.gov

ISBN 978-0-8077-5871-7 (paper)
ISBN 978-0-8077-7666-7 (ebook)

Printed on acid-free paper
Manufactured in the United States of America

25 24 23 22 21 20 19 18   8 7 6 5 4 3 2 1

Contents

Foreword—Education, Wisdom, and Agency: The Need to Reinvent,
Rethink, and Reconnect Leadership in Schools ... vii
William Ayers

Introduction—Leading Against the Grain: Listening to Leaders
from Around the Globe and Throughout Time ... 1
Jeffrey S. Brooks and Anthony H. Normore

1. A Woman for All Seasons:
Learning from the Wisdom of Antonia Pantoja ... 4
Sonia Nieto

2. Grassroots Leadership for Ecological Sustainability,
Empowerment, and Political Change: Wangari Maathai
and the Green Belt Movement ... 14
Melanie C. Brooks

3. In the Shadow of Totalitarianism: Tsunesaburo Makiguchi
and the Struggle for Value-Creating Educational Leadership ... 23
John M. Heffron

4. Sun Yat-sen: A Boundary-Crosser ... 32
Haiyan Qian and Allan Walker

5. Peter McLaren's Liberation Theology:
Karl Marx Meets Jesus Christ ... 39
Peter McLaren and Petar Jandrić

6. Saul Alinsky: The Magnificent Rebel ... 49
Lisa Catherine Ehrich and Fenwick W. English

7. The Resurrection of Educational Leadership:
Lessons from Rev. Dr. Samuel DeWitt Proctor ... 57
Atiya S. Strothers and Catherine A. Lugg

8. José Rizal:
   Leadership Lessons from the National Hero of the Philippines   64
   Jeffrey S. Brooks and Anthony H. Normore

9. A Life Lived Well:
   American Indian Educator, Scholar, and Leader
   Dr. John W. Tippeconnic III (Comanche/Cherokee)   72
   Susan C. Faircloth (Coharie)

10. Jimmy Carter: A Portrait of Moral and Ethical Leadership   80
    Michelle D. Young and Bryan A. VanGronigen

11. Harold Gatensby: Tlingit Peacemaker and Leader   90
    Polly Hyslop and Brian Jarrett

12. Golda Meir: A Leader for National Revival and Social Justice   96
    Izhar Oplatka

13. Passing the Torch: The Legacy of Fannie Lou Hamer   104
    Gaëtane Jean-Marie

14. Incrementalism Beats Flamboyance: Ethel M. Smith   115
    Catherine M. Marshall and Becca Merrill

15. Ella Flagg Young:
    Individuality, Freedom for the Teacher, and
    Freedom For the Pupil   124
    Jackie M. Blount

16. Aung San Suu Kyi:
    A Leadership Journey Toward Peace and Democracy   131
    Whitney McIntyre Miller and Margaret Grogan

17. Understanding Real "Black Girl Magic":
    Anna Julia Cooper as a Thought Leader   140
    Gloria Ladson-Billings

About the Contributors   147

Index   153

FOREWORD

Education, Wisdom, and Agency
The Need to Reinvent, Rethink, and Reconnect Leadership in Schools

The word *leadership* brings with it considerable cultural baggage that's all about hierarchy and power. One of the things that I very luckily learned as a young teacher was that the strongest leadership—the strongest leadership in the classroom—is a leadership that rejects notions of hierarchy and power. This book introduces many new ways to think about leadership in education, and we desperately need to reinvent, rethink, and reconnect leadership in schools in new and innovative ways.

For my entire life as a teacher, I've felt that the biggest challenge to myself and other teachers is to discover how to recognize and then unleash the wisdom in the room—to create the conditions that will allow the wisdom in the room to assert itself. I feel that it's true in kindergarten, it's true in elementary school, and it's true in graduate school. How do you create an environment based on dialogue, with the potential to undermine and undo the power that's built into the institutional structures we inhabit? How do we teachers come to see ourselves not as more powerful, wiser, or smarter people than those "beneath us" but as associates and co-learners? Seeing one's self as an "associate teacher" offers two fundamental lessons: First, I have nothing to teach you—I'm not your leader. Second, and intimately linked to the first, you, the student, have within yourself the agency and the power to learn, the power to take control of your life, the power to change the world. You can change yourself, and in changing yourself you change the world.

It takes enormous energy to work within institutions that are based on the assumption that what you are there to do is climb to the top of the pyramid, to progress in a linear manner, and to one day become the "leader"—the powerful one, the wise one, the successful one. It's a necessary effort to resist all of that, to create the conditions in which your students (or your staff) can develop the sense that it's their own power and wisdom that must be foregrounded, that we're all in this together, and that although each of our experiences is different, none is superior. I've tried in a thousand ways over many years to communicate to my students: I'm not here to teach you;

I'm here to go on a voyage with you. Leaders might think about their work in the same way.

It's important to remember that when people become administrators in schools, they learn a new language, one that is fundamentally different from the language of teaching, learning, and loving—it's mainly a language of efficiency, power, and authority. But let's not put that all onto administrators. It's equally important to remember that we do that to classroom teachers as well—we have them talking about accountability, ranking students against one another, comparing their outcomes to those of other teachers, and saying that they are better or worse than their neighbor, their colleague, and their friends down the hall or in the school on the next block. We've imposed a language onto schooling that has helped bureaucrats write reports, but it is not a language that has helped make education meaningful or relevant for teachers or students or the larger communities we must stand in solidarity with. If you are a classroom teacher who has found ways to resolve this, or better yet to resist this movement toward neoliberalism—toward thinking about kids as percentage points and quartiles instead of as complex human beings—then you are subversive. Yes, teachers who believe that students are idiosyncratic, complex individuals who learn in unique ways are subversive.

There are for me two major lessons I hope to pass along to teachers, and these lessons are also relevant for leaders. The first is that I want them to understand their agency and to understand that the source of that agency is drawn from within; it isn't bestowed on them by a leader, a title, or by a system. It is there to be realized and cultivated; it isn't a prize you get when you take on the title "teacher" or "principal." Second, I want them to understand that there is always a great deal of wisdom in any classroom, and that their job is not to teach students in some kind of top-down way but is rather to go on a journey with people that encourages them to share that wisdom and to draw from the wisdom of others as a way to grow and develop. If you understand these two basic lessons as a schoolteacher and recognize that the way these lessons look from semester to semester, year to year, or even day to day is different, then you have a chance to really make a difference in people's lives (your own included). Teachers can take those same two lessons with them as they transition into formal leadership roles in schools.

The best principals that I've known are principals who do exactly what I just described as good teaching—they gather people together, they give the message that they see the wisdom in the room, and they practice leadership in a collaborative and transparent way that brings people in rather than pushing them out. They understand that the answers don't rest at the top of an organizational chart or at the front of a classroom—the answers are in the brotherhood and sisterhood of the school community, in open and honest dialogue, in collective problem solving, and in individual support.

Great principals are constantly looking for ways to let their faculty and staff experience and realize their own agency and to let them exercise their own internal power in ways that benefit the school and community.

Among the things I learned from studying and practicing anarchy is that one of our greatest obstacles to transforming society is that we and nearly everyone we know lacks the confidence that we can run our own affairs. As an example, several years ago my city was having a mayoral election. I was hanging out with the progressives, who kept coming together to discuss which candidate we should support. They wanted to talk through policies, but I had a different question—why do we need a mayor? At the time, they looked at me like, "What the hell, Bill? We're trying to have a productive conversation here. Of course we need a mayor!" But the more we talked about it, the more it became clear that not many people knew what the mayor actually did. Everyone could name a few basic functions, but when you pressed people, they really didn't know what the mayor's work was, beyond a few symbolic purposes and positional responsibilities. The fact that we don't know what a mayor does or what a chief of police does while nevertheless assuming that we would be rudderless and lost without them is absolute nonsense. There are societies, cities, and communities all over the world that get on just fine without any of those sorts of leaders. You'll read about many of these communities and organizations in this book. Again, I think it comes down to confidence—we don't believe in ourselves enough, and we've come to believe in institutions that dominate the entire landscape and each of our lives without either interrogating or really understanding what they do.

As a school reform leader, the principle I try to keep in the forefront of my mind is that I can't teach you anything—all I can do is try to help you see your own wisdom and the wisdom of others. I can suggest things we might do and experience together, but in the end the only authentic learning, the only authentic leadership, comes from within.

When you get out of the bubble of radical, critical educators, most people think that teachers teach and students learn; that teachers tell and students take it in. Even the most progressive people will say that critical approaches, wisdom, and talk of love and empowerment are fine, but don't you have to teach students the basics? They have to achieve something to get to the next step, don't they?

I remember the birth of our first son. After 36 hours of labor, we wrapped him in a blanket and put him to his mother's breast. My wife had prepared by taking classes, reading up on nursing, and talking with friends, and there was a midwife present, but the surprise was that our son, at 5 minutes old, was teaching my wife some important things as well—the right angle, what was too much and what was too little, what was too hard and what was too soft. They were in dialogue, and the agency of each, the wisdom of each, was essential for the dialogue to proceed. What that moment and a lifetime of teaching made me recognize was that living and learning are identical—they are the same thing. If you are alive, you are learning, and the idea that we need to overdesign learning and create arbitrary benchmarks or standards for people's learning doesn't make sense. You can see this with babies or toddlers—if you put them in an environment that nourishes them, that supports them, that challenges them, nearly all of them will learn to walk, talk, think, eat, love, read . . . everything. But no two will do it in exactly the same way. Put differently, it comes from within—we need to get out of the way more than we need to tell anyone at any age what to do.

In some ways, leading is harder than following and teaching is harder than learning precisely because leaders and teachers need the discipline to be quiet and get out of the way. That can be a very hard thing to do. It presents a paradox in that for followers to develop their wisdom and agency, they need leaders to develop a comfort and respect for vulnerability, both in themselves and others. The way that we do all of this is through dialogue. Dialogue—speaking with the possibility of being heard and listening with the possibility of being changed—is the fundamental character of education and of leadership, and because honest dialogue is always unrehearsed and uncertain, it always has the potential to come off the tracks. That's a good thing because this is where we find real discovery, exploration, and authentic learning—but it can also be terrifying. That means you have to be open to change, and change is hard.

Think about the current use of pronouns in our modern age of gender fluidity—we are being taught a whole new way of speaking and listening by members of the LGBTQ community that I, at least, had never considered. It is a way of speaking that honors people's identity and the ways they want to live in the world, but until recently, I seldom thought about pronouns and sexuality in that way—certainly not 20 years ago. Perhaps 10 years ago I began to gain some understanding, but now my education is full-on and I understand so much better why it's important to be respectful and loving with language in this space. Now, people are telling us to stop making assumptions about gender, and rejecting the idea that gender is a binary construct. That's a good thing, and humanizing for all concerned. It allows us to discover new ways of knowing and being, and also of helping people discover new things about themselves, about one another, and about the world.

We've accepted a reductionist, functionalist idea of what leadership is about for a long time. It's not only misguided, it is violent to most people who work and study in educational systems. The basic idea that there is something monolithic we should aspire to become is nonsense. We cannot predict the kind of leaders we will become or the kinds of leaders that schools need; we can only seek wisdom in ourselves and in others. This kind of leadership education will take us into places we can't imagine, but it should not take us down the path of becoming a standardized and watery version of someone who invented some set of standards or who has a list of 20 things that great leaders supposedly do. Show me any list like that and I'll show you 20 amazing leaders who don't do those 20 things. There is no universal linear path of development for children, teachers, and certainly not for leaders. We have to see the human condition as complex and ever-changing. Administrators have a huge responsibility to run schools in a way that honors people, but few do; they instead run schools that honor processes. Consider that humanity in schools often disappears under a blizzard of one-dimensional labels: The Teachers, The Students, The School, The Quartile, That Sub-Group, and so on. Why do we accept this? It's dehumanizing.

I've been reading Halberstam's (2011) book *The Queer Art of Failure*, and he makes the point that when things are "normal," you never need to question anything. On the other hand, when things come off the rails, you need to question everything; that which was calm and normal becomes abnormal. We have to accept and at times even encourage things to go off the rails or we will never know the potential of ourselves, our followers, and our institutions. Now, I would not wish Donald Trump on anyone, but he's disrupting the system in a way that is waking people everywhere; there is now an urgency to resist and to change for many that wasn't there under President Obama. We're not only questioning Donald Trump, but we're all questioning our country—what is this place all about that I felt was something different? It's disorienting, and for many it will have immediate and terrible consequences, but it will also create a generation of new activists who are watching mobilization on a larger level than we've recently seen. It's pointing out to many that the Democratic Party has been in collusion with the Republican Party for 4 decades, creating a system of permanent war, mass incarceration, a militarized police presence—a system that erodes the public space and eclipses the public as it advantages some and oppresses others in a way that transcends left and right. We can see now that the Democrats can't lead the resistance because they are part of the problem.

As I read this book, I reflected on people I think are great leaders in education. One is Karen Lewis, who is a leader in the Chicago Teachers Union. She didn't come to her position grasping for political power or self-promotion, she came out of a group of teachers who showed up to protest and picket school closings over the past decade. She is a consensus builder, a listener, and, more important, she is one with those she leads—she knows that the organization is led by all, not by one. What Karen Lewis and her fellow teachers had been building together—through collective wisdom, through partnerships with communities, and through persistence and support for the oppressed—is a leadership that brought many people together who were not formerly united. They could see that she was one of them, not over them, and they could see that when the chips were down, she was there with them. Now her union is strong and gaining friends and supporters every day. She is a new type of leader, and the group is not just a teachers' union in the traditional sense—it's a union of social justice, a union of people who recognize that their community is under attack, and their solidarity is the thing that will save it, not a heroic savior or figurehead.

Leaders can be a big part of change, but they can only ever be a part. Lyndon Johnson was never part of the Civil Rights Movement, but he passed the most far-reaching civil rights legislation since Reconstruction in the United States. He was responding to fire from below, to millions of people rising up and demanding change. Franklin Roosevelt was a patrician from the Hudson Valley, but he supported far-reaching labor legislation because a mass movement of workers was on the move. The forces that create change that matters come from below—from people getting together to demand change. Formal leadership has a part, but it is secondary to the will of the people. The most powerful forms of leadership are grown at the grassroots levels, not in the upper branches of the tree. We shouldn't think of it as something immediate or something distant—we need to be looking at the principal's office or the school board as something that is an extension of our own agency, wisdom, and power. We are part of leadership and followership at the same time.

—William Ayers

REFERENCE

Halberstam, J. (2011). *The queer art of failure*. Durham, NC: Duke University Press.

INTRODUCTION

Leading Against the Grain
Listening to Leaders from Around the Globe and Throughout Time

Jeffrey S. Brooks
MONASH UNIVERSITY, AUSTRALIA

Anthony H. Normore
CALIFORNIA STATE UNIVERSITY, DOMINGUEZ HILLS, UNITED STATES

This book began, like so many others, as a conversation after listening to some particularly insightful school leaders speak about their work. We were attending a school leadership conference in Los Angeles and had just left a session in which newly appointed and experienced principals were discussing their inspirations. For some, their inspiration had been a person in their family—perhaps a caring parent, grandparent, or sibling who had been a role model or guide. Other educators pursued a career path in leadership after a professional colleague encouraged or recruited them to join a leadership development program. These people explained that someone had seen their potential as they worked in a school, and that they had moved toward leadership thanks to the backing of that supportive person. As the conversation developed, each participant eventually mentioned an iconic leader whom he or she hoped to emulate: Andrew Jackson, Martin Luther King Jr., Abraham Lincoln, Mahatma Gandhi, George Washington, Nelson Mandela, and the list went on. Over the following years, we asked our students and the leaders with whom we worked if any iconic leaders had inspired them and the list continued, but it didn't increase much in number or diversity—we realized that although people sought inspiration, there were many incredible leaders whose stories were unknown.

For this book, we asked authors to choose inspirational leaders outside of the mainstream Western canon of leaders. Our aim was to introduce readers to leaders with whom they might be unfamiliar or about whom they might have misconceptions. *Leading Against the Grain: Lessons for Creating Just and Equitable Schools* includes brief profiles of outstanding leaders paired with succinct explanations of what their experiences can teach contemporary school leaders. Importantly, *Leading Against the Grain* includes leaders from around the world, which helps facilitate a sharing of innovative and classic ideas across national and cultural boundaries.

In addition to drawing from exemplars across the globe, we were also careful to maintain an equitable balance between women and men, an important dynamic that books of this ilk have at times neglected. Some of the leaders highlighted in chapters include Aung San Suu Kyi (Burma), Wangari Maathai (Kenya), José Rizal (Philippines), Tsunesaburo Makiguchi (Japan), Golda Meir (Israel), Antonia Pantoja (Puerto Rico), John W. Tippeconnic III (Comanche/Cherokee), and many others. In addition to gender and demographic diversity, readers will find that authors explain and interpret the lessons these leaders offer from a variety of theoretical and practical perspectives. Each chapter is structured in a similar manner, in an effort to give the book an overall cohesion and balance. Chapters focus on a single leader rather than a group or movement, even though nearly all of the chapters describe leadership that is in some ways collaborative, distributed, and complex.

Save for a few, each chapter follows roughly the same structure:

1. **Introduction and biographical sketch.** Each chapter introduces the basic details of the leader's life. This typically includes information such as date and places of birth and death, education, career milestones, and the leader's importance within her or his country.
2. **Discussion of context and activities as a leader.** This section includes a discussion of the context in which the leadership activity occurred, meaning a consideration of societal dynamics, organizations, and people with whom the leader interacted as well as actions that the leader took that defined his or her work. The emphasis here is on both the processes and outcomes that the leader was able to facilitate and the way his or her specific approach was effective, depending on the aims of the leadership activity.
3. **A list of the key lessons readers can learn from the leader.** In this section, authors will list a number of lessons that readers can learn from the leader's work and life. The list format is meant to make the lessons specific and clear. In doing this, we do not intend to downplay or eschew complexity; instead, we are thinking of the chapters as an introduction to a way of thinking about and enacting leadership. References at the end of each chapter offer additional resources and information for curious readers.
4. **Explanation of how this leader's lessons are relevant for today's educational leaders.** This section connects the leadership lessons of the previous section directly to contemporary educational leadership practice. The emphasis here is on practical application, and authors have attempted to translate research, theory, and

ideas from disparate contexts into practice of the key lessons that practitioners can use in their schools tomorrow.

In summary, *Leading Against the Grain* is an invitation and an introduction. It is an invitation in the sense that it is full of exciting stories of heroic leadership that are concise and selective rather than deep and exhaustive. Our aim here is to pique curiosity. The book is also an introduction in that we are guessing that several of the leaders in this book may be new to readers, even to scholars and practitioners seeking to learn something new. One of the great joys of editing this book was reading and commenting on drafts of the chapters as they came through. Many of these leaders were new to us, and even chapters about those with whom we were familiar were shown in a new light.

It is important to point out that the book includes many of our sheroes and heroes, among both the subjects of the chapters and the chapter authors themselves. It represents a roll call of outstanding and innovative thinkers writing about leaders who excite and challenge them. For example, Peter McLaren's chapter, singular for both its interview format and its theoretical perspective, looks closely at one of the most influential leaders in the Western world, Jesus Christ (considered together with Karl Marx, which makes for a fascinating read). It is curious that this leader who inspires so many is so seldom written about in academic discourse. Gloria Ladson-Billings's chapter about Anna Julia Cooper is an outstanding contribution to our understanding of an important thought leader who helped shape our thinking and urgency around intersectional issues of race and gender as they relate to Black girls. Jackie Blount's chapter extends and revisits her work on Ella Flagg Young published in the germinal 2004 book *Fit to Teach*. Melanie C. Brooks examines Wangari Maathai and the Green Belt Movement, and John M. Heffron introduces us to important Japanese thinker Tsunesaburo Makiguchi. Haiyan Qian and Allan Walker discuss renowned leader Sun Yat-sen, while Sonia Nieto offers a remarkable chapter on Puerto Rican leader Antonia Pantoja. Lisa Catherine Ehrich and Fenwick W. English revisit *Rules for Radicals* author Saul Alinsky, and Atiya S. Strothers and Catherine A. Lugg provide an excellent chapter about the Reverend Dr. Samuel DeWitt Proctor. Coharie scholar Susan C. Faircloth reflects on the life and work of Dr. John W. Tippeconnic III (Comanche/Cherokee), and Michelle D. Young and Bryan A. VanGronigen take an uncommon look at the principled life and presidency of Jimmy Carter. Polly Hyslop and Brian Jarrett discuss the peace-focused efforts of Tlingit leader Harold Gatensby, and the outstanding Israeli scholar Izhar Oplatka examines the importance of Golda Meir's leadership. Gaëtane Jean-Marie examines the leadership of civil rights icon Fannie Lou Hamer's contributions, while Catherine M. Marshall and Becca Merrill consider the work of women's rights leader Ethel M. Smith.

Whitney McIntyre Miller and Margaret Grogan contribute an interesting chapter about Burmese leader Aung San Suu Kyi.

Collectively considered, these contributions help expand our conceptualization of leadership, expanding our familiarity with new leaders as we learn new lessons and allowing school leaders to reflect on their practice. We hope you enjoy learning about these leaders as much as we have, and we entreat you to use their stories and lessons as a point of departure for learning about them, not as a final destination.

CHAPTER 1

A Woman for All Seasons
Learning from the Wisdom of Antonia Pantoja

Sonia Nieto
UNIVERSITY OF MASSACHUSETTS–AMHERST, UNITED STATES

> My life has been one of action, learning, and teaching, a life of building with others, a life of fighting injustice and trying to change conditions and relations that are wrong because they deny people their rights and destroy their potentialities.
>
> —Antonia Pantoja, *Memoir of a Visionary*, 2002

These words, written by Antonia Pantoja in the introduction to her memoir (2002, p. xvii), define a remarkable life of leadership, innovation, and commitment to the Puerto Rican community. Published in 2002, the first copies were delivered to her home shortly before she died. In her 80 years, Pantoja had indeed lived a full life of fighting inequality and bigotry by creating organizations that would provide opportunities for her beloved Puerto Rican community, especially for young people. The legacy she left has been both rich and significant.

Though she was born and lived in Puerto Rico until the age of 23, Antonia Pantoja later became an icon of the Puerto Rican community in the United States. During her lifetime, Pantoja worked as a factory worker, artist, teacher, social worker, and, most significantly, as a community organizer and activist. It was in New York, the largest stateside population of Puerto Ricans, where she made her mark. Shortly after moving there, she found her way to the Puerto Rican community, where she began her life's work as a community organizer and institution builder.

It was said of Antonia Pantoja that she never saw a problem that couldn't be addressed by creating the appropriate institution. Many educational and social justice efforts among Puerto Ricans in the latter half of the 20th century can be traced directly to her vision (see Perry, 1998, for an interview with Pantoja). She received numerous awards in recognition of her extraordinary service to the Puerto Rican and other underserved communities, including five honorary doctorates, and in 1996 she received the Presidential Medal of Freedom from President Bill Clinton, the highest award given to civilians. Pantoja was the first Puerto Rican woman to receive this prestigious honor.

ANTONIA PANTOJA'S WORK AND LEGACY

Antonia Pantoja was born in 1921 in Puerta de Tierra and raised in Barrio Obrero—two neighborhoods mired in poverty—in San Juan, Puerto Rico. As a teenager, she gained admission and a scholarship to the University of Puerto Rico's premier campus in Río Piedras. Obtaining a normal degree after 2 years, she was an elementary school teacher in the mountains of Puerto Rico. In 1944, given her difficult life and family constraints, she moved to New York to pursue further education and explore new adventures and possibilities.

Pantoja's life and work were influenced by numerous philosophers and activists, including Søren Kierkegaard, José Ortega y Gasset, Eugenio Maria de Hostos, Paulo Freire, Frantz Fanon, Charles Frederick Menninger, Erik Fromm, and above all, Miguel de Unamuno. Clearly, their writings and ideas, along with her own experiences with racism, sexism, and class discrimination, helped create a fierce sense of advocacy and justice in the young activist. Nevertheless, as she wrote in her memoir, as a Black Puerto Rican female, she felt there were no role models for her, nor were there places where she could learn about and be proud of her identity, history, culture, and experiences. She wanted to help young people develop pride and a sense of purpose, and she especially wanted them to pursue higher education and community service. For these reasons, she set about, with other young Puerto Rican professionals, creating institutions and programs to achieve these goals.

When Pantoja arrived in New York, she worked at sundry jobs until she found her calling as a community activist and institution builder. Continuing her education in the city, Pantoja first earned a BA at Hunter College of the City University of New York and later, a master's degree at the Columbia University School of Social Work. She made it clear, however, that she did not want to be a typical social worker, a profession she believed co-opted communities rather than helping to liberate them. She wanted, instead, to become an agent of change.

The presence of Puerto Ricans in New York had grown from about several hundred at the turn of the century to more than 1,000 by 1920. The numbers increased exponentially after World War II when cheap flights, more work opportunities in New York City than on the island, and a Puerto Rican government initiative to encourage emigration set the stage for mass migration to the United States. By 1957, 550,000, or fully a quarter of all

Puerto Ricans, lived in the United States. Between 1940 and 1970, more than 835,000 moved to the U.S. mainland on a net basis, making it one of the most massive emigration flows in the 20th century. In spite of the growth of the Puerto Rican community, there were few services to help its members confront the harsh conditions they faced (see Nieto, 2004, for a summary of this history). It was a community ripe for development.

In addition, by the early 1960s, the United States was experiencing growing political turmoil, both because of opposition to the Vietnam War and because of the civil rights movement, with African Americans and other disenfranchised groups at the forefront of demands for economic, educational, and political justice. Pantoja became a leader in the Puerto Rican community by confronting these issues. Consequently, from 1950 to 1960, she was instrumental in helping to organize and create grassroots organizations focused on Puerto Ricans. Though for a number of decades there had been organizations that served the Hispanic community in general, none was specifically focused on the needs of Puerto Ricans, which Pantoja insisted were different from those of other Hispanic groups because of Puerto Rico's colonial relationship with the United States.

Pantoja's first community development effort was to mobilize a group of young activists to start the Hispanic Young Adult Association (HYAA), whose name was later changed to the Puerto Rican Association for Community Affairs, also known as PRACA. Pantoja was elected president by acclamation. PRACA would go on to sponsor many community development projects, including a shelter for homeless men, a voter registration drive in East Harlem (also known as El Barrio), and a high school youth conference that became the precursor to ASPIRA (Spanish for "aspire"), Pantoja's most enduring legacy. Antonia Pantoja was called the "inspiration and guiding spirit" of these early movements (Fitzpatrick, 1971).

The character of Puerto Rican self-help and advocacy organizations, the trademark of a community bent on defining itself and seeking its own solutions to problems, invariably centered on education. Antonia Pantoja was influential in working with other young activists to create the Puerto Rican–Hispanic Leadership Forum in 1965 (later changed to the Puerto Rican Forum), an organization she viewed as a potential founder of other institutions to help develop young leaders for the New York City Puerto Rican community. It was, she would later write:

> an instrument for us, as Puerto Ricans, to create institutions that would fight to eliminate the problems that were making our community weak, poor, silenced, submissive, and convinced that they were the cause of their own poverty and exclusion. (Pantoja, 2002, pp. 91–92)

Among its many activities, the Puerto Rican Forum gathered information, conducted studies, and held symposia and discussions about oppressive conditions in the New York Puerto Rican community. Within a few years, it had started a number of important organizations, including the Puerto Rican Development Project, the Agency for Business and Career Development (ABCD), the Puerto Rican Institute for Political Participation (PRIPP), and others. As a result of research conducted by the Puerto Rican Forum, the idea for an organization that would inspire young people to seek postsecondary education was born. It was ASPIRA that cemented Pantoja's reputation as an incomparable community organizer and inspiration to millions.

ASPIRA was an organization of clubs, mostly located in high schools throughout the city with substantial Puerto Rican student populations. Created in 1961, ASPIRA is still a significant organization in many high schools and communities in New York City and beyond. But ASPIRA was not, Pantoja (2002) insisted, a service agency, but rather a movement. Now known as the ASPIRA Association, it has since expanded to eight states and Puerto Rico, with headquarters in Washington, DC. Antonia Pantoja became the first executive director of the organization.

The organization engaged in numerous activities. It sponsored leadership study trips to Puerto Rico, an annual conference, and other activities created by club members, or *Aspirantes* ("those who aspire"). ASPIRA is dedicated to teaching young people about their culture, history, and reality. By doing this, the organization's overall goal is to motivate young people to pursue educational opportunities and become future leaders in their communities. In addition, ASPIRA has engaged in significant advocacy work. The prime example of this advocacy was taking the case for bilingual education to the U.S. Supreme Court (*ASPIRA v. New York City Board of Education*, 1974), resulting in the ASPIRA Consent Decree, to provide bilingual education to all students requiring such services in the New York City public schools regardless of ethnicity or home language.

Throughout her life, and in spite of the many other institutions she helped start and the tremendous difference they all made, Pantoja always considered ASPIRA her most important legacy and contribution to the community. Though focused on Puerto Ricans, ASPIRA also serves Latin@s of other ethnic backgrounds, as well as African Americans, Haitians, Asians, Arab Americans, and Whites, among others. About 55,000 students a year are served by the organization, with 95% graduating from high school and 90% going on to college, far higher rates than among students who have not had the ASPIRA experience. The outcome? ASPIRA is proud to claim that "Virtually every second generation Hispanic leader, in the Northeast, Chicagoland, Southeast and Puerto Rico, has been an *Aspirante*" (ASPIRA Association, 1991).

Even after leaving New York City for visits to Puerto Rico that lasted a number of years; a brief stint in Washington, DC; and an extended stay in San Diego, Pantoja continued to create and support additional community-based institutions. She helped found, for instance, the Graduate School for Community Development, a freestanding school for leadership and community development in San Diego; an ASPIRA affiliate in Puerto Rico that would join the several states that had begun their own branches; the Puerto Rican Research and Resources Center in Washington, DC (for which she served as the first executive director); Universidad Boricua (later Boricua College) in New York City, of which she was also the first president; and PRODUCIR, a community development project in Puerto Rico. Pantoja was also a professor at her alma mater, Columbia University, as well as at the California State University School of Social Work, where she served as the undergraduate director, and a Multicultural Arts Institute in Puerto Rico, among other institutions of higher learning.

Despite the fact that she was born and raised in Puerto Rico, Antonia Pantoja struggled to define her identity. Near the end of her life, she was at peace with who she was. Her memoir ends by declaring that her most important achievement in the process of integrating her identity was finding her self-definition as "Nuyorican," that is, a Puerto Rican New Yorker: "I now know that home is New York City. I have returned and resumed my work in my community with old friends and new friends. I am a Nuyorican!" (Pantoja, 2002, p. 197).

LEARNING FROM ANTONIA

Antonia Pantoja's model of community development was based on integrity, a passion for justice, and deep respect for those with whom she worked. There are numerous lessons to be learned from her long life of service, lessons that can be useful for other individuals and institutions, whether they focus on education or not.

First, Antonia Pantoja had a deep **belief in people, particularly in those who had been left behind, marginalized, and oppressed by society**. She made it a priority to work *with* rather than *for* the communities in which she was engaged. As a result, she never started institutions or programs without first developing relationships with the people involved, listening to and collaborating with them each step of the way.

Second, Pantoja believed that **everyone learns and develops best in communities**. She understood that all people, and particularly young people, need a sense of belonging and pride. At the time ASPIRA was founded, the dropout rate among Puerto Rican students was tremendously high, and most young Puerto Ricans knew little about postsecondary education. (These problems continue to exist, especially in schools and communities without ASPIRA

Clubs or other organizations that provide similar services and experiences.) Concerned that the growing number of gangs in New York City was attracting Puerto Rican youngsters who felt alienated and invisible in their schools and communities, Pantoja sought to create an alternative to gangs that would fill the same need but in a positive and productive way. She addressed this point in a 2009 film by Lillian Jimenez, saying:

> I had a vision that you would organize groups of young people. . . . The club would be like a gang, kind of family. And I thought, "It has to be a movement, and you have to give them the things that the gang would bring: *identification*, with a jacket, with symbols, with ceremony." (Jimenez, 2009)

Thus, ASPIRA, according to Pantoja (2002), was grounded "in the knowledge and value that people are born, grow up, and develop fully and best in a community" (p. 106; see also ASPIRA Association, 1991). Creating institutions that provide people with a sense of belonging and purpose was one of Pantoja's greatest achievements.

A third lesson is that **one must both mentor and learn from young people**. Antonia Pantoja's dedication to the young was unsurpassed. Her goal was always to nurture youths to become leaders in their own right. Because of this strong belief, she often spoke about the importance of dialogue with the young. She was, for instance, proud of the fact that all the activities of ASPIRA were created and developed by the *Aspirantes*.

Another important lesson to be learned from Antonia Pantoja is that **leadership needs to be shared, not hoarded.** For example, despite the fact that she considered ASPIRA her greatest accomplishment, in 1965 she voluntarily left as the organization's executive director. Her reasoning was that the top person of an organization needs to eventually step aside in order to promote new leadership. She did the same with other organizations, choosing to have the institutions she founded become incubators for young leaders who would, in turn, know when it was time to step down.

CONCLUSION

Though Antonia Pantoja is best remembered for her leadership and service, she also was a scholar. Though I knew about her service and inspiration for many years, it was not until I was a doctoral student that I read a book she had coedited (Pantoja & Blourock, 1976), a book that left an indelible impression on me and influenced my own research, teaching, and advocacy. Also, with her longtime partner and fellow dreamer, Dr. Wilhelmina (Mina) Perry, she wrote several important articles and book chapters, many of which spell out their goals and aspirations for the communities they served (e.g., Pantoja & Perry, 1976, 1993, 1998).

Throughout her life, Antonia Pantoja was the embodiment of service, respect for the community, and passion for justice. If we were to follow her example not only in education, but also in other nonprofit areas and in the corporate world, our society would be much better for it. For example, what would happen if public schools were to follow Antonia Pantoja's life lessons? For one, schools would honor the cultures, languages, and lived experiences of all young people through the curriculum, pedagogy, and other school policies, practices, traditions, rituals, and values. Schools would make serious attempts to hire faculty and staff that reflected the diversity of students and their communities. If they saw themselves reflected in the books they read, the curriculum they study, outreach to families, and in meaningful inclusion in school matters, no student would feel alienated, invisible, or unworthy.

Antonia Pantoja's life exemplified service as a noble goal. She believed that teachers, police officers, health care professionals, and others first and foremost need to think of themselves as *servants* of the communities in which they work rather than as superior to those communities. Doing this would mean working in partnership with communities and having a deep respect for people instead of dictating how they should live their lives. If this were the case, for example, the Black Lives Matter movement might never have had to be created.

Both public- and private-sector groups would also be dramatically different were they to follow Pantoja's model of leadership. She exemplified that elusive combination of strength and humility. If others were to follow this example, there would be more sharing of responsibility and power. Even in for-profit organizations—though the profit motive would still be important—sharing decisionmaking would make these organizations more humane and collaborative.

In spite of her tremendous accomplishments and accolades, Antonia Pantoja was also reserved and unassuming. Lillian Jimenez, a friend of hers who also made the film *Antonia Pantoja: Presente!*, recalled many occasions on which Antonia was embarrassed by all the attention she received. Lillian said:

> At the San Juan Airport, this woman came up to her and thanked her for all the work she had done on behalf of the Puerto Rican community in New York and Puerto Rico. This would happen frequently and it always disquieted Toni as she was a very private person and very humble. Also, I remember that Toni and Mina had organized a bilingual education conference at the CUNY (City University of New York) Graduate Center and a young Polish American man went up to the microphone and thanked Puerto Ricans

for establishing bilingual education because he could speak English because of our efforts. Toni was just so excited that her pioneering work had helped other immigrant groups. (Jimenez, personal communication, July 16, 2016)

Even after her death in 2002, Antonia Pantoja has remained a formidable model of strength and perseverance in the Puerto Rican community. Several years after her death, artist Manny Vega created a stunning mosaic of Pantoja at the Corsi Houses Senior Center in the heart of El Barrio in New York City. It is a striking reminder of her ongoing influence, an influence that will live on for many years. At the age of 80, when reflecting on her life, Pantoja (2002) wrote, "If I had not guided my life by these principles of integrity and honesty, I believe that I might have lived a life of self-serving mockery" (p. x), words that other individuals and organizations would do well to live by.

NOTE

I wish to thank Dr. Wilhelmina Perry and Ms. Lillian Jimenez for their feedback and suggestions on a first draft of this chapter.

REFERENCES

ASPIRA Association. (1991). *The ASPIRA story: 1961–1991*. Washington, DC: Author.

Fitzpatrick, J. P. (1971). *Puerto Rican Americans: The meaning of migration to the mainland*. Englewood Cliffs, NJ: Prentice-Hall.

Jimenez, L. (Director & Producer). (2009). *Antonia Pantoja: Presente!* (film). USA: Latino Public Broadcasting.

Nieto, S. (2004). Puerto Rican students in U.S. schools: A troubled past and the search for a hopeful future. In J. A. Banks & C. A. M. Banks (Eds.), *Handbook of research on multicultural education* (2nd ed., pp. 515–541). San Francisco, CA: Jossey-Bass.

Pantoja, A. (2002) *Memoir of a visionary: Antonia Pantoja*. Houston, TX: Arte Público Press.

Pantoja, A., & Blourock, B. (1976). Cultural pluralism redefined. In A. Pantoja, B. Blourock, & J. Bowman (Eds.), *Badges and indicia of slavery: Cultural pluralism redefined* (pp. 2–24). Lincoln, NE: Cultural Pluralism Committee, Study Commission on Undergraduate Education and the Education of Teachers.

Pantoja, A., & Perry, W. (1976). Toward the development of theory: Cultural pluralism redefined. *Journal of Sociology and Social Welfare, IV*, 125–146.

Pantoja, A., & Perry, W. (1993). Cultural pluralism: A goal to be realized. In M. Moreno Vega & C. Greene (Eds.), *Voices from the battlefront: Achieving cultural equity* (pp. 135–148). Trenton, NJ: Africa World Press.

Pantoja, A., & Perry, W. (1998). Community development and restoration: A perspective and case study. In J. L. Ehrlich & F. G. Rivera (Eds.), *Community organizing in a diverse society* (pp. 220–242). Boston, MA: Allyn & Bacon.

Perry, W. (1998). *Memorias de una vida de obra* (Memories of a life of work): An interview with Antonia Pantoja. *Harvard Educational Review, 68* (2), 244–258.

CHAPTER 2

Grassroots Leadership for Ecological Sustainability, Empowerment, and Political Change
Wangari Maathai and the Green Belt Movement

Melanie C. Brooks
MONASH UNIVERSITY, AUSTRALIA

> It's the little things that citizens do. That's what will make the difference. My little thing is planting trees.
>
> —Wangari Maathai

Dr. Wangari Maathai led a grassroots environmental movement focused on social justice, environmental sustainability, democratic governance, and peace. In doing so, she changed the lives of rural Kenyan women and became renowned as a remarkable and influential African leader. Her activism began in the mid-1970s when she became aware of the struggles that rural poor women faced in securing food, water, and fuel for their families. Colonial and postcolonial development saw Kenya's population grow from 2 million at the turn of the 20th century to 8.5 million in 1962, a year before Kenyan independence from British colonial rule (Ofcansky, 1984). As the population swelled, forests were culled for farmland and fuel, with just 3% of forested land remaining (Ofcansky, 1984). For Maathai, the solution was simple: Plant trees to renew the land. On Earth Day in 1977, Maathai established the Green Belt Movement (GBM). Today, this grassroots organization comprises more than 100,000 women activists, 600 community networks, and 6,000 tree nurseries, and boasts more than 51 million trees planted (Green Belt Movement, 2016). Originally a tree-planting movement, the GBM expanded to become inextricably linked to rectifying social and economic injustice throughout Kenya. In honor of her life's work, in 2004, Maathai became the first African woman awarded the Nobel Peace Prize, for her "strong voice speaking for the best forces in Africa to promote peace" (Nobel Committee, 2004). Maathai was also awarded 15 honorary doctorate degrees, received dozens of awards for her professional achievements, worked in leadership positions in numerous international environmental organizations, and served as a member of the Kenyan parliament from 2002 to 2007 (Green Belt Movement, 2016). Maathai died on September 25, 2011, from ovarian cancer.

A SIMPLE VISION: PLANT TREES

Wangari Maathai was born on April 1, 1940, in a small village in the central highlands of British colonial Kenya. Her father worked on White-owned farms and Maathai lived apart from him because there was no school for her to attend near his work. She attended a rural primary school, and when she was 11, her mother placed her in St. Cecilia's Intermediate Primary, a boarding school. Maathai's time at the boarding school sheltered her from the Mau Mau Uprising (1956–1960), and upon completion of her studies, she enrolled in the only Catholic high school for girls in Kenya. While there, she learned English and converted to Catholicism. Maathai performed at the top of her class and was selected as one of 300 students to study in the United States through the Joseph P. Kennedy Jr. Foundation. She earned a bachelor of science degree in 1964, a master of science degree in 1966, and was appointed research assistant in the zoology department at the University College of Nairobi. Upon her arrival, she learned that the position had been given to another and blamed gender and tribal bias for the duplicity. Two months later, she obtained a position as a research assistant in microanatomy at the School of Veterinary Medicine at the University College of Nairobi, and thereafter met and married Mwangi Mathai. In 1971, she earned a PhD in veterinary anatomy at the University of Nairobi, becoming the first East African woman to earn a doctorate.

While teaching anatomy at the University of Nairobi, Maathai's activism took root. She led a campaign to secure equal rights for women in higher education in Kenya. She wrote, "I had never anticipated that I would be discriminated against on the basis of my gender as often as I was. . . . I found myself challenging the idea that a woman could not be as good as or better than a man" (Maathai, 2007, p. 117). During her time as a lecturer, her husband ran for parliamentary election in 1974. As Maathai worked for his election, she observed firsthand the struggles facing rural poor women in Kenya. She was surprised by this, as she remembered that during her own early years in the central highlands, "there was more than enough food, the food itself was nutritious and wholesome, people were healthy and strong, and there was always enough firewood to cook with" (Maathai, 2006, p. 123). Her observations were confirmed when she attended a lecture hosted by the National Council of Women in Kenya that discussed the rise of disease and malnutrition afflicting children in central Kenya (Cesar, 2010). As a response to this crisis, Maathai founded Envirocare Limited, a company focused on tree planting and overall environmental renewal. She started with few resources and based the organization out of her home. The company struggled. Supported by the United Nations Environment Program, Maathai attended the first United Nations Conference on Human Settlements in Vancouver, Canada, in 1976. The conference focused on actionable plans for sustainable urban development, a topic that renewed her enthusiasm, energy, and commitment to environmental sustainability. Upon her return, she began work to develop a tree nursery at her home. Her husband disapproved of her initiative and, because of a drought, the saplings died (Maathai, 2006). Maathai didn't give up on her vision, however. She was asked to speak about the United Nations Conference on Human Settlements to the National Council of Women of Kenya (NCWK) and was soon thereafter selected to be an executive committee member. With the support of the NCWK, Maathai re-envisioned her tree-planting campaign, naming it Save the Land Harambee—the Swahili word *harambee* meaning "let us all pull together" (Maathai, 2006, p. 20).

The first Save the Land Harambee tree-planting ceremony honored seven deceased Kenyans who had made significant contributions to Kenyan society. The second tree-planting ceremony took place during the United Nations Conference on Desertification in Nairobi in 1977. Maathai organized delegates to plant a second green "belt." Following the conference, she led a mass communication campaign to educate Kenyans about the dangers of desertification and the importance of community action. She organized additional tree-planting ceremonies throughout Kenya using her NCWK connections, but many of the trees died as a result of communities failing to care for the saplings. Maathai learned that she needed to find a way to gain the interest of local people, and for them to invest in sustaining the trees. Save the Land Harambee also needed seedlings if it was going to continue, and Maathai turned to the Kenyan forestry department for help. During the 1970s, the Kenyan government expanded the forestry department by employing extension officers (Otieno, 2008). Maathai tapped these extension officers to help with supplying seedlings, but when the demand for seedlings exceeded the supply, Maathai encouraged women to obtain seeds from indigenous trees, grow their own saplings, and share knowledge about tree planting and care (Maathai, 2006). Relations with the forestry department waned and Maathai galvanized women to develop local community nurseries to source seedlings. Women became creative in propagating trees. She called the women "foresters without diplomas" (Maathai, 2006, p. 29). Maathai saw this as an important shift toward self-efficacy and a significant turning point in the Green Belt Movement (Maathai, 2006).

THE GREEN BELT MOVEMENT

Maathai developed a grassroots organization rooted in five values: (1) love for environment conservation; (2) self- and community empowerment; (3) volunteerism; (4) strong sense of belonging to Kenya's Green political party; and (5) accountability, transparency, and honesty (Maathai, 2006). As the movement expanded, Maathai hired staff members to direct project management, administration, and finance, and to coordinate programs (Maathai, 2006). International donors, such as the United Nations Fund for Women, the Danish Voluntary Fund for Developing Counties, Mobil Oil, and many others, supported the GBM thanks in large part to Maathai's ability to speak in a way that "underscored intersections between environmental and social justice for peacebuilding" (Gorsevski, 2012, p. 292; Hayanga, 2006). International support allowed the GBM to expand its reach and employ thousands working in various capacities throughout Kenya (Maathai, 2006). Through the simple vision of planting trees, Maathai tapped into the emotional concept of home and belonging (Kirkscey, 2007), while also emphasizing the importance of girls and women in sustainable development (Hayanga, 2006). Yet this movement was not without conflict, and it "grew from a tree-planting program into one that planted ideas" (Maathai, 2007, p. 173).

Maathai (2007) felt it was important to educate rural communities about the linkages between environmental degradation, poverty, and democracy to promote responsible governance and environmental sustainability. She encouraged communities to take action to improve their livelihoods by caring for the environment and investing in themselves. She explained:

> It soon became clear that responsible governance of the environment was impossible without democratic space. Therefore, the tree became a symbol for the democratic struggle in Kenya. Citizens were mobilized to challenge widespread abuses of power, corruption and environmental mismanagement. ("Wangari Maathai - Nobel Lecture", 2004)

For 2 decades, then–Kenyan president Daniel arap Moi actively fought against Maathai's work. Moi called Maathai "a threat to the order and security" of Kenya and had Maathai arrested several times, harassed, and intimidated (Gorsevski, 2012, p. 291). Moi viewed her as an opponent to the progress and development of Kenya; however, she continued to fight deforestation from illegal logging and land sales, stating, "I wouldn't be silenced or deterred from telling the truth" (Klopp, 2012; Maathai, 2007, p. 221). Maathai's grassroots movement symbolized an egalitarian, participatory democracy, which ran counter to Moi's neoliberal autocracy. Maathai became a political figure, a foil to Moi's government. By 1991, Moi had Maathai (2007) arrested for "spreading malicious rumors, sedition, and treason" (Maathai, p. 213). As a result of international pressure, he later dropped the charges. Moi left office in 1992 and Maathai continued to lead the Green Belt Movement and engage in democratic activism. Through Maathai's authentic grassroots leadership, Kenyan women began to have a voice and agency in directing their lives (Hayanga, 2006). Reflecting on her political activism, Maathai stated, "I started out planting trees and found myself in the forefront of fighting for the restoration of democracy in my country" (Mohamed, 2011).

MAATHAI'S AUTHENTIC GRASSROOTS LEADERSHIP

Maathai's grassroots leadership empowered communities to take action in reforesting their land, yet it was not an easy process (Presbey, 2013). She had to teach women how to plant and care for trees. She reflected:

> In the beginning it was difficult because the women felt that they had neither the knowledge, the technology, nor the capital to [plant trees]. But, we quickly showed them that we did not need all of that to plant trees, which made the tree-planting process a wonderful symbol of hope. Tree-planting empowered these women because it was not a complicated thing. It was something that they could do and see the results of. They could, by their own actions, improve the quality of their lives. (Maathai, 2000)

Maathai led from outside hegemonic patriarchal and authoritarian power structures. When the forestry department failed to help secure enough seedlings, Maathai (2007) taught women to identify saplings and replant them in used containers. Through her work in the field, she encouraged poor rural women to see the value of civic participation. She modeled democratic change and demanded accountability from elected leaders. Her leadership of the Green Belt Movement helped women become agents of change to improve the well-being of their families, communities, and nation.

Yet Maathai was also an authentic leader. Shamir and Eilan (2005) defined authentic leaders as genuine, principled, and original. Eagly (2005) described authentic leadership as emerging from the reciprocal interpersonal relationships between leaders and followers. Avolio and Gardner (2005) found that authentic leadership develops over time and often in response to major life events. Elements of these definitions are all present in Maathai's leadership; however, George (2003) presented five characteristics of authentic leadership that are especially relevant to Maathai's leadership: (1) having a clear purpose, (2) having strong ethical values, (3) establishing trusting relationships, (4) demonstrating self-discipline and action, and (5) having passion. As an authentic leader, Maathai cared about environmental sustainability and democratic empowerment. She acted ethically and built trusting relationships. She faced challenges with self-discipline and acted on her passion to empower Kenya's rural poor. She showed great passion. When the complexity of Maathai's leadership is considered, it is clear that she was an authentic grassroots leader.

AUTHENTIC GRASSROOTS LEADERSHIP

Maathai's authentic grassroots leadership suggests a unique form of leadership that couples authentic leadership with grassroots leadership to enable positive social change (see Figure 2.1). What can educational leaders learn from the authentic grassroots leadership of Wangari Maathai, an African environmentalist and peace activist?

Figure 2.1 aims to show that educational leaders can apply authentic grassroots leadership in their school contexts to influence positive change. Just as Maathai's authentic grassroots leadership highlights the need to build trusting relationships with followers, be passionate about your work, be self-disciplined, be consistent, and be goal-oriented, so must school leaders have passion for their work (Fullan, 2003), behavior that reflects their values (Starratt, 2012), the capacity to build relationships (Eacott, 2015), and the necessary self-discipline and consistency to lead others toward achievable goals (English, 2015). Moreover, Maathai's authentic grassroots leadership was grounded in her ability to remain positive during critical life events. She did not surrender to governmental pressures and

Figure 2.1. Authentic Grassroots Leadership Model

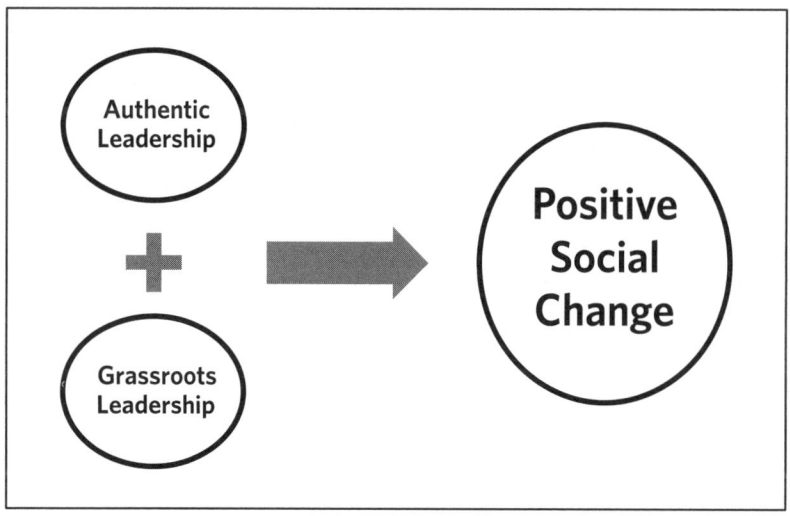

maintained an internalized moral perspective, resiliency, and confidence to continue with her work despite the challenges. Authentic school leaders are similarly led by strong moral grounding (Shapiro & Stefkovitch, 2016) and are resilient and confident in their knowledge that they can see their way through challenges (Moos, Johansson, & Day, 2011). Like Maathai, authentic school leaders focus on the welfare of the community over individual differences (Furman, 2002).

Maathai's (2006) authentic grassroots leadership was grounded in a philosophy of "*by* the people rather than *for* the people" (p. 72). Like Maathai, authentic school leaders have compassion for those they lead, are reflective (Begley, 2003), and consider the needs of the organization while staying true to themselves. Maathai (2000) stated that her program was a "strategy to empower people and to give them a sense of taking their destiny into their own hands, removing their fear, so that they can stand up for themselves and for their environmental rights." Likewise, authentic grassroots school leaders provide opportunities for stakeholders to lead from the bottom up, allow for the development of local programs to enact positive educational change, and are genuine, morally grounded, and honest in their day-to-day work. Maathai's example of authentic grassroots leadership has bearing on the work of school leaders in that in both contexts, the empowerment of others is central to their work.

CONCLUSION

Maathai's authentic grassroots leadership enriched both the people and the environment of Kenya. In the years that followed the establishment of the GBM, her vision expanded to include peace activism, empowerment, good governance, and ecological and economic sustainability. Maathai began the GBM with strong conceptual and technical skills. Her knowledge of environmental issues allowed her to understand deeply technical issues and also identify innovative solutions. Maathai went from having an idea, to creating a small movement, to making a difference nationally, to influencing not only a continent but the whole world. As the scope of her work increased, she remained an authentic grassroots leader. Leadership is a lifelong journey rather than a destination, and Maathai's work will help leaders keep in mind the value of grassroots authenticity, working with passion, and cultivating relationships to build an equitable and sustainable future.

REFERENCES

Avolio, B. J., & Gardner, W. L. (2005). Authentic leadership development: Getting to the root of positive forms of leadership. *Leadership Quarterly, 16*, 315–338.

Begley, P. T. (2003). In pursuit of authentic school leadership practices. In P. T. Begley & O. Johansson (Eds.), *The ethical dimensions of school leadership* (pp. 1–12). New York, NY: Kluwer Academic Publishers.

Cesar, D. (2010). Jane Addams and Wangari Maathai: Nobel Laureates on education and organizing women for local food security. *Vitae Scholasticae, 27*(2), 123–141.

Eacott, S. (2015). *Educational leadership relationally: A theory and methodology for educational leadership, management, and administration*. Rotterdam, The Netherlands: Sense Publishers.

Eagly, A. H. (2005). Achieving relational authenticity in leadership: Does gender matter? *Leadership Quarterly, 16*, 459–474.

English, F. W. (Ed.). (2015). *The SAGE guide to educational leadership and management*. Thousand Oaks, CA: Sage Publications.

Fullan, M. (Ed.). (2003). *The moral imperative of school leadership*. New York, NY: Corwin Press.

Furman, G. (Ed.). (2002). *School as community: From promise to practice*. Albany: The State University of New York Press.

George, B. (2003). *Authentic leadership: Rediscovering the secrets to creating lasting value*. San Francisco, CA: Jossey-Bass.

Gorsevski, E. W. (2012). Wangari Maathai's emplaced rhetoric: Greening global peacebuilding. *Environmental Communication, 6*(3), 290–307.

Green Belt Movement. (2016). Tree planting and water harvesting. Retrieved from www.greenbeltmovement.org/what-we-do/tree-planting-for-watersheds

Hayanga, A. (2006). Wangari Maathai: An African woman's environmental and geopolitical landscape. *International Journal of Environmental Studies, 63*(5), 551–555.

Kirkscey, R. (2007). Accommodating traditional African values and globalization: Narrative as argument in Wangari Maathai's Nobel Prize lecture. *Women & Language, 30*, 12–17.

Klopp, J. M. (2012). Deforestation and democratization: Patronage, politics and forests in Kenya. *Journal of East African Studies, 6*(2), 351–370.

Maathai, W. M. (2000). *Speak truth to power*. Retrieved from greenbeltmovement.org/wangari-maathai/key-speeches-and-articles/speak-truth-to-power

Maathai, W. M. (2009). *The challenge for Africa*. London, England: Routledge.

Maathai, W. M. (2006). *The green belt movement: Sharing the approach & the experience*. New York, NY: Lantern Books.

Maathai, W. M. (2007). *Unbowed: A memoir*. New York, NY: Knopf.

Mohamed, A. (2011). Our planet. *United Nations Development Programme*. Retrieved from www.unep.org/ourplanet/2011/dec/en/star.asp

Moos, L., Johansson, O., & Day, C. (Eds.). (2011). *How school principals sustain success over time: International perspectives*. Dordrecht, The Netherlands: Springer.

Nobel Committee. (2004). The Nobel Prize for 2004 to Wangari Maathai [Press release]. Retrieved from www.nobelprize.org/nobel_prizes/peace/laureates/2004/press.html

Ofcansky, T. P. (1984). Kenya forestry under British colonial administration, 1895–1963. *Journal of Forest History, 28*(3), 136–143.

Otieno, A. O. (2008). *Forest politics in colonial and postcolonial Kenya, 1940s–1990s* (Unpublished doctoral dissertation). Northwestern University, Evanston, Illinois.

Presbey, G. M. (2013). Women's empowerment: The insights of Wangari Maathai. *Journal of Global Ethics, 9*(3), 277–292.

Shamir, B., & Eilam, G. (2005). "What's your story?" A life-stories approach to authentic leadership development. *Leadership Quarterly, 16*, 395–417.

Shapiro, J. P., & Stefkovich, J. A. (2016). *Ethical leadership and decision making in education: Applying theoretical perspectives to complex dilemmas.* New York, NY: Routledge.

Starratt, R. J. (2012). *Cultivating an ethical school.* New York, NY: Routledge.

Wangari Maathai - Nobel Lecture. (2004, December 10). Retrieved from www.nobelprize.org/nobel_prizes/peace/laureates/2004/maathai-lecture-text.html

CHAPTER 3

In the Shadow of Totalitarianism
Tsunesaburo Makiguchi and the Struggle for Value-Creating Educational Leadership

John M. Heffron
SOKA UNIVERSITY OF AMERICA, UNITED STATES

The fact that by the 1930s, Japan had become a thoroughly militarized society, with its schools made to serve the imperialistic aims of the government from the emperor on down, is more or less common knowledge. Less well known are the contemporaneous efforts of one obscure Japanese elementary school principal, Tsunesaburo Makiguchi (1871–1944), to keep alive a democratic stream of philosophical thought in education, which had all but dried up (Kobayashi, 1964). In contrast to the militant nationalism underlying the relations of school and society in Japan at least since the Imperial Rescript of 1890, an edict making loyalty to the Emperor the test of good citizenship, one finds in the life and work of Makiguchi a very different kind of militancy, a peaceful but no less strident cultural and intellectual revolution, redefining those relations in new and radically humanistic ways (Anderson, 1959, p. 15). This revolution, which has significance today for how we think about educational leadership, arose under the name of *Soka*, or value-creating education. It wasn't long before this countervailing educational and philosophical movement—aligned after 1930 with the no less iconoclastic egalitarian Buddhism of 13th-century Japanese religious reformer Nichiren—came to the attention of Japanese counterespionage, the notorious "Thought Police" (Hoyt, 2001, p. 113). Everything Makiguchi stood for—individualism (although not, to be sure, in the Western European tradition), internationalism, and pacifism—was allied with treason. In 1943, along with his long-time protégé, Josei Toda, Makiguchi was arrested for the crime of *lèse-majesté*, offending the emperor, in particular for his opposition to government-supported State Shinto. Makiguchi died a year later in Sugamo Prison at the age of 73 (Bethel, 1984; Goulah & Gebert, 2014).

Born at the dawn of the Meiji Era (1868–1912) in a remote farming village in northwestern Japan, Makiguchi experienced a youth that was turbulent, not unlike the times. Abandoned by his father, nearly killed in a suicide attempt by his mother, placed under the custody at different times of two different uncles, and unable to complete a college-preparatory education, Makiguchi, like many other young, aspiring teachers, managed nevertheless, with the support of a patron, to enroll in Sapporo Normal School, one of a growing number of schools in Japan dedicated to educating the "foot-soldiers of modernization" (Goulah & Gebert, 2009, p. 119). One of the results of the 19th-century opening of Japan was an influx of Western educational ideas and practices, an uncritical hodgepodge of competing ancient and modern influences from Plato and Aristotle to Montaigne and Comenius to Rousseau, Pestalozzi, and even a recapitulationist like Herbart. Cosmopolitan in his reading tastes, Makiguchi was nevertheless "particularly disturbed," according to Gebert and Joffee (2007), "by the sight of teachers struggling to absorb and implement the latest theories from Europe and the United States," encouraging them as both a teacher educator and later as a school principal instead to "inductively establish principles" of praxis based on their own experiences (p. 73). Although never fully accepted by the educational establishment of his time, Makiguchi, in addition to working for over 20 years as an elementary school teacher and principal, was a prolific writer; his collected works today extend to 10 volumes.

THE CONTEXT

As a school principal, Makiguchi was prohibited by Japanese law from direct political involvement, and yet the four books he published over the course of his lifetime (and was able to get past government censors) are a testimony to the political power of his ideas. They provide a clue to Makiguchi's unique approach to problems of educational administration, a view that resists simple categorization as either progressive or traditional, Eastern or Western. Makiguchi published his first major work in 1903, *A Geography of Human Life*, followed in 1912 by *Community Studies as the Integrating Focus of Instruction*, and 4 years later by *Research into Methods and Content of Geography Instruction*. These works and the thought that went into them helped lay the foundation for his masterwork, *The System of Value-Creating Pedagogy*, appearing in four volumes, the first in 1930 and the second, third, and fourth in 1931, 1932, and 1934, respectively. *The System of Value-Creating Pedagogy* is considered the first pedagogical system in Japan to be born out of day-to-day educational practices in the actual classroom (Takeuchi, 1986), but in Makiguchi's philosophy, it was a classroom without walls, a semi-permeable membrane for the exchange and ultimately for the equalization of forces within it and without it. The local community was not something "out there" to be served, nor did parents' responsibility for the education of their children stop at the school door. School, community, and society, as well as animate and inanimate nature, all shared a single universe of overlapping influence and dependence. It was the role of education to tease out these interconnections and utilize them for the promulgation of good, beauty, and gain (economic or otherwise), the triad of human values that Makiguchi proposed as the basic ends and means of value creation.

At the heart of Soka education is the belief that human beings have an intrinsic capacity to generate value and meaning both personally and interpersonally, under the worst no less than the best of times and circumstances. "To live to the full realization of one's potential," Makiguchi wrote almost a century ago, "is to attain and actualize values. Helping us to learn to live as creators of value is the purpose of education" (Makiguchi in Bethel, 1989, p. 54). Makiguchi placed heavy emphasis on what he called "personality integration" and "self-reflection" as prerequisites to value creation. Self-reflection, however, would, in his words, have to go "beyond the infantile or primitive state of nondiscrimination of self and others or of sheer other-awareness, to come back . . . to examine oneself in light of what one has contributed to that point, for better or worse, to the lives of those who share one's communal existence" (pp. 86–87). In this sense, Soka education is not so much a philosophy of education as it is a philosophy of life, one in which the creation of value for the sake of oneself and others constitutes the highest form of meaning. Today, nearly three-quarters of a century since Makiguchi's death in 1944, K–12 and tertiary Soka schools that pursue these ideals encircle the globe, stretching from Japan and Singapore to Brazil and the United States. As Ikeda (2001), the founder of these schools, writes: "The ultimate goal of Soka, or value-creating, education is to foster people of character who continuously strive for the 'greatest good' of peace, who are committed to protecting the sanctity of life, and who are capable of creating value under even the most difficult circumstances" (p. 115).

KEY LESSONS FOR EDUCATIONAL LEADERS

1. The local community as a site of interpenetrating micro and macro worlds (Gebert, 2009; Goulah, 2010a & 2010b), and their "sympathetic interaction" as an educational imperative (Makiguchi, 2002, p. xiv). The link between education and democracy was at the level of cooperative living—"social living focused on spiritually uplifting the community," wrote Makiguchi. But not even this was possible without having "awakened to an awareness of the meaning and importance of society in the life of the individual person" (quoted in Bethel, 1989, p. 43). As he wrote in *A Geography of Human Life*, "Each member shares duties necessary for the continued activity of the group, similar to the functioning of organs in a living body" (2002, p. 31).

In teaching children an appreciation, especially in our global world, of all the many people and forces at work in the creation of a single article of clothing or piece of furniture, we teach them, asserted Makiguchi, that the community is a microcosm of the world:

> If we encourage children to observe directly the complex relationships between people and the land, between nature and society, we will be able to help them grasp the realities of their homes, their school, the town, village or city, and to understand the wider world. (Makiguchi in Garrison et al., 2014, p. 148)

It was important to plan educational experiences—direct, firsthand experiences in the child's immediate environment—designed explicitly to foster this "deeper way of seeing and learning about the world" (Makiguchi, 2002, p. 23).

2. The centrality of value and value creation in a world of facten sammler (fact gatherers, the popular epithet hurled against German historicism). The truths of nature and society were less important for Makiguchi than what people were able to make of them for the creation of value. Unlike the discovery of truth, the production of values was just that—an act of creation. As Makiguchi wrote in *The System of Value-Creating Pedagogy*, in a natural extension of *A Geography of Human Life*:

> When we speak of creation, we refer to the process of bringing to light whatever has bearing on human life from among elements already existing in nature, evaluating these discoveries, and through the addition of human effort further enhancing that relevancy. In other words, creation reworks the "found order" of nature into an order with special benefits for humanity. Strictly speaking, then, creation applies only to value and not to truth, for truth stops at the point of discovery. (quoted in Bethel, 1989, pp. 56–57)

The distinction between truth and value was an important one for Makiguchi, and not simply for philosophical reasons but for sound educational ones as well. He bemoaned the fact that educators, especially educational leaders, too often confused cognition (apperception of the facts) with evaluation (interpretation of the facts). It's not simply that they mistake what "is" for what "should be" or what "should be" for what actually "is," cloaking value judgments in statements of truth and vice versa; they also fail to understand that the facts themselves do not say anything, do not impose any meaning. It is the educator guided by particular purposes—good or bad, relevant or irrelevant—who imposes a meaning.

3. *First Do No Harm.* Makiguchi placed the blame for this epistemological state of affairs not only on the confusion of cognition and evaluation or on the nationalist goals of the Shinto state, but on the kind and degree of educational leadership in Japan. His approach to the reform of educational administration was twofold: It called on the one hand for stricter standards for entering the profession—in other words, for the greater professionalization of principals and school inspectors—and, on the other hand, for greater community responsibility and control over the management and supervision of schools, including, under important safeguards, the hiring and firing of principals. Teachers needed to come down from their thrones to meet students as equals in the learning process, but so too did school leaders need to work collaboratively with teachers and parents. Principals had administrative duties to uphold "passively" certain rules and regulations, but this role was secondary to "actively working to increase the effectiveness of the teachers under them" (Makiguchi in Bethel, 1989, p. 111). This was to be accomplished not by imposing performance standards on teachers, but by essentially getting out of the way, "removing obstacles that would otherwise prevent dedicated and motivated teachers from taking the initiative in implementing their skills" (p. 111). The important thing was "to create a horizontal structure of equally and mutually supportive relations between teaching and administration, instead of the present vertical hierarchy" (Bethel, 1989, p. 134). This was a clarion call in the 1930s from which we still have much to learn today for the reform of education and educational leadership.

4. *The duty to "bring a peaceful order to the school."* "No matter how well external appearances are glossed over," wrote Makiguchi, "even the most celebrated principal will fall from popularity and soon vanish in ignominy if no lasting, fundamental order is established" (Bethel, 1989, p. 112). Makiguchi compared the principal to the head of the household, whose job it was, he believed, to maintain peace and harmony among family members, and to the head of state, who had responsibility for ensuring the security of the nation. This was best achieved, however, not by establishing elaborate rules and regulations but by "setting down basic standards" of common decency and right behavior and through "active value creation . . . [the] active provision of optimal conditions for value creation in children's education" (pp. 111–112).

5. *Empower families to take greater personal responsibility for the education of their children and the community.* The time had come, Makiguchi believed, for parents and local groups to begin to take greater direct responsibility for the quality of children's education. "For better or worse," wrote Makiguchi, "it is now the community's own school, understood as an extension of home life" (quoted in Bethel, 1989, p. 131). On par with parents' other household and childrearing duties was the need to make "educational studies figure into their common knowledge" and for parents to familiarize themselves with the contents of the curriculum; issues of grading, testing, and evaluation; and different types of pedagogy and their effectiveness (p. 132).

6. The happiness of the learner as "the raison d'être of education." According to Makiguchi, the greatest happiness for a human being, and the goal of all education, was to discover one's own natural inclinations, develop them, and bring them to fruition. In the process of fulfilling one's inborn talents, skill, and mission, the individual would begin to contribute naturally to the happiness of others, to humankind's common quest for principles of right living in the home, at work, in the community, and in nature.

7. Value creation is not a fait accompli. It requires purposive and directive action and behavior. "Creation," as Makiguchi said, "reworks the 'found order' of nature into an order with special benefits for humanity" (quoted in Bethel, 1989, p. 57). The "found order" confronting any principal or school superintendent in any country and under any political system is not nor should it be interpreted as an *a priori* "given" but rather as working materials for the challenge of value creation. Education for value creation is a deliberate process of educating individuals to challenge and rise above their inexperience, any slavish dependency on the work and thought of others, a reliance on secondhand knowledge, their habituation to "momentary or circumstantial terms"—a euphemism for immediate results—and an ignorance of past successes and failures of every hue and cry (pp. 88–89). Strong personal character was cause and effect of the ability to create value, beginning with the acquisition of "mature core beliefs and a sense of purpose in life." This, in turn, would lead to the two most important prerequisites for value creation—"mind and body unity" and "psychological consistence over time" (pp. 87–89). A person of strong character is not one person one day and another person the next, his or her disposition under the sway of ever-changing circumstances. This is what Makiguchi meant by having a core set of beliefs and a clear sense of purpose in one's orientation to life. A mind lacking unity, a unity of thought and action, is more likely to fall prey to a psychological *inconsistency* over time. And here was Makiguchi's worry: that "inconsistencies in someone's [read: educational leader] mental state as reflected in divergent behavior from one day to the next will cause others to distrust that character," disrupting the peaceful and harmonious school order that it was the leader's job to safeguard (p. 87).

RESEARCH AND THEORY INTO PRACTICE

The shift that began to occur in the United States in the 1960s from preparing school plant managers to preparing educational leaders, and more recently, from preparing professional administrators to preparing so-called transformational leaders, has involved a number of largely unresolved controversies over "the knowledge most worth having"—and thus, worth teaching—in graduate-level educational leadership preparation programs. What would a Makiguchian curriculum look like if it were designed to develop leaders for tomorrow's schools? What would our schools look like under such leadership? And, finally, what would have to change in the traditional training of educational leaders to achieve such a vision?

As the seven key lessons bequeathed by Makiguchi indicate, only a combination of respect for the community and respect for the individual, as an object of the "rediscovery of the I in the Thou" (Dilthey, 1961, p. 67), as well as an understanding of the limitations of executive leadership, can lead to schools in which there is equal opportunity for all—students, parents, and staff alike. This being the case, students of educational leadership will likewise get their best education in the community, in sympathetic interaction with students and teachers, and in a formal education that stresses, as Makiguchi says, the affective qualities of "mind and body unity" and "psychological consistence over time," as well as the acquisition of "mature core beliefs and a sense of purpose in life." It may be time, as English (2006) and others (Crow & Grogan, 2005; Donmoyer, Imber, & Scheurich, 1995; Littrell & Foster, 1995) have argued, to abandon the search for "a new center of gravity" in the knowledge base of educational administrators. In the conviction that "all that is solid melts into air," these researchers see the concept of a knowledge base as essentially "a myth." More than anything else, writes English (2006), "the creation of a knowledge base is an exercise of political power," resulting in a curriculum that "remains truncated, ahistorical, decontextualized, and, most important, immobile" (pp. 462 & 465). English (2006) prefers the notion of a "knowledge dynamic," one that is fluid and unpredictable, neither stable nor fixed, an "expanding universe with very porous borders, if there are borders at all" (p. 466). Almost by default, the development of a knowledge base has become an "exercise in exclusion," not simply for what is left out but for what is left in, the result being a narrowing and crimping of the knowledge and skills necessary for good educational leadership (p. 467).

The postmodern backlash against a knowledge base in educational administration notwithstanding, the question still remains: "What knowledge is most worth having?" The answer to this question, applied to the principal or the superintendent whose job has never been more complex or more nuanced, requires the broadest and most inclusive affective cognitive knowledge, skills, and abilities. In addition, it requires that special *"je ne sais quoi"* that is difficult to teach. There is no one book or teaching available that will help a person develop the natural curiosity and disposition to answer this question; it takes a more holistic set of idiosyncratic experiences. Most important, we need educational leaders, and with them schools, that will make it their mission to confront and create value out of the many problems and difficulties of our age. We also need students and parents, no less than teachers and administrators, with broadly expansive, cultivated personalities; sensitivity and appreciation for the cultures and value systems of other peoples; great skill in dialogue; and a commitment to peace and nonviolence. As Makiguchi makes clear, the education of the community and the education of leaders go hand in hand, the one determining and reinforcing the other in a closed loop of mutual interdependence. The sense of disempowerment shared today by students, parents, teachers, and educational leaders alike is a vicious cycle that only such a realization of our interconnectivity, confidently asserted in unity, can break. Herein lies at once the ultimate goal and expression of value creation.

REFERENCES

Anderson, R. S. (1959). Japan: Three epochs of modern education. *Bulletin 1959*, 11.

Bethel, D. M. (1984). *Makiguchi the value creator: Revolutionary Japanese educator and founder of Soka Gakkai*. New York, NY: Weatherhill.

Bethel, D. M. (Ed.). (1989). *Education for creative living: Ideas and proposals of Tsunesaburo Makiguchi* (A. Birnbaum, Trans.). Iowa City, IA: Iowa State University Press.

Crow, G., & Grogan, M. (2005). The development of leadership thought and practice in the United States. In F. English (Ed.), *The Sage handbook of educational leadership: Advances in theory, research, and practice* (pp. 110–129). Boston, MA: Pearson.

Dilthey, W. (1961). *Pattern and meaning in history: Thoughts on history and society*. New York, NY: Harper and Row.

Donmoyer, R., Imber, M., & Scheurich, J. J. (Eds.). (1995). *The knowledge base in educational administration: Multiple perspectives*. Albany: The State University of New York Press.

English, F. W. (2006). The unintended consequences of a standardized knowledge base in advancing educational leadership preparation. *Educational Administration Quarterly, 42* (3), 461–471.

Garrison, J. W., Hickman, L. A., & Ikeda, D. (2014). *Living as learning: John Dewey in the 21st century*. Cambridge, MA: Dialogue Path Press.

Gebert, A. (2009). The role of community studies in the Makiguchian pedagogy. *Educational Studies, 45*(2), 146–164.

Gebert, A., & Joffee, M. (2007). Value creation as the aim of education: Tsunesaburo Makiguchi and Soka education. In D. T. Hansen (Ed.), *Ethical visions of education: Philosophies in practice* (pp. 65–82). New York, NY: Teachers College Press.

Goulah, J. (2010a). From (harmonious) community life to (creative) coexistence: Considering Daisaku Ikeda's educational philosophy in the Parker, Dewey, Makiguchi, and Ikeda "reunion." *Schools: Studies in Education, 7*(2), 253–275.

Goulah, J. (2010b). (Harmonious) community life as the goal of education: A bilingual dialogue between Tsunesaburo Makiguchi and Francis W. Parker. *Schools: Studies in Education,7*(1), 64–85.

Goulah, J., & Gebert, A. (2009). Tsunesaburo Makiguchi: Introduction to the man, his ideas, and the special issue. *Educational Studies, 45*(2), 115–132.

Goulah, J., & Gebert, A. (Eds.). (2014). *Tsunesaburo Makiguchi (1871–1944): Educational philosophy in context*. London, England: Routledge.

Hoyt, E. P. (2001). *Japan's war: The great Pacific conflict*. New York, NY: Cooper Square Press.

Ikeda, D. (2001). *Soka education: A Buddhist vision for teachers, students, and parents*. Santa Monica, CA: Middleway Press.

Kobayashi, V. N. (1964). *John Dewey in Japanese educational thought*. Ann Arbor, MI: Malloy Lithoprinting.

Littrell, J., & Foster, W. (1995). The myth of a knowledge base in educational administration. In R. Donmoyer, M. Imber, & J. J. Scheurich (Eds.), *The knowledge base in educational administration: Multiple perspectives* (pp. 32–46). Albany: The State University of New York Press.

Makiguchi, T. (2002). A geography of human life. D. M. Bethel (Ed.). (Katsusuke Hori et al., Trans.). San Francisco, CA: Caddo Gap Press. (Original work published 1903)

Takeuchi, Y. (1986). Theory of value as the fundamental principle of Soka pedagogy. *The Journal of Oriental Studies, 25*(2), 1–17.

CHAPTER 4

Sun Yat-sen
A Boundary-Crosser

*Haiyan Qian &
Allan Walker*
THE EDUCATION UNIVERSITY OF HONG KONG

Sun Yat-sen (1866–1925) was a Chinese revolutionary and one of the greatest leaders of modern China. Sun distinguishes himself from other 20th-century Chinese political leaders for being widely respected by people on both sides of the Taiwan Strait. In the Republic of China (ROC) in Taiwan, he is referred to as the "Father of the Nation" (*guofu*). Across the strait in the People's Republic of China (PRC), he is the "forerunner of democratic revolution."

Sun was born into a peasant family in coastal Guangdong Province. At the age of 13, Sun left home to join his elder brother, Sun Mei, in Hawaii in 1879. Sun Mei sent him to a missionary school in Honolulu, where he learned English, religion, and Western history. Sun Yat-sen was sent back to China 4 years later and then went to Hong Kong to continue his studies. From 1887 to 1892, he studied medicine at the first College of Medicine for Chinese in Hong Kong.

The travels, encounters, and education that Sun received overseas initiated him into the modern world and aroused in him a desire to set China on its own path to modernity (Wang, 2011). Seen as a revolutionary by the Qing monarchy, Sun had to spend many years in exile. Sun and other revolutionaries successfully ended over 2,000 years of imperial rule in China in 1911, and Sun became the first provisional president of the Republic of China in 1912. He later cofounded the Kuomintang (KMT) and formulated his political philosophy, Three Principles of the People (*sanmin zhuyi*), which included nationalism (*minzhu zhuyi*), democracy (*minquan zhuyi*), and the people's livelihood (*minsheng zhuyi*). Since his death at the age of 58 in 1925, Sun has become a symbol of democracy and a pioneer of the revolution, and he is remembered by Chinese around the world.

A BOUNDARY-CROSSER: CONTEXT AND PRACTICES

When Sun was born, China was in a perilous state, and was forcibly opened up to foreigners (Bergère, 1998). The ruling Qing Dynasty, suspicious of all things foreign, had been unable to reinvent itself (Patrikeeff & de Cure, 2004). The government's stance was to maintain the principle of "Chinese learning as the substance, Western learning as the function" (*zhongxue weiti, xixue weiyong*) (Tan & Chua, 2015, p. 697). This did not help China out of the crisis; instead, in the early 1900s, Western armies from, for example, the United Kindom and France, marched into Beijing, and Chinese people were angry, bewildered, and in despair (Wang, 2011).

Sun was brought up in a mixed environment that ultimately made him a "globe-trotter with a cause" (Bergère, 1998, p. 6). He was not adequately trained in the Chinese classics nor sufficiently steeped in traditional ideas and practices to be able to resist Western influence in the way that children from Chinese literati families might have done (Wang, 2011). Instead, his early years were open to foreign influences. He was born in a coastal area with a lively foreign presence and booming foreign trade. His missionary teachers in Honolulu, Hawaii, gave him access to textbooks and foreign languages, and in Hong Kong, he learned from British medical scientists at the college. Sun's experiences made him believe that China needed to learn from the more advanced Western administrative and economic systems.

Adapting to the challenging modern values without abandoning the traditions that people needed to retain their self-respect presented a challenge (Wang, 2011). Sun Yat-sen took up that challenge. He looked at the politics and society of China "with the critical perspective of a cosmopolitan observer, but without the detachment" (Bergère, 1998, p. 6). He assumed the mission of saving his country and devoted his life to that ambition.

Sun spent most of his political life in exile in different parts of the world, including Japan, Southeast Asia, and London, England. His geographic mobility nurtured his equally great versatility of mind. He took his ideas from wherever he found them and spread them wherever he happened to be, pleading his cause with different groups of people over the years (Bergère, 1998). In formulating the ideas that eventually became central to his political party after the 1911 revolution, he brought together a wide range of ideas that had converged in his mind. He proposed choosing a number of Western political ideas, including concepts such as sovereignty, democracy, and the citizen state and concerns about people's welfare and livelihood, and combining them with some of China's own popular ideas of legitimate authority and governance (Wang, 2011). Sun was the first to take his ideas for change onto a political stage that was rooted in Chinese practice and to apply Western knowledge to enhance and help preserve his Chinese heritage (Patrikeeff & de Cure, 2004; Wang, 2011).

Sun was a boundary-crosser in the sense that he crossed cultural boundaries as easily as geographical ones; he could speak the language of the people with whom he was dealing, and he was able to discover and draw knowledge from the outside world without breaking with Chinese civilization (Bergère, 1998; Wang, 2011).

KEY LESSONS ABOUT SUN'S LEADERSHIP

Multiple lessons can be drawn from Sun Yat-sen's political life and his leadership style.

Sun had a strong will and unshakable faith to save China and he set China on its own path to modernity. Having witnessed the vulnerability of the Chinese government in the face of growing Western power, Sun developed a deep and unshakable sense that it was his mission to save his country. Sun was an ardent champion of modernization (Bergère, 1998). He recognized early that if China hoped to survive modernity, it had to rid itself of all notions of empire and become more modern politically and economically (Patrikeeff & de Cure, 2004). Sun devoted his life to fighting for the modernity of China until his death. In his last words, he reflected that he had committed himself to revolution for more than 40 years to make China a free and equal society. The most widely known last words were that the work of the revolution was not yet done, so his party members needed to strive to complete it (*Geming shangwei chenggong, tongzhi rengxu nuli*) (Bergère, 1998).

Sun had a strong concern for people's livelihood rather than personal gain. Sun Yat-sen advocated fraternity, which he interpreted as mutual support among people and countries. All of his revolutionary efforts aimed at continuing the life and existence of China and improving the lives of Chinese people (Heng, 2011). To this end, he sacrificed personal gains. For example, Sun was elected as the first provisional president of the new Provisional Government of the Republic of China. However, at the time, some major forces had not made declarations against the Qing monarchy. To make China a united nation, Sun promised Yuan Shikai, who controlled the military force in northern China, the position of president if he could get the Qing court to abdicate. In February 1912, the last emperor, Puyi, abdicated the throne, and Sun stepped down as president and gave the post to Yuan as promised. Sun did not care about his personal position and status when the collective and societal welfare was threatened.

As a resilient leader, Sun was not defeated by failures. Sun Yat-sen has been cited as "a failed politician but a great leader" (Wang, 2011, p. 1). This revolutionary leader's political life was filled with many failures. However, he was also a man of action who never stopped struggling in different forms to replace the dynastic system with a modern nation-state. He founded the Restore China Society (*Xingzhong hui*) in Hawaii in 1894 and in Hong Kong in 1895 (Wang, 2011). He then led the first Guangzhou uprising in 1895. Because the plan of the uprising was leaked, Sun had to spend time living in Japan in exile. In 1900, he launched the Huizhou uprising, which was also a failure. Sun again had to live in exile in Japan and Europe. His life was constantly under threat, but he never gave up his revolutionary mission and kept bouncing back after failures.

Sun was a communicator with strength in persuasion. As "a globe-trotter with a cause" (Bergère, 1998, p. 6), Sun spent most of his life in different parts of the world pleading for support for the Chinese revolution. He was talented in persuasion. For example, while he was in exile in Japan, he made friends with many Japanese who were motivated by his warning of encroaching Western imperialism. He also sought support from overseas Chinese in Southeast Asia, from his teachers and friends in the United Kingdom, and from the Soviet Union in his later years. He was multilingual in the sense that he used different languages to plead his cause with different people. He was as capable of operating in missionary circles as in the lodges of secret societies, in merchant guilds, and in students' cultural societies, and he was as active in Tokyo, London, and San Francisco as he was in Hong Kong, Hanoi, and Singapore (Bergère, 1998).

Sun had strong and deep roots in Chinese tradition and practice. For Asian leaders during Sun's time, Western power was a reality. The question was how far to Westernize if they were to defend their countries against being dominated, conquered, or colonized (Wang, 2011). Sun Yat-sen is a remarkable figure in the political history of China because he successfully blended the pursuit of modernity with traditional Chinese utopian philosophy (Patrikeeff & de Cure, 2004). Sun had the unique ability to project his mixed vision onto an increasingly insecure and uncertain Chinese people; this led him to carve out a life in politics (Wang, 2011). At the heart of Sun's ideology was a universalism/cosmopolitanism, and a comfortable acceptance of hybridity in China's economy and socio-polity—the blending of modern and ancient, traditional and progressive (Patrikeeff & de Cure, 2004). Although he was exposed to Western influences, he never lost sight of what China and the Chinese people needed. Sun Yat-sen judged China as an outsider but loved it as a son (Bergère, 1998).

IMPLICATIONS FOR TODAY'S EDUCATIONAL LEADERS

The social environment has substantially changed since Sun Yat-sen's era. However, many of Sun's leadership lessons still have strong implications for contemporary educational leadership practices in today's increasingly globalized world.

First, Sun's example confirms the importance of vision and shared purpose. Sun was not born into an elite family, and for most of his political life he did not have his own military force. What Sun did have was a strong faith in fighting for China's modernity and freeing Chinese people's lives from war and poverty. This vision sustained him during his years in exile and helped him bounce back from the multiple failures he faced in his political struggles. His vision won him wide support from his fellow comrades, international friends, overseas Chinese businessmen who sponsored the revolution, and the desperate Chinese people, who also supported the Three Principles of the People. Sun's ideas were not profound or dogmatic, but they provided an alternative vision of China's future that was worth fighting for (Wang, 2011). Today's educational leaders also need to inspire, motivate, and expect high performance from others based on strongly held core values (House & Javidan, 2004; Lussier & Achua, 2013). This kind of leadership involves being visionary, inspirational, self-sacrificing, trustworthy, and decisive (House & Javidan, 2004). For example, policymakers and school reformers have increasingly pointed to the school principal as the most important agent of needed change in our schools (Day et al., 2010; Robinson, Lloyd, & Rowe, 2008). When principals are overloaded by more and more expectations, there is a need to arouse their passion and ingenuity to fight for something big and to establish conditions, cultures, and commitment so that others become willing to fight for the vision of the organizations, too (Fullan, 2008).

Second, globalization has created a need for leaders to become competent in cross-cultural awareness and practice (Kumer, Anjum, & Sinha, 2011). Sun Yat-sen left a legacy in this area. He traveled across geographical and cultural boundaries easily and seemed able to adapt to different societies and types of people. He was always open and tolerant of other people's cultural traditions and practices, which made him a boundary-crosser. In today's globalized society, schools are becoming increasingly intercultural, and diversity is a reality (Walker, Qian, & Chen, 2007). Rather than simply clarifying and articulating personal values, beliefs, and purposes, school leaders must be sensitive to the value orientations of various educational stakeholders (Begley, 1996; Starratt, 2005). Today's leaders must be adept at leading people of different cultures; they must listen to the "voices of the people" and understand what those voices may actually be telling them (Kumar et al., 2011). As Sun's case shows, it is important for global leaders to be skilled in creating transcultural visions; there is a need for leaders to develop communication competencies that enable them to articulate and implement their vision in a diverse workplace (Kumar et al., 2011; Ting-Toomey, 1999).

Third, Sun left a legacy in his search for balance and his willingness to borrow and incorporate elements he found useful while not breaking with Chinese tradition and civilization (Patrikeeff & de Cure, 2004). Sun's approach differed from the blind borrowing of Western modern administrative and political ideas without giving due consideration to the realities and needs of the local context. This approach also has profound implications for today's educational leaders. Because of the growing pressure of large-scale international tests such as the Program for International Student Assessment (PISA) and Trends in International Mathematics and Science Study (TIMSS), there is a global move to find out what high-performing societies are doing and what others can learn from them (Jensen, 2012; Sellar & Lingard, 2013). Based on international comparisons, various reports have suggested some solutions that are attractive to regional governments because of their simplicity and applicability regardless of local contexts (Ball, 2012). Schools and school leaders are often encouraged to adopt solutions or "best practices" drawn from these international reports (Phillips & Ochs, 2003; Rizvi & Lingard, 2010). The challenge for educational leaders is to recognize both the homogenizing forces and the profound differences between and across different contexts (Qian, Walker, & Bryant, 2017). Caution must be exercised to avoid adopting practices exclusively from borrowed models rather than those based on local realities or hybrids that contextualize empirically sound practices.

REFERENCES

Ball, S. J. (2012). *Global education inc.: New policy networks and the neo-liberal imaginary.* New York, NY: Routledge.

Begley, P. T. (1996). Cognitive perspectives on values in administration: A quest for coherence and relevance. *Educational Administration Quarterly, 32* (3), 403–426.

Bergère, M-C. (1998). *Sun Yat-sen* (Janet Lloyd, Trans.). Palo Alto, CA: Stanford University Press (Original work published in 1994).

Day, C., Sammons, P., Hopkins, D., Harris, A., Leithwood, K., Gu, Q., & Brown, E. (2010). *10 strong claims about successful school leadership.* Nottingham, UK: National College for Leadership of Schools and Children's Services. Retrieved from dera.ioe.ac.uk/2082/1/10-strong-claims-about-successful-school-leadership.pdf

Fullan, M. (2008). *What's worth fighting for in principalship?* (2nd ed.). New York, NY: Teachers College Press.

Heng, T. S. S. (2011). Sun Yat-sen's Three Principles of the People. In L. T. Lee & H. G. Lee (Eds.), *Sun Yat-sen: Nanyang and the 1911 revolution* (pp. 28–43). Singapore: ISEAS Publications.

House, R. J., & Javidan, M. (2004). Overview of GLOBE. In R. J. House, P. J. Hanges, P. J. Javidan, M. Dorfman, P. W. Gupta, & Associates (Eds.), *Culture, leadership and organizations: The GLOBE study of 62 societies* (pp. 9–24). Thousand Oaks, CA: Sage.

Jensen, B. (2012). *Learning from the best school systems in Asia*. Carlton, Australia: Grattan Report.

Kumar, R., Anjum, B., & Sinha, A. (2011). Cross-cultural interactions and leadership behavior. *Journal of Arts, Science & Commerce, II*(3), 151–160.

Lussier, R. N., & Achua, C. F. (2013). *Leadership: Theory, application & skill development*. Mason, OH: Cengage Learning.

Patrikeeff, F., & de Cure, G. (2004). Sun Yat-sen and greater China. Paper presented at APSA (Australian Political Studies Association) Conference, September 29–October 1, University of Adelaide, Australia.

Phillips, D., & Ochs, K. (2003). Processes of policy borrowing in education: Some explanatory and analytical devices. *Comparative Education, 39*(4), 451–461.

Qian, H. Y., Walker, A., & Bryant, D. (2017). Global trends and issues in the development of educational leaders. In M. D. Young & G. M. Crow (Eds.), *Handbook of research on the education of school leaders* (2nd ed., pp. 53–73). New York, NY: Routledge.

Rizvi, F., & Lingard, B. (2010). *Globalizing education policy*. London, England: Routledge.

Robinson, M. J., Lloyd, C. A., & Rowe, K. J. (2008). The impact of leadership on student outcomes: An analysis of the differential effects of leadership types. *Educational Administration Quarterly, 44*(5), 635–674.

Sellar, S., & Lingard, B. (2013). Looking east: Shanghai, PISA 2009 and the reconstitution of reference societies in the global policy field. *Comparative Education, 49*(4), 464–485.

Starratt, R. J. (2005). Cultivating the moral character of learning and teaching: A neglected dimension of educational leadership. *School Leadership and Management, 25*(4), 300–411.

Tan, C., & Chua, C. S. K. (2015). Education policy borrowing in China: Has the west wind overpowered the east wind? *Compare: A Journal of Comparative and International Education, 45*(5), 686–704.

Ting-Toomey, S. (1999). *Communicating across cultures*. New York, NY: Guilford.

Walker, A., Qian, H. Y., & Chen, S. Y. (2007). Leadership and moral literacy in intercultural schools. *Journal of Educational Administration, 45*(4), 379–397.

Wang, G. W. (2011). Keynote address—Sun Yat-sen and the origins of modern Chinese politics. In L. T. Lee & H. G. Lee (Eds.), *Sun Yat-sen: Nanyang and the 1911 revolution* (pp. 1–16). Singapore: ISEAS Publications.

CHAPTER 5

Peter McLaren's Liberation Theology
Karl Marx Meets Jesus Christ

Peter McLaren
CHAPMAN UNIVERSITY, UNITED STATES

Petar Jandrić
ZAGREB UNIVERSITY OF APPLIED SCIENCES, CROATIA

This chapter is written in the form of a conversation between Peter McLaren and Petar Jandrić.

Petar Jandrić (PJ): Peter McLaren (PM) is distinguished professor in Critical Studies and codirector of the Paulo Freire Democratic Project at the College of Educational Studies, Chapman University; emeritus professor of urban education at the University of California, Los Angeles; emeritus professor of educational leadership at Miami University of Ohio; and honorary director of the Center for Critical Studies in Education at Northeast Normal University in China, where he also holds the position of chair professor. Between 1974 and 1979, as a fresh graduate in English literature, Peter worked as an elementary teacher in suburban Toronto housing projects. In 1980, he wrote one of Canada's top-selling nonfiction books of the year, *Cries from the Corridor*. Later on, he expanded it into the classic textbook of critical education *Life in Schools: An Introduction to Critical Pedagogy in the Foundations of Education* (2014), which is now in its sixth edition and was named one of the 12 most significant writings by foreign authors in the field of educational theory, policy, and practice by the Moscow School of Social and Economic Sciences. In 2007, Peter debuted as a poet in *MRZine*.

Peter has published more than 50 books and hundreds of scholarly articles and chapters that have been translated into more than 20 languages. His name has slowly but surely become almost synonymous with the contemporary project of critical education. Among numerous accolades, five books written by Peter have won American Educational Studies Association Critics' Choice awards, and his work has been the foundation for several dedicated institutions, including La Fundación McLaren de Pedagogía Crítica, Instituto Peter McLaren in Mexico, and La Catedra Peter McLaren at the Bolivarian University in Caracas. Peter received an honorary doctorate from the University of Lapland in Finland (2004) and from La Universidad del Salvador in Buenos Aires, Argentina (2010). He also received the Amigo Honorífica de la Comunidad Universitaria de esta Institución from La Universidad Pedagógica Nacional, Unidad 141, Guadalajara, Mexico. In 2016, Peter's book *Pedagogy of Insurrection: From Resurrection to Revolution* (McLaren, 2015) received the Division B Outstanding Book Recognition Award from the American Educational Research Association and the Society of Professors of Education Book Award.

As the "intellectual relative" of Paulo Freire (1995, p. x), and one of the leading architects of contemporary critical pedagogy, Peter has left an invaluable mark on the past and present of the educational left. Yet Peter has never looked backward. Instead of lulling in the well-deserved secure position of a senior intellectual, in 2015 he published the groundbreaking book *Pedagogy of Insurrection* (McLaren, 2015), which develops a new emancipatory praxis at the crossroads between revolutionary critical pedagogy and liberation theology. This conversation discusses some of Peter's most recent and deepest insights into the relationship between revolutionary critical pedagogy and liberation theology, and outlines the main directions of development of his thought during and after *Pedagogy of Insurrection* (McLaren, 2015).

THE IDOLATRY OF MONEY

PJ: Theology and (social) science are written using radically different languages—therefore, we need to read them in radically different ways. Most of our readers will be familiar with reading one or another language of science. How should we go about reading the Gospels?

PM: Both Jesus and Marx maintained a commitment to the poor and the powerless. In the case of Jesus, his story is the embodiment of the word of God. Theology helps us to gain a deeper understanding of the meaning of Jesus's life. Jesus brings to the encounter with the divine a new praxis, an incarnation that radiates love through a concretization of prophetic justice. Of course, when we attempt to fathom the paschal mystery, we are guided by our own history, our own formation, what the Germans refer to as *Bildung*. Here, we adhere to historico-critical exegesis with an understanding that a purely scientific exegesis does not eliminate divergent interpretations because it is impossible to rid ourselves of all of our theologio-dogmatic presuppositions. When we read the scriptures, we have to acknowledge that our interpretations are guided by our own biographies and by suffering Christian communities throughout the ages who read the Gospels through contextually specific eschatological, soteriological, and Christological themes—mainly with a kerygmatic intention. As Leonardo Boff (1987) would put it, reading the Gospels is not the same as reading facts of history because in such a reading, you are dealing with history, the interpretation of history, and a profession of faith working together to understand the totality of Christianity from an apologetical viewpoint. Christ destroys all of our previous images of God, as Christ suffers for all the crucified of history. As Boff (1987) notes, this is a mystery inaccessible to discursive reason but capable of being understood through human praxis. We are resurrected through our refusal to cooperate with the social sin of this world.

Remember, Petar, that Paulo Freire (1973) wrote that the prophetic position of the Church "demands a critical analysis of the social structures in which . . . conflict takes place. This means it demands of its followers a knowledge of socio-political science, since this science cannot be neutral; this demands an ideological choice" (p. 14). Here, Freire admits to the notion that all science is a form of ideology and that there is an ideological choice in choosing particular types of science with which to clarify and deepen our understanding of the struggle for liberation. Part of the prophetic vision of the Church demands an engagement with social science that can help unpeel the veneer of mystification that keeps us from knowing reality. Freire (1973) writes that a prophetic perspective "does not represent an escape into a world of unattainable dreams. It demands a scientific knowledge of the world as it really is" (p. 14). But note that for Freire, this scientific understanding of the world is found through praxis, through revolutionary praxis. Freire warns that "to denounce the present reality and announce its radical transformation into another reality capable of giving birth to new men and women, implies gaining through praxis a new knowledge of reality" (p. 14). Freire criticizes the petit bourgeois dimension of the Church today and urges theologians to consider in their work the so-called Third World that exists within their own so-called First World—in the outskirts of their cities. And I would add—within our segregated inner cities.

PJ: What is the main point of convergence between teachings of Jesus Christ and Karl Marx?

PM: According to Miranda (1980), Jesus was the first human being in history to denounce money as the object of idolatry, which centuries later, Marx referred to variously as the biblical idols of Baal, Mammon, and Moloch. In fact, when discussing the commodity form of production, he used these terms as much as he did the word *fetish*.

When Saint Paul talks about the "lust which is idolatry," he is referring to money. Book Three of *Capital* (Marx, 1981) makes clear that the capitalist mode of production is not the origin of class violence in capitalist society. As Miranda (1980) notes, the class division is created outside the sphere of production, when money becomes god, and it was this god that created the conditions of possibility for the capitalist mode of production. Money as exchange value stands outside production and circulation, and yet dominates both. Money represents the autonomous existence of value as the concretization of human labor. It is when money no longer represents commodities, but when commodities represent money, that money becomes a god. Money is the god of all people living under the commodity mode of production, and money had already become a god during the time of Jesus. In other words, the accumulation of capital is not enough to automatically create the mode of production we know today as capitalism, because it takes a certain type of historically produced civilization. The transformation of money into capital requires a certain kind of historical circumstances. Today, capitalism still functions as the institutionalization of the worship of Mammon.

Marx does a brilliant job of explaining how money was transformed into a god that rules human beings. Marx reveals how money is both the object and fountainhead of greed, of *auri sacra fames*, the product of a historically conditioned environment. According to Miranda (1980), Marx perceived the switching of the subject into an object and the transformation of the ends into the means as the centerpiece of the making of a false religion. Marx then applied this "conversion" to economics, to the production of value. Capital finds a way to exchange itself for a commodity that produces more value than the commodity itself—labor power. Capital moves into production through an exchange with labor power, via wage labor, which brings about the separation of the direct producers from the owners of the means of production. Interest-bearing capital is a fetish, is self-expanding value, and it expands its value independently of reproduction, which is a reversal of the relationship between persons and things—all pointing to Marx's anathematization of the worship of money as god. Miranda (2004) points out that at the very central point of his analysis of capital, at the very point where he uncovers the birth of money as a commodity, Marx cites two entire verses from the apocalypse (Revelation, 17:13, 13:17, King James Version). Marx offers a scientific elaboration of Christ's teaching about the god Mammon.

PJ: Poverty is a central point of departure for Jesus, Marx, and Paulo Freire. Yet the answers seem to collide. For Jesus, the poor will inherit the Kingdom of God; for Marx and Freire, the poor will should take matters in own hands here and now . . .

PM: Jesus did not sacralize poverty or preach resignation to it because there will be some extraterrestrial compensation for it in the afterlife. That would be a glib and cynical assessment, and it erases the prophetic nature of such a pronouncement. To say the poor are blessed is not an involuntary justification of the relations and structures of exploitation. The poor are blessed because the coming of the Kingdom of God in the fullness of history will put an end—in the concrete sociological sense—to their poverty and suffering. Poverty is a form of structural sin that is incompatible with the Kingdom of God. I am not trying to reduce the Gospels to a manual for attaining political consciousness but maintaining that the Gospels have an inherent political dimension. As Gustavo Gutierrez (1988) notes:

> This conscienticizing of the preaching of the Gospel, which rejects any aseptic presentation of the message, should lead to a profound revision of the pastoral activity of the Church . . . the oppressed themselves should be the agents of their own pastoral activity. (pp. 154–155)

Freire was a Christian and sympathetic to Marx, and although I never had a chance to discuss with Paulo the topic of liberation theology, I believe that it would have been a fascinating dialogue. For me, critical consciousness is something that is central to the movement of liberation theology, in the sense that Christians come to recognize not only their preferential option for the poor but, as I would put it, their preferential obligation and commitment to the poor. Critically conscious Christians come to recognize their political formation as subjects—their standpoint epistemology—in relation to others, but also gain ontological and ethical clarity on their role as Christians.

BETWEEN THE MATERIAL AND THE SPIRITUAL

PJ: Are there any theoretical and/or practical dissonances between Marxism and Christianity in your theory? If there are, how do you deal with them?

PM: Though some might argue that traditional nonreligious Marxism is not as equipped as theological traditions to engage fundamental questions pertaining to the hermeneutics of spirituality, there are numerous Marxist theorists who have written profoundly about issues of the spirit—here, I am thinking of Ernst Bloch, Walter Benjamin, and Erich Fromm, just to name a few. I think Marxism does address issues of the human spirit, but what interests me, in particular, is an engagement with a tradition that deals with a triune god. Of course, liberation theology comes in many forms: Chicano liberation theology, Latinx liberation theology, Native American liberation theology,

African American liberation theology. Therefore, I do not want to limit liberation theology to the political theology that comes out of Europe, or to the Latin American liberation theology that is primarily Catholic and pastoral.

I work as a Marxist materialist, but I believe there is a world beyond physicalism. That is a world of hope. Hope is conjugated in opposition to injustice and gestated in the struggle of humanity against inhumanity. Rubem Alves writes of hope as follows:

> Hope is the presentiment that the imagination is more real, and reality less real, than we had thought. It is the sensation that the last word does not belong to the brutality of facts with their oppression and repression. It is the suspicion that reality is far more complex than realism would have us believe, that the frontiers of the possible are not determined by the limits of the present, and that, miraculously and surprisingly, life is readying the creative event that will open the way to freedom and resurrection . . . (cited in Boff, 1987, p. 124)

Hope does not deliver us from suffering. But hope, I believe, can deliver us from the fear of suffering. It does this by giving us the courage to believe that we are not fated to live in misery, that light does shine through the cracks of the day-to-day sepulcher in which we find ourselves, in this cold and damp undercroft, in this darkness of inevitability.

PJ: An important aspect of Christian mysticism—and one of the main intersections between Christianity and Marxism—is the eschatological aspect of history. For Christians, this eschaton is the (arrival of) the Kingdom of God; for Marx and Engels, it is utopian socialism predicted as early as in the *Communist Manifesto* (1848). Can you elaborate this eschaton a bit deeper? What, for you, is the Kingdom of God?

PM: We have to honor the victims, speak to their lives of suffering in their theological reality. As Sobrino (2001) notes, the crucified peoples of this Earth must not be remembered as some historical add-ons to our Sunday sermons but as those who were victims of the anti-Kingdom. After all, the anti-Kingdom is the Kingdom of Capital, of Wall Street, and the world of value production (i.e., monetized wealth), of profit, of the exploitation and alienation of human labor, of private ownership of the means of production, of the market mechanism that forces capitalists (regardless of whether or not they are good people) to exploit workers, of the emergent transnational capital consolidated in a global capitalist historic bloc and the pillage zones of Latin America and of the deregulated, informalized, and de-unionized capital–labor relations and the worldwide subordination of labor.

But here I need to emphasize something Sobrino (2001) has discussed at length in his many important writings. While we focus on the divine in Christ, we have forgotten the Kingdom of God of which Christ speaks. So, when we identify as Catholics, why have we forgotten the primacy of creating the Kingdom of God and bringing it forth as Christ exhorted us to do? In my view, it is because our entire system operates as the anti-Kingdom. Christianity itself is undergirded by the imperatives of the anti-Kingdom in that it has attached itself to the imperatives of capitalism. To create the Kingdom of God means seeking the creation of a social universe outside of value production, or the production of profit for the rich. Creating the Kingdom of God means liberating the poor, and this means ending the brutal war against the poor unleashed by the deregulation of the market. It means challenging the anti-Kingdom that stands against immigrants seeking a better life, against migrant workers, against refugees, and the intergenerationally reproduced barrios of planet slum! We focus instead on eternal life, on gnostic mysteries, and distance ourselves from the Kingdom of God with reality TV and the hundreds of TV channels we have at our disposal. We confuse the drive to increase material wealth with the drive to produce value, or create endless profits that can be expanded indefinitely.

In our forays into the hinterlands of mysticism, we cannot forget that the Kingdom of God is, in Sobrino's (2001) terms, a "type of historical-social-collective reality" (p. 334) and not, as the old union song has it, a "pie in the sky when you die." The Kingdom of God is not some metaphor for an unearthly paradise, some ecclesiastical makeover of the Earth in terms of the divine Christ or such that the holy and apostolic Church becomes the prime sign or marker of the Kingdom. Clearly, for me, the Kingdom of God is not some place where well-heeled and aristocratic-looking souls lounge about in togas and golden wreaths. For me, the Kingdom of God is more likely found on the picket lines, in the temple cleared of the money-lenders, in a world where the rich no longer dominate, a world where death squads do not murder peasants with impunity, and where poor tenants do not confront racist landlords and developers do not build themselves towers in glorious homage to their wealth and power while others are forced to sleep under bridges.

THE SOCIALIST KINGDOM OF GOD

PJ: Can you link the Kingdom of God to Marx's prophecy of the future socialist society?

PM: I do see socialism as fitting in with the Kingdom of God announced by Jesus. Socialists in the past of sometimes made such a connection. Take the case of Helen Macfarlane. In 1850, Scottish governess

Helen Macfarlane wrote polemical treatises supporting the Chartist movement. She was the first person to translate Hegel's philosophical writings into English and the first person to translate *The Communist Manifesto* into English. The Chartists were the first working-class movement to fight the British establishment in order to secure rights for the working class. For a time, Macfarlane supported Chartist leader Julian Harney in rebuilding the movement from a socialist and international perspective and refused to moderate the movement to win over the radical liberals. She allied herself with Marx and Engels and took on literary giants such as Thomas Carlyle and Charles Dickens. She interpreted Hegel as a humanist pantheist and she defined pantheism in humanistic terms. Her work reflects the Hegelian pantheism of David Strauss, and her engagement with Marx and Engels helped her to radicalize Strauss's critical Hegelianism. For Hegel, the importance of the Gospels was their symbolic content. For David Strauss, what was important about the Gospels was their historicity—as myths that contained the messianic desires of the early Christian communities (Black, 2004).

Feuerbach believed that theological knowledge was subjective and that the final criterion for the truth was to be found in the senses. Here, the ego remains passive and determined by objective reality. For Marx, truth was found through historical praxis, through the negation of the negation. What is interesting about Macfarlane was her ability to merge the idea of socialism, left Hegelianism, and Marxism with the teachings of Jesus and, in doing so, spiritualize the struggle for social justice. In 1850 she wrote:

> We Socialist-democrats are the soldiers of a holy cause; we are the exponents of a sublime idea; we are the apostles of the sacred religion of universal humanity. We have sworn by the God who *"made of one blood all nations of the Earth"*, that we will not pause till we have finished the great work—begun by the Nazarean—of man's redemption from the social miseries which destroy body and soul. (quoted in Black, 2014, p. 22)

PJ: If the Kingdom of God is a "type of historical-social-collective reality" (Sobrino, 2001, p. 334), why should we not just stick to Marx and Engels's utopian socialism? Why, in this context, do we need a god?

PM: As a species on the verge of biological extinction, we have an ongoing obligation today to commit ourselves to build a network among the working class, the peasantry, and the urban cognitariats and precariats in order to break down the immutable hierarchies of power and privilege concomitant with the workings of capitalist society. In our struggle to achieve this, God will be revealed. As Miranda (1977) writes: "Only in a world of justice will God be" (p. 45). The revolution, therefore, depends not on man himself or woman herself or on the collectivity (which would be merely expanded egoism) but on the Other. Providing for each according to his or her needs presupposes caring for people simply because they exist and are God's children. The social relations of capitalist exploitation can force us to yield, but they cannot oblige us to obey. God is the moral imperative itself, the imperative to struggle against injustice and innocent suffering. God's presence in history, the true revelatory intervention of the God of the Bible in human history, occurs when we take up the struggle for social justice.

It is interesting to note that Marx and Engels entered an organization in 1872 that was founded by Wilhelm Weitling, the founder of German communism. Weitling's organization was based on a communism grounded entirely in the Gospels, as can be seen in his 1845 book, *The Gospel of a Poor Sinner* (Miranda, 1980). Marx was a great admirer of the Peasants' War organized and directed by Thomas Munzer in the 16th century. This was, in effect, the first anticapitalist revolution. Munzer argued that the Kingdom of God is a condition of society without class differences, without private property, and without state powers opposed to the members of society.

PJ: You often talk about the development of critical consciousness among students. What does this mean?

PM: A commitment to the oppressed leads to action in and on the world on behalf of the aggrieved of this world. Critical reflection on that action leads to what I refer to as protagonistic agency, a praxis of liberation. Protagonistic agency pulls out of the darkness of probability and potentiality the reality of social change, bringing it into the realm of actuality. Through a concentration of will—a type of hyper-intentionality—critical educators can submerge their ideas in their unconscious, where they can confront their fears and traumas surrounding the risks and reprisals that they may face in their struggle for social justice. Such a struggle in the Golgotha of their hearts can direct their ideas into the light of reflective awareness without overidentifying with their feelings because these ideas have now been conditioned to ratify a new reality rather than remaining trapped by the old. This is fundamentally a dialectical process, an embrace of absolute negativity, which leads to new beginnings.

ACKNOWLEDGMENTS

This text is based on previously published conversations between Peter McLaren and Petar Jandrić. We would like to thank the editors of *Policy Futures in Education* for their permission to republish parts of the following articles:

McLaren, P., & Jandrić, P. (2014). Critical revolutionary pedagogy is made by walking—in a world where many worlds coexist. *Policy Futures in Education, 12*(6), 805–831.

McLaren, P., & Jandrić, P. (2017). From liberation to salvation: Revolutionary critical pedagogy meets liberation theology. *Policy Futures in Education, 15*(5). doi:10.1177/1478210317695713

A small part of this text was also published in:

Jandrić, P. (2017). *Learning in the Age of Digital Reason*. Rotterdam, Netherlands: Sense.

REFERENCES

Black, D. (Ed.). (2014). *Helen Macfarlane: Red republican*. London, England: Uncant Publishers.

Boff, L. (1987). *Passion of Christ, passion of the world: The facts, their interpretation and their meaning yesterday and today* (R. R. Barr, Trans.). Maryknoll, NY: Orbis Books.

Freire, P. (1973). Education, liberation and the church. *Study Encounter, 38*, 9(1), 1–16.

Freire, P. (1995). Preface. In P. McLaren (Ed.), *Critical Pedagogy and Predatory Culture* (pp. ix–xi). London, England: Routledge.

Gutierrez, G. (1988). *Atheology of liberation: History, politics, and salvation* (C. Inda & J. Eagleson, Trans.). Maryknoll, NY: Orbis Books.

Jandrić, P. (2017). *Learning in the age of digital reason*. Rotterdam, Denmark: Sense.

Marx, K. (1981). *Capital, Vol. III*. New York, NY: Vintage.

Marx. K., & Engels, F. (1848). *The Communist Manifesto*. Retrieved from www.marxists.org/archive/marx/works/1848/communist-manifesto/index.htm

McLaren, P. (2014). *Life in schools: An introduction to critical pedagogy in the foundations of education* (6th ed.). Boulder, CO: Paradigm.

McLaren, P. (2015). *Pedagogy of insurrection: From resurrection to revolution*. New York, NY: Peter Lang.

McLaren, P., & Jandrić, P. (2014). Critical revolutionary pedagogy is made by walking—in a world where many worlds coexist. *Policy Futures in Education, 12*(6), 805–831.

McLaren, P., & Jandrić, P. (2017). From liberation to salvation: Revolutionary critical pedagogy meets liberation theology. *Policy Futures in Education, 5*(5). doi:10.1177/1478210317695713.

Miranda, J. P. (1977). *Being and the Messiah: The message of St. John*. Maryknoll, NY: Orbis Books.

Miranda, J. P. (1980). *Marx against the Marxists: The Christian humanism of Karl Marx* (John Drury, Trans.). Maryknoll, NY: Orbis Books.

Miranda, J. P. (2004). *Communism in the Bible* (R. R. Barr, Trans.). Eugene, OR: Wipf & Stock.

Sobrino, J. (2001). *Christ the liberator*. Maryknoll, NY: Orbis Books.

CHAPTER 6

Saul Alinsky
The Magnificent Rebel

Lisa Catherine Ehrich
QUEENSLAND UNIVERSITY OF TECHNOLOGY, AUSTRALIA

Fenwick W. English
UNIVERSITY OF NORTH CAROLINA, UNITED STATES

Saul Alinsky (1909–1972) was a Jewish American political activist and writer, considered the founding father of "community organizing." Community organizing can be understood as "a type of social action that brings powerless . . . people together in solidarity to defend and advance their interests and values" (Miller & Schutz, 2015, p. 2). Alinsky lived most of his life in Chicago. He was raised by Russian immigrant parents who were both Orthodox Jews. Alinsky had good grades in school and went on to complete an undergraduate degree in sociology at the University of Chicago. Following graduation, he won a fellowship to study criminology, where he spent many hours in the field gaining the trust and respect of members of teenage gangs and juvenile delinquents who became the focus of his investigations (Horwitt, 1989). He established himself as a community organizer when he worked in the Back of the Yards neighborhood in Chicago, an area that covered livestock yards and a meatpacking center. This neighborhood was home to many poor families of differing ethnicities. Each ethnic group had its own school and church parish, and there was great animosity among the different groups. The aim of Alinsky's work was to create unity among very divided community members so that they could work together to improve their social and economic circumstances. There, he established a neighborhood council with representatives from local parishes, unions, and businesses, and from across various ethnic groups. The motto of the Back of the Yards Neighborhood Council was "we the people will work out our own destiny" (www.bync.org/about-us/history). Under the guidance of Alinsky as community organizer, the Neighborhood Council used a variety of confrontational strategies against the stockyard owners and government in its quest for change (www.bync.org/about-us/history). Based on his success in bringing about stability and social welfare programs for the community, Alinsky replicated his methods of community organizing in other disadvantaged communities across the country. Described by one biographer as "a fascinating character whose life suggests . . . that one can be heroic without being saintly" (Horwitt, 1989, p. xvi), Alinsky used both unconventional and controversial tactics in his pursuit of democracy and social justice for the underdog.

DISCUSSION OF CONTEXT AND ACTIVITIES AS A LEADER

The context in which Alinsky developed his ideas and saw them through to fruition was a period of significant change and social upheaval in the United States. His working life spanned the 1930s (which saw the Great Depression that crippled much of the nation) through to the early 1970s. In those years, he honed his skills as a community organizer. He was shaped by (and in turn shaped) a number of the social movements sweeping through the United States, including the labor movement of the 1930s and the civil rights movement of the 1950s and 1960s, during which he worked in Black neighborhoods and with members of the Hispanic community (Horwitt, 1989).

An early influence on Alinsky's thinking and development as a community organizer was John L. Lewis, leader of the Congress of Industrial Organizations (CIO), which was a large federation of unions in the United States. In the 1930s, Lewis was hailed as an excellent strategist and hero who fought tirelessly for (and succeeded in) achieving better pay and conditions for both Black and White workers (von Hoffman, 2010). Alinsky adopted many of the strategies he saw Lewis using, including "humor, surprise and theatrics on a national stage" (von Hoffman, 2010, p. 90).

In his capacity as a community organizer working for the Industrial Areas Foundation, an organization he helped establish, Alinsky employed democratic processes to empower disadvantaged members of communities to find their voice and seize power. He achieved this by helping to set up grassroots organizations, or "People's organizations," in communities where local people could discuss their discontent about economic and/or social injustices affecting their lives. Alinsky and other community organizers provided training to the local leaders within these organizations and helped guide their actions and decisions. These actions often took the form of protest rallies and demonstrations that gave the locals a voice, resulting in heightened public awareness of the issue and, in some cases, wins or concessions for the local community (Perazzo, 2008).

Because of the great cultural, economic, and social diversity to be found within local communities, Alinsky "encountered and worked with Communists, socialists, capitalists, small 'd' democrats and religionists who didn't identify with these categories but thought of justice in theological and moral terms" (Miller, 2015, p. 17). Central to his belief was the idea that "once people get to know each other as human beings rather than as impersonal symbols representing diverse philosophies and organizations, then a new set of relationships composed of a genuine understanding and real sympathy will arise" (Alinsky, quoted in Horwitt, 1989, p. 106).

Over many years, Alinsky's two greatest allies were the Catholic Church and the unions (Miller & Schutz, 2015). He also worked with Protestant churches and, by the mid-1960s, the majority of Protestant churches across the country had made a commitment to fund community organizing projects because of his influence (Miller, 2015).

Alinsky's great strength lay in the way he was able to build upon existing formal and informal social relationships within a community (Perazzo, 2008). In his various projects as a community organizer—whether it was the Back of the Yards neighborhood; the Temporary Woodlawn Organization (TWO), which was the first African American organization he led; or the Rochester campaign, in which he secured more employment for African Americans by the Eastman Kodak Company (Horwitt, 1989; von Hoffman, 2010)—Alinsky cultivated relationships with local leaders. He saw those local leaders as having not only an inside understanding of their community but also as holding the respect and trust of their people, which was important currency in bringing about change.

According to Miller (2015), community organizers are involved in four main processes: listening, challenging (or agitating), thinking through, and training (Miller, 2015). In *Rules for Radicals*, Alinsky (1971/1989) refers to the importance of organizers *listening* carefully to the problems identified by community leaders, posing questions to them so that they can arrive at their own understandings and conclusions. This active listening approach and two-way form of communication was considered important for developing an agenda and identifying strategies and tactics.

Challenging is seen as a process whereby the community organizer stirs leaders by encouraging them to pour out their dissatisfaction and resentments (Alinsky, 1971/1989). As Alinsky (1971/1989) writes, "through action, persuasion, and communication the organizer makes it clear that organization will give them the power, the ability, the strength, the force to be able to do something about these particular problems" (p. 119).

Another important process of the community organizer is *thinking through*, and this involves persuading local leaders that something can be done (Miller, 2015). Often, this takes the form of the organizer telling a story to the community leaders that is relevant to the current situation, connects to their experience, and provides a way forward for action.

The fourth process is to provide *training* in order to build capacity within the members of the community (Miller, 2015). This is essential for the community to become self-supporting and sustaining. Training opportunities might include teaching leaders how to conduct effective meetings, how to undertake research on strategies and power structures, how to handle the media and negotiate with others, how to carry out campaigns, fundraising, how to reflect on actions, and how to create a story of the project (Miller, 2015). An important part of Alinsky's work was facilitating workshops on community organizing to leaders, mentoring associates who worked with him on various projects, and providing training for people wishing to become community organizers (Miller, 2015).

KEY LESSONS ONE CAN LEARN FROM ALINSKY

Alinsky identified practical lessons about community organizing in his two books, *Rules for Radicals* (1971/1989) and *Reveille for Radicals* (1946, 1969). Most of these rules or lessons are concerned with ways of empowering local communities to challenge their current circumstances and bring about change. Below is a range of lessons that can be gleaned from his work:

No two situations are ever the same—all situations are unique. Although Alinsky identified "rules" for community organizers and radicals to follow in their quest to bring about change, he saw these more as principles to guide or inform rather than step-by-step instructions. For Alinsky, every community and situation was different and the tactics employed depended greatly on the people concerned, the times, the context, and the situation (von Hoffman, 2010).

Conflict is necessary for change. According to Alinsky (1971/1989), "conflict is the essential core of a free and open society" and "new ideas arise from conflict" (pp. 62, 79). Not surprisingly, one of Alinsky's central tactics was conflict. He believed not only in the importance of questioning injustice but also in pursuing confrontational action such as protest marches, strikes, and sit-ins to bring about a reaction in an individual or group to ultimately create change. Alinsky (1971/1989) believed passionately in collective action drawing upon democratic processes to work within the system in order to change it.

The people who are most affected by a problem are best able to resolve it. Alinsky believed in putting control in the hands of the people who were most affected by the issues or problems (Seal, 2008), because they were the ones best placed to resolve the problem. Alinsky (1971/1989) said that people:

> cannot be denied the elementary right to participate fully in the solutions to their own problems. Self-respect arises only out of people who play an active role in solving their own crises and who are not helpless, passive, puppet-like recipients of private or public services. (p. 123)

Alinsky held that if change is to take place, then those people most affected by the change need to be united in their vision and their strategy for bringing about the change. He believed the role of the organizer was to "suggest, maneuver, and persuade the community" (Alinsky, 1971/1989, p. 91) to work together and in alliance with others to strengthen their platform and power base.

Organizing a community requires the leader to have a good understanding of members of that community, its values, and its beliefs. A key role of community organizers is spending time getting to know local leaders in the community, as well as their values, beliefs, and motivations (Alinsky, 1971/1989). For this to occur, building strong interpersonal relationships with local leaders is critical. For community organizing to succeed, local leaders need to have faith in the community organizer and his/her ability to "provide the opportunity for action, power, change" (Alinsky, 1971/1989, p. 99). The community organizer needs to have a sense of what the issues are (the details as well as the big picture) and be able to communicate those persuasively to local leaders. Alinsky (1971/1989) said, "as an organizer I start from where the world is . . . not as I would like it to be" (p. xix). Here, it could also be added, starting "where the people are at," an expression that comes from Myles Horton (2003, p. 261), a civil rights advocate and an associate of Alinsky's (von Hoffman, 2010) who trained community leaders and activists around the same time Alinsky was working.

Democracy is the best political means to attain values or ends. Alinsky (1971/1989) believed that democratic processes are the best way of achieving change because "the spirit of democracy is the idea of importance and worth in the individual, and faith in the kind of world where the individual can achieve as much of his [*sic*] potential as possible" (p. xxiv). He lamented that "there can be no darker or more devastating tragedy than the death of man's [*sic*] faith in himself and in his power to direct his future" (p. xxvi). Miller (2015) described Alinsky as a "radical democrat" because of his belief in the importance of a civil society built on a vision of equality, social justice, and participation.

Understand how power works and tactics of confrontation. Alinsky (1971/1989) saw power as a dynamic life force ubiquitous in everyday life that can be used to empower or disempower. He believed that power and confrontational strategies should not be feared but rather employed to bring about change. Over the years, community organizers have been known to use a variety of strategies, including strikes, protests, rallies, demonstrations, and passive resistance (Ehrich & English, 2012). Among Alinsky's (1971/1989) power tactics was the rule of ridicule, which he saw as a "most potent weapon" because it angers the enemy and usually causes a reaction (p. 128). Alinsky (1971/1989) was not afraid of using ridicule or other tactics that "revealed the hypocrisy and arrogance of the powerful" (Miller, 2015, p. 32) if it meant gaining the upper hand in a confrontation.

An example of ridicule Alinsky provides was during the Rochester campaign, the aim of which was to secure employment for more African Americans from the biggest employer in the city, Eastman Kodak Company. Alinsky (1971/1989) recalled the time when he was visiting Rochester and reporters asked him what he thought about the city. He replied, "It's a huge southern plantation transplanted north" (p. 137). When they questioned him why he was "meddling" in the black ghetto, he replied "Maybe I am innocent and uninformed of what has been happening here, but as far as I know the only thing Eastman Kodak has done on the race issue in America has been to introduce color film" (p. 137). When his remarks were printed in the newspapers, there was resentment, anger, and shock from Eastman Kodak at Alinsky's statement. By ridiculing the company, Alinsky achieved his goal of drawing attention to the injustice of its hiring policy.

Just as Alinsky drew upon a range of confrontation tactics, he also saw that there was a place for compromise, as it is an important tool and "always present in the pragmatics of operation" (Alinsky, 1971/1989, p. 59).

RELEVANCE FOR TODAY'S EDUCATIONAL LEADERS

Real educational change is about power; it is messy and emotional. Alinsky understood that real change, change that signals a profound alteration of the status quo, is never a tidy process. Furthermore, it is not a purely rational endeavor. Reason alone will not prevail. Meaningful change involves conflict, and that means it will be emotional and will involve the full array of human reactions. Change, therefore, involves the application of power and the use of power as leverage. Alinsky was fond of quoting Frederick Douglass (1857), who said, "Power concedes nothing without a demand. It never did and it never will." The educational leader who is considering using Saul Alinsky's model to promote social change must thoroughly understand that there is no polite way to promote change. Alinsky reminded his acolytes that "Change means movement; movement means friction; friction means heat; and heat means controversy" (quoted in Horwitt, 1989, p. 523). Although some educational leaders desire change, many are averse to controversy, believing that their job is all about running a "smooth ship" where conflict is not present and everyone is happy. Pursuing a real educational change agenda is not likely to produce a school of "happy campers." Change is also unlikely to please central office superiors who don't want to deal with protests, disenchanted parents, or a community embroiled in conflict. Only superficial change that actually changes little will not rock the boat. Alinsky (1971/1989) dourly observed that "To pander to those who have no stomach for straight language, and insist upon bland, non controversial sauces, is a waste of time" (p. 49).

Leading from the back of the room is an art form. Saul Alinsky practiced community organizing in which the main emphasis was discerning who the real leaders were in the community and empowering them to become the community's change agents. The real leaders were not necessarily members of the Rotary Club, businesspeople, or other professionals who did not actually live in the community. They were the so-called "informal leaders"— the ones without formal bureaucratic positions. They were people whom other community members listened to and whose opinions were sought out. Often, these leaders had no college degree and did not speak the King's English or observe other upper-class customs of appearance or dress. But most often they possessed a solid state of an idea for justice and fairness. They understood power and opportunity. An educational leader who is leading from the back of the room is looking for faculty and community leaders to become empowered and to become spokespersons for true educational reform that enhances social justice for all children.

There are no rules or checklists to guarantee success. Alinsky's approach to leadership was fluid and often impromptu. He let circumstances dictate his choice of strategies. He taught community organizers to understand that much of human behavior is irrational and that "life is a quest for uncertainty; that the only fact of life is uncertainty," that "all values are relative, in a world of political relativity" (Alinsky, 1971/1989, p. 79). Because of this stance, a community organizer "is unlikely to disintegrate into cynicism and disillusionment, for he [sic] does not depend on illusion" (p. 79).

Educational leaders who look to Saul Alinsky for a model will find a serious, dedicated person who took up the cause of procuring and securing power to change inequalities of those people who had little to no power in the larger social arena. Alinsky had a mission that was thoroughly rooted in democratic participation. He was not an ideologue but a pragmatist. He had a powerful sense of irony and a keen sense of humor. He understood organizational life and what made organizations tick. He forged ways to find leverage against those who squashed the little people. He mastered the means to perform "organizational jujitsu," in which one opponent uses the energy of the other against him/her. For educational leaders, learning that lesson means coming to understand how schools and educational bureaucracies work and how to find the internal pressure points to change their ways. Some have called it "creative insubordination"—it means one has to know how to break the rules when necessary (Morris, Crowson, Porter-Gehrie, & Hurwitz, 1984, p. 149).

REFERENCES

Alinsky, S. D. (1946). *Reveille for radicals.* Chicago, IL: University of Chicago Press.

Alnsky, S. D. (1969). *Reveille for radicals* (Updated ed.). New York, NY: Vintage Books.

Alinsky, S. D. (1989). *Rules for radicals: A pragmatic primer for realistic radicals.* New York, NY: Vintage Books. (Original work published 1971)

Douglass, F. (1857). West Indies emancipation. Speech delivered at Canandaigua, New York, August 3, 1857. Retrieved from genius.com/Frederick-douglass-west-india-emancipation-speech-annotated

Ehrich, L. C., & English, F. W. (2012). What can grassroots leadership teach us about school leadership? *Halduskultuur—Administrative Culture, 13*(2), 85–108.

Horton, M. (2003). *The Myles Horton reader: Education for social change.* Knoxville, TN: University of Tennessee Press.

Horwitt, S. D. (1989). *Let them call me rebel: Saul Alinsky—his life and legacy.* New York, NY: Alfred A. Knopf.

Miller, M. (2015). Saul Alinsky and his core concepts. In A. Schutz & M. Miller (Eds.), *People power: The community organizing tradition of Saul Alinsky* (pp. 17–42). Nashville, TN: Vanderbilt University Press.

Miller, M., & Schutz, A. (2015). Editor's introduction. In A. Schutz & M. Miller (Eds.), *People power: The community organizing tradition of Saul Alinsky* (pp. 1–16). Nashville, TN: Vanderbilt University Press.

Morris, V. C., Crowson, R. L., Porter-Gehrie, C., & Hurwitz, Jr. E. (1984). *Principles in action: The reality of managing schools.* Columbus, OH: Charles E. Merrill Publishing Company.

Perazzo, J. (2008). Saul Alinsky. Retrieved from the Discover the Networks website: discoverthenetworks.org/individualProfile.asp?indid=2314

Seal, M. (2008). Saul Alinsky, community organizing and rules for radicals. *The encyclopaedia of informal education.* Retrieved from www.infed.org/thinkers/alinsky.htm

von Hoffman, N. (2010). *Radical: A portrait of Saul Alinsky.* New York, NY: National Books.

CHAPTER 7

The Resurrection of Educational Leadership
Lessons from Rev. Dr. Samuel DeWitt Proctor

Atiya S. Strothers
UNIVERSITY OF PENNSYLVANIA, UNITED STATES

Catherine A. Lugg
RUTGERS UNIVERSITY, UNITED STATES

Rev. Dr. Samuel DeWitt Proctor (1921–1997) was born and raised in Norfolk, Virginia. His parents were Velma Hughes and Herbert Proctor. Proctor's grandparents on both sides had received a college education, which was uncommon for Blacks at the time. This demonstrated the importance of education to the Proctor family. As a child, Proctor attended the family church, founded by his great-grandfather Zechariah Hughes. Proctor's Christian faith and religion were central to his upbringing and understanding of the world about him. Growing up during segregation, the hope for racial justice was central to Proctor's (1995) being. This hope was anchored in humanity and morality—the belief that every person was valuable in the eyes of God and should be treated with fairness and justice.

Proctor spent one year at Virginia State University and one year at the Norfolk Navy Yard. He would go on to complete his studies at Virginia Union University (VUU), receiving a bachelor's degree in 1942. As a college student, he was baptized and married his sweetheart, Bessie Tate. He then received a second bachelor's degree in divinity from Crozer Theological Seminary in 1945 and, following graduation, he accepted the call as pastor of Pond Street Baptist Church in Providence, Rhode Island, along with a fellowship to study ethics at Yale. After a short time commuting and splitting his responsibilities, Proctor enrolled at Boston University and received a PhD in theology in 1950. Later, Proctor served as president of VUU and North Carolina A&T University (A&T). He had strong ties to the Kennedy and Johnson administrations and served as an advisor to the federal Office of Economic Opportunity and as the associate director of the Peace Corps in Nigeria (Bond, 2013).

After serving as a leader in religion, politics, and education, Proctor came to Rutgers University in 1969 in an effort to advance racial justice and enhance the presence and experience of African American students. He served as the Martin Luther King Jr. chair in education. During his time at Rutgers, Proctor also became the pastor of the historic Abyssinian Baptist Church in New York City (Proctor, 1995). As the endowed chair at Rutgers, Proctor would mentor and teach a number of students pursuing a career in education. His classes were often filled to capacity with standing room only. Proctor was a highly respected pastor, educator, and advocate who had a way of imparting wisdom through stories. During his career, he was a mentor to Dr. Martin Luther King Jr., Jesse Jackson, Jeremiah Wright, and a host of other prominent religious, educational, and political leaders (Bond, 2013; Proctor, 1995). Rev. Dr. Samuel DeWitt Proctor received more than 40 honorary degrees and died in Mount Vernon, Iowa, while delivering a speech at Cornell College. The Samuel DeWitt Proctor School of Theology at VUU and an endowed chair called the Samuel DeWitt Proctor Chair in Education at Rutgers University were established to honor his career and legacy.

DISCUSSION OF CONTEXT AND ACTIVITIES AS A LEADER

In the United States, the notion of leadership is important and yet highly contested. As we embark upon the administration of a new president, one cannot help but ask: What makes someone a leader? Is leadership attached to charisma and influence? Is it based upon experience or a collection of followers? We argue here that Proctor connected leadership to service, to the service of bettering and strengthening others in building a more just and ethical world. However, how does one measure such a leader? "And he shall be like a tree planted by the rivers of water, that bringeth forth his fruit in his season; his leaf also shall not wither; and whatsoever he doeth shall prosper" (Psalms 1:3). The measure of such a leader is seen in his or her legacy and good works—both of which remain fruitful for Proctor.

The fruit of Proctor's labor is seen in those who continue to carry his legacy of service. Although he held various leadership roles across many institutions with differing institutional missions, we cannot fully understand him as a leader without understanding the context in which he led. In 1955, Proctor was appointed as the fifth president of VUU at the tender age of 33. This was a fairly young age for one to be responsible for leading such an important and historic institution. Virginia Union, being a historically Black college (HBCU), was central to Black life in Richmond (Proctor, 1995). It was a hub of Black scholarship and intelligentsia. Gaining national attention, the Montgomery Bus Boycott was under way at this time as well, a formative event in the civil rights movement. While leading VUU, Proctor invited his mentee, Dr. Martin Luther King Jr., to campus to discuss civil rights and the boycott. At the same time, Dr. King requested that Proctor deliver the so-called Spring Lecture Series at his church in Montgomery, Alabama (Asante, 2012). At a time when the civil rights movement was starting to reach its peak and society was in a state of unrest, President Eisenhower invited Proctor and other Black leaders to the White House to discuss civil rights and suggested that they relent in their pursuit of racial justice. The leaders rejected this notion.

Another presidential meeting Proctor attended happened with John F. Kennedy (prior to his election) and 40 United Negro College Fund presidents in 1959. This meeting reflects the influence and power that HBCU presidents had during this time. HBCUs served as a hub for Black scholarship, advancement, and community organizing, and the leaders of such institutions had a certain prestige, honor, and presence about them. As the second Black president of one of the most revered HBCUs, Proctor was still met with White supremacy, as a cross was burned on campus by the Ku Klux Klan and civil unrest continued to grow in the South and other places in the country.

After 5 years of leadership at VUU, Proctor became the president of North Carolina A&T University (A&T) in 1960. The context in which he assumed this post is critically important. He went to A&T during the height of the Greensboro sit-ins, a nonviolent protest by four A&T students occupying the all-White lunch counter at a Woolworth's department store, requesting to be served. It ended in the policy of racial segregation being removed. Proctor's approach to these sit-ins and fulfilling the civil rights agenda was one of strategy and less direct confrontation. Because of this, some criticized him for not being as vocal on the events unfolding in the public. Instead, he focused more on the behind-the-scenes work, such as counseling and advising his students and mentees, including Martin Luther King Jr., Jesse Jackson, and a host of others who were involved. As A&T's president, he also ensured that students on the Freedom Ride buses were fed and had a place to sleep. Proctor also made himself available to speak and organize the masses for the greater good. He may not have been on the front line, but he was concerned about the individual. He stated, "While earthshaking events raged around us, I tried not to lose sight of the personal needs of individual boys and girls. Like my mother I had a habit of poking into the lives of the young people, a kind of pastoral spillover into my academic role" (Proctor, 1995, p. 92). Proctor was not a confrontational type of leader. In fact, he was known by many as a "quiet activist," which was evident during his time at A&T (Pace, 1997).

While serving as president of A&T, Proctor received an offer to serve as associate director of the Peace Corps in Africa. He had built a meaningful relationship with Sargent Shriver, an American politician, founder of Job Corps, and driving force behind the Peace Corps. Dr. Proctor had close ties with President Kennedy as well. Proctor took a 1-year leave of absence from A&T in 1962 to lead and direct the Peace Corps in Africa. After being at A&T for just a few years, Proctor resigned in 1964 and began government work as Shriver's special assistant in the Office of Economic Opportunity. During the years of 1967–1969, Proctor served in various positions, including as a speechwriter for Vice President Humphrey and as a dean at the University of Wisconsin. In 1969, he and his family (his wife and their four sons) settled in New Jersey as Proctor assumed a leadership role at Rutgers University as the Martin Luther King chair in education. He then became pastor of the historic Abyssinian Baptist Church in Harlem, New York, in 1972. While at Abyssinian, he helped lead and facilitate economic and housing development for the community. Under his leadership (1969–1984), Rutgers saw more than 100 Black students graduate with doctoral degrees (Pace, 1997). With Proctor's guidance and the work exhibited by his students, this is truly the fruit of his labor.

From oral interviews and archival research, it is clear that Proctor was a no-nonsense type of leader. He set high expectations for those around him and firmly believed in the moral good of humanity. At the core of his leadership was his faith and religion. Religion was rooted in his family from past generations, and his sense of justice and equality was possibly linked to one of the many lessons he learned from his grandmother. As Proctor (1995) wrote, "God created all people; any inequalities among us were due to unequal opportunity" (p. 2). His belief in Christ allowed for his belief in justice. He possessed an innate ability to share wisdom through the method of storytelling or moral parables, a technique rooted in Christianity, particularly the Black church. Proctor was able to draw connections, whether he was telling a personal story or one from the Bible. Proctor was the type of leader who commanded attention with just a few words, and his humor made people feel comfortable and at ease. Most important was his service to people and the calmness he carried with him. As some have said, "There was just a presence about him" (Pace, 1997). At Proctor's funeral, the representative from Rutgers stated that Proctor was a gifted speaker, but he was also a gifted "doer" (Pace, 1997).

LIST OF THE KEY LESSONS READERS CAN LEARN FROM THE LEADER

In Proctor's last book (1995), he posed the question: "Can these bones live again?" This question is based in a biblical framing from the prophet Ezekiel that tells the story of the prophecy of dry bones in the valley revealed to Ezekiel. As the prophet, it was his responsibility to revitalize these dry bones, save them from captivity, and allow restoration to happen. Proctor recontextualized this question and posed it to African American leaders in all sectors, including education. It was asked in hope and faith, providing the right choices were made to allow the "bones to live again." In his final text, Proctor provided an answer—not *the* answer—for advancing the Black community and allowing God to breathe life into these dry bones. Here, we offer the five-point plan he developed, to be "blended together" (Proctor, 1995), as lessons to be learned for advancing education and the Black community.

The first point is individual involvement. Proctor highlights the importance of one-on-one work and the uplifting of children, particularly in the African American community. The little things are often the ones we take for granted, but they are also the things that add up. He calls for people from all occupations and trades to reach out and pour something positive into the next generation.

The second point is family rejuvenation. Family structure is critical; it is "rehearsal for life" (Proctor, 1995, p. 205). This is where Proctor identifies certain morals and values that are instilled through the nucleus of family. Characteristics such as trust, forgiveness, self-esteem, vulnerability, mutual responsibility, and accountability are vital for families. Proctor calls for the involvement of both parents to provide for their family, beyond government assistance, to break the cycle of poverty and offer a haven for rejuvenation. Proctor says reform takes compassion without condemnation.

The third point is specialized teacher training for public schools. To support this effort, Blacks need to have a thirst for knowledge and the desire to learn, which is connected to the quality and commitment of teachers. In building the pipeline of teachers, Proctor called for recruiting people from the community without college degrees and providing them with access to education and teacher certification. The program he put in place at Rutgers produced 120 new teachers over a span of 3 years to serve in the communities from which they came. With the rise of charter schools and private education today, it is important to prevent the destruction of public schools. Public education needs to invest in specialized training for teachers, along with pay incentives, longer school terms, and added personnel for discipline, which should be separate from teaching responsibilities.

The fourth point is committed church leadership. Proctor believed that religion and faith drive purpose, direction, and destiny. He believed that the Black church needed an intervention. On a national level, it must rid itself of ornamental value and have real meaning with one voice. Church leadership should rid itself of "old-boy connections" that result in stagnant leadership and join together across all denominations to provide appropriate resources for the community and bring about national change.

The final point is a national program to reclaim failing and lost youth. This is found in building and restructuring the economy so that the conditions of the poor change. Given the seemingly intractable issues involved with generational poverty, Proctor proposed a National Youth Academy modeled after the Peace Corps to serve children who need a home, surrogate parents, and an education. The nation's top educators would develop a 6-year curriculum starting at the 7th grade for all children. However, creating this type of program would require government support and exceptional leadership.

The above lessons are offered in hopes that each individual will find his or her place in one of the five efforts listed. We are not all connected to each one, but we have the ability to push forward where we have the opportunity and responsibility to do so.

EXPLANATION OF HOW THIS LEADER'S LESSONS ARE RELEVANT FOR TODAY'S EDUCATIONAL LEADERS

As we embark with a new presidential administration, many have expressed a sense of fear and uncertainty about the future. Those persons on the margins are deeply concerned about their own lives and, again, the notion of leadership is in question. This chapter has explored a historical figure, but we are facing a certain level of civil unrest, even today. Having long battled racial injustice and ignorance, we can learn how to advance education from Proctor; even though the contexts may be packaged differently, they are still related.

If we modeled education today after Proctor's approach, one practice that would be emphasized is the concept of what we now call mentoring. Mentioned earlier as one-on-one interactions and individual involvement, mentoring was a critical part of Proctor's leadership. Applying this to education today would provide students with an additional resource to help them succeed. Due to his various leadership roles in politics and religion, Proctor's mentoring required significant personal sacrifice and involved communication, accessibility, advocacy, and expectation. He was the pastor of a 15,000-member church in Harlem during his tenure at Rutgers and still made time for his students. It was an investment he was very proud of because he knew the return would be invaluable. This type of mentoring or highly personal attention is necessary in schools, the community, church, and higher education. It is a communal approach to achievement and the development of the next generation of leaders.

Another practice that would be emphasized is the development of moral character of individuals. Proctor would focus on ethics and humanity for all stakeholders involved: parents, teachers, students, and administrators. Creating just and noble citizens was a priority for Proctor. What good is individual advancement if you are not a person of good character? Mandating ethics in high school and college would help create a culture of service to all mankind.

Finally, educational leaders would take a communal approach in leadership practice. Students do not live only in the classroom. There are many moving parts that shape their academic success, things such as family, community, belief systems, and so forth. A communal approach would incorporate the community into the educational process. It would provide community leaders with a role in the school. It would also focus on the family and providing resources to help rejuvenate families. This approach will demonstrate a deeper investment, proving to the students that they are cared for and that much is expected of them, regardless of where and how they begin.

In a speech (Proctor, 2011), Proctor discussed the "scratch line" where everyone starts the race of life. Some of us inherit benefits that allow us to start life above the scratch line—benefits such as a productive family life, art, culture, education, faith, and so on. Others inherit deficits, such as absent parents, alcoholism and drug abuse, and a lack of values or moral grounding, that force them to start life beneath the scratch line. These things make a difference in how children run the race of life and are very telling of their future.

Although Proctor served and led just over 30 years ago, we face a context today in which educational leaders must concern themselves with a new approach to leadership for the sake of our children, our society, and all of humanity.

> If we want these bones to live again, those of us who have inherited benefits that we did not earn or deserve need to turn around and help those who inherited deficits that they did not earn or deserve, and help them to rise up to the scratch line—where we are. So that they may earn and enjoy all of the benefits that we so take for granted. Can these bones live again, O Lord? Thou knowest. These bones can live. (Proctor, 2011)

REFERENCES

Asante, M. K. (2012). *The African American people: A global history*. New York, NY: Routledge.

Bond, A. (2013) *The imposing preacher: Samuel DeWitt Proctor and Black public faith*. Minneapolis, MN: Fortress Press.

Pace, E. (1997, May 26). Samuel Proctor, 75, dies. *New York Times*. Retrieved from www.nytimes.com/1997/05/26/us/samuel-proctor-75-dies-led-abyssinian-baptist-church.html

Proctor, S. D. (1995). *The substance of things hoped for: A memoir of African-American faith*. New York, NY: G. P. Putnam's Sons.

Proctor, S. D. (2011, Jan. 21). *"The Scratch Line" Rev. Dr. Samuel Dewitt Proctor--SDPC* [video]. .Retrieved from www.youtube.com/watch?v=X1la3TAxu8w_

CHAPTER 8

José Rizal

Leadership Lessons from
the National Hero of the Philippines

Jeffrey S. Brooks
MONASH UNIVERSITY, AUSTRALIA

Anthony H. Normore
CALIFORNIA STATE UNIVERSITY, DOMINGUEZ HILLS, UNITED STATES

José Rizal, the national hero of the Philippines, was born José Protasio Rizal Mercado y Alonso Realonda on June 19, 1861, in Calamba, a small town in the Laguna Province. As a young boy, he showed special academic promise and moved to Manila for additional schooling, eventually completing his secondary schooling at Ateneo de Municipal Manila. He continued his studies at the university level, pursuing a career in law at Santo Tomas University in Manila. However, Rizal's talent and wanderlust brought him to study in Spain, France, and eventually Germany, where he earned acclaim in the medical field with a specialization in ophthalmology (Palma, 1949; Rizal, Blumentritt, & Alzona, 1962).

However, although Rizal was obviously gifted with a scientific mind, he was also endowed with an artist's soul. He excelled as a poet, sculptor, painter, and as a novelist, where he made his greatest impact. While completing his studies in Europe, he wrote two great novels, *Noli Me Tangere* (1886/2006) and *El Filibusterismo* (1891/2009), that inspired reformists and revolutionaries in the Philippines to speak out and then rise up against the Spanish. In addition to these major works, Rizal also penned a series of important articles in the Spanish newspaper *El Solidaridad* that raised consciousness about unjust Spanish rule and the value of Filipino culture, identity, and intellect. However, Rizal was more than a distant social critic. In 1892, he returned to the Philippines, knowing that he would be a high-profile target for the Spanish government. With that risk in mind, he returned home to take part in efforts to reform the colonial system, with a long-term goal of a return to sovereignty for the Filipino people. In 1896, he was arrested, tried, and executed (Constantino, 1975; Palma, 1949). To this day, Rizal stands alone as the greatest and most revered symbol of the potential and achievement of Filipinos. The lessons of leadership we can learn from his erudite and courageous life stand the test of time.

JOSÉ RIZAL: HIS CONTEXT AND LEADERSHIP ACTIVITIES

Rizal's main contributions as a leader were through his insightful and inspirational writing and, to a lesser extent, his role as a reformist and a symbol of hope. In order to better understand the importance of his work, it is important to understand the context into which he was born and raised. Rizal lived during a time of Spanish colonization that lasted from 1521 to 1898. Spanish rule was heavy-handed, and stretched into every aspect of Philippine life, from economics to politics, to culture and religion (Anderson, 1988; Kramer, 2006). Education under the Spanish brought a certain uniformity and organization to the country, but as Brooks and Sutherland (2014) argued:

> Spanish colonial schools, 1565–1898, were designed to convert and indoctrinate national Filipinos, and provide basic education (Schwartz, 1971). The Spanish colonial education did little in and of itself to provide an actual educational value to Filipinos, but it introduced policy and leadership influence that led to the inception of secular private education, a formal curriculum, and a free public education (Fox, 1965). The progression of Spanish educational development would later lead to the establishment of universities, colleges, and vocational schools (Fox, 1965; Schwartz, 1971). (p. 342)

Given the oppression embedded within government education, Rizal's own educational path—which took him from a small town in the Philippines to study with some of Europe's leading minds—is itself an act of inspiration and revolution (Abinales & Amoroso, 2005; Counts, 1925). Considered as a whole, his scientific achievements, artistic acumen, and keen aptitude for social critique made him the perfect leader to inspire a nation, and he did so mainly via his two novels and a series of articles in a Spanish newspaper.

Noli Me Tangere

Rizal's novel *Noli Me Tangere* chronicles the story of Crisostomo Ibarra, who (like Rizal) returns to the Philippines after years of study abroad. Ibarra sees the Spanish colonizers differently from the way he did when he left. Where once he thought the leaders were benign or even benevolent, he comes to see them as inequitable and cruel oppressors who deny Filipinos their culture, traditions, language, religion, identity, and intellectual potential. The book shows how colonization has taken pride away from Filipinos and instilled in them a shame and powerlessness that keeps them from developing themselves academically and spiritually (Coates, 1968).

In the book, Ibarra has both subtle exchanges and overt confrontations with various archetypal characters that represent and illustrate the institutionalized oppression and hegemony that keeps Filipinos in their place at the bottom of the social order. This includes interactions with cruel Franciscan friars, corrupt government officials, and even Filipinos who have adopted their oppressors' mannerisms and values as a way to curry favor with the powerful Spaniards. Through his adventures, Ibarra cuts a heroic and principled figure, one who is willing to stand up for what is right. In the end, he pays for his insolence by losing nearly everything he has fought for and feigning his own death. The novel is a brilliant social commentary that manages, at once, to communicate a complex analysis of social inequity, microaggressions, and institutional violence while also reaching great heights in terms of literary quality. The tone is somewhat hopeful, despite everything Ibarra suffers.

Of particular interest to those interested in leadership, and particularly those interested in school leadership, is the chapter "Adventures of a Schoolmaster." In this chapter, Rizal shifts his point of view from that of Ibarra and instead takes the perspective of a schoolmaster in a small village. This serves to provide an exemplar for the ways that Franciscan friars and government agents (both Spanish and Filipino) work together to suppress learning and take authority and dignity away from Filipino elders. In one passage, the schoolmaster laments:

> Do you want to know the stumbling blocks to teaching? Well, in our current situation, without powerful assistance, teaching will never amount to anything, in the first place because childhood itself contains neither incentive nor stimulation, and in the second place, when they do exist, just finding the means to live and other similar concerns kills them. (Rizal, 1886/2006, p. 108)

He goes on to show how Filipino elders are denigrated, thereby eroding traditional values related to respect and reverence that are a feature of traditional Filipino society:

> A child does not respect a schoolmaster when he has seen him mistreated, his prerogatives, given no value. For a schoolmaster to be heard and his authority not called into question, he needs prestige, a good name, moral force, a certain freedom. (Rizal, 1886/2006, p. 109)

Yet Rizal doesn't stop with naming the problem; he also suggests a solution. Later in the chapter, the schoolmaster takes it upon himself to learn Spanish, to educate himself through reading and analysis, and to understand the things around him on a deeper level. This is an excellent example of Rizal's use of storytelling as a way to awaken in the reader a revolutionary imagination, and illustrates how a novel can raise awareness in an oppressed people who cannot see a path out of their situation.

El Filibusterismo

El Filibusterismo was the sequel to *Noli Me Tangere*. It is a decidedly darker novel that suggests revolution and revolt as a way of liberating the Philippines from its Spanish colonizers. The plot centers around Ibarra, who returns (after faking his death in Rizal's previous book) as a violent subversive bent on undermining Spanish rule through force and guerrilla tactics. At the climax, Ibarra attempts to murder many high-ranking Spaniards attending a party, but is foiled by one of his own comrades, whose love for a woman at the party overrides his love for country and revolution. This betrayal leads to Ibarra being wounded and ultimately dying after losing his certainty about whether what he was doing was really selfless liberation or petty revenge.

Taken as a whole, Rizal's books might be seen as a meditation on the various paths that one might take to change an oppressive system. On the one hand, *Noli* puts faith in the goodness of man and in the idea that the truth will eventually carry the day. *Filibusterismo*, on the other hand, assumes the worst and sees only violent revolution as a means to change. In the end, Rizal leaves it to the reader to decide which course of action is best, although he does not allow that accepting the status quo is a viable option—Filipinos should either work to reform the system through peaceful means or take back their country by force (Hau, 2000).

Rizal the Revolutionary, Peacemaker, and Martyr

In addition to writing, Rizal felt a strong need to act as well as inspire. In 1892, he returned to the Philippines knowing that he would likely be imprisoned or killed. Indeed, he was labeled an enemy of the state and exiled to an island off of the southern island of Mindanao. Interestingly, his response to this was to become increasingly an advocate for peaceful social change and to speak out against violence. Nevertheless, when a revolution did break out, authorities used it as an opportunity to accuse Rizal of inciting resistance. Though he spoke out for peace and denounced the revolution, Rizal was nonetheless executed in 1896. The Philippines was liberated from Spanish colonization 2 years later when Americans invaded Manila as part of the Spanish-American War. Sadly, one colonizer was replaced with another—the United States and then Japan colonized the country until the Philippines finally earned independence in 1946 (Constantino, 1970).

LEADERSHIP LESSONS FROM JOSÉ RIZAL

Although there are many lessons leaders might take from José Rizal's writings and life, we focus here on four: public intellectualism, visible critique, leadership for social justice, and the possibility of both soft and hard revolution.

Public Intellectualism. José Rizal is perhaps one of the greatest exemplars of public intellectualism the world has seen. He combined insightful social analysis with artistic expression in a manner that stirred a nation to rise up against oppression, instilled in people a great sense of national identity, and illustrated the power of standing up for one's principles. Sandlin, O'Malley, and Burdick (2011) offer a useful and nuanced way of thinking about public intellectualism as something that is at once individual and communitarian. That is, Rizal practiced one form of public intellectualism in writing books that offered a diagnosis and explored treatments that might prove useful in thinking about forms of resistance against the oppressive Spanish colonialism. However, it is not altogether accurate to suggest that intellectuals stand alone with their critique—they are simultaneously one with those with whom they communicate. Herein may lie the key to public intellectuals who actually influence others to act: They are ready to act themselves, because they are one with their audience. In this sense, though Rizal's writing was a catalyst for change, it is likely that it was equally important and powerful that he stood on principle and with his audience, taking part in the change, even though it cost him his life.

Visible Critique. Another key lesson from Rizal is that he not only conducted his own social, cultural, and political analysis, but he sought and found the correct audience for his work and offered his thoughts in an engaging manner. It is important that he wrote *Noli Me Tangere* and *El Filibusterismo* as novels, because that would allow people to connect to an issue that had cognitive and affective dimensions through a medium suited to convey messages about both. Rizal was perfectly capable of writing his work as technical, philosophical, and political treatise, but he chose to write novels instead of textbooks and he chose to publish his work in newspapers instead of academic journals. This made his ideas not only accessible but engaging to both reason and the imagination (Giroux, 2004).

Leadership for Social Justice. The purpose of Rizal's work was liberation—the telling of truths to power and teaching a beaten-down people that they not only deserved better treatment, but were capable of excellence and should take a great deal of pride in their traditions and achievements. José Rizal was a leader for social justice in that he put the needs and freedom of others ahead of his own and recognized that anti-oppression education would ultimately set free a colonized and seemingly powerless people.

Leadership for social justice demands a deep engagement across sectors and organizations—it is an approach to leadership that embraces science, art, community, and relationships, and takes on barriers to equality and equity wherever they are found (Brooks, Jean-Marie, Normore, & Hodgins, 2007; Jean-Marie, Normore, & Brooks, 2009).

Soft Revolutions and Hard Revolutions. *Noli Me Tangere* and *El Filibusterismo* embody Postman and Weingartner's (1971) notions of soft and hard revolutions. Soft revolution is what Rizal espoused in *Noli Me Tangere*, an approach to changing the system by working on it from within. Soft revolutionaries identify leverage points in the system and then use these to shift the system itself. For example, in *Noli*, Ibarra sought to change society by engaging the country's elite and by working with government officials and friars. To a certain extent, he saw them as partners and believed that he could convince them to change the system for the good of the people. By the time we meet Ibarra in *El Filibusterismo*, he is a hard revolutionary, ready to reject the system and blow it up from the outside. Rizal understood that change likely happens by exploring both of these possibilities and plotting a course of action that incorporates both forms of revolutions. Put differently, there is a time to vote and a time to picket, a time to go through the proper channels and a time to go around them.

JOSÉ RIZAL AND CONTEMPORARY SCHOOL LEADERSHIP: WHAT CAN TODAY'S PRINCIPALS LEARN FROM THE NATIONAL HERO OF THE PHILIPPINES?

Reflecting on José Rizal's leadership legacy is daunting, but we have identified five principles that might be helpful for principals to consider.

1. Principals Must Identify and Engage Oppression. Schools are data rich, which gives leaders the opportunity to identify and engage inequity and inequality in ways they never have before. For example, it is unacceptable for school leaders to perpetuate inequitable discipline referrals for African American boys when they see the disproportionate numbers in their school. Upon seeing such inequity, school leaders should engage it and seek to identify possible causes and alternate courses of action, for themselves and others. Remember that Rizal did not offer a single solution but explored alternatives once he saw that there was a problem (Scheurich & Skrla, 2003).

2. Principals Are Public Intellectuals. Given their agency and unique position in schools, principals have a strong influence on the intellectual nature of their own work and the school's work (Merchant & Shoho, 2006). Do principals keep up with the latest research and local practices? Do they engage others in what they find? Do they facilitate the intellectual development and engagement of others while keeping a focus on equity, equality, excellence, and justice?

3. Leadership Is Both Art and Science. Rizal was both scientist and artist, and school leaders would do well to embrace both aspects in their work. The artistic side might be thought of as relational and communicative. Whether this means communicating emotion, information, or expectations, it is important to consider that people need to be invited into the work of education in engaging ways. Principals would do well to (re)think the ways that they communicate with people individually and collectively (Brooks & Normore, 2010). The science, of course, comes in the form of generating and using multiple forms of evidence to inform practice in a structured and measured manner.

4. Talk the Talk and Walk the Walk. Rizal was ready to go to the Philippines and stand shoulder to shoulder with the revolutionaries he inspired, no matter the cost. This is a reminder to school leaders that what they say is less important than what they do—action must follow understanding and intent (Normore, 2004).

5. Put Others Before Yourself. Rizal's life and work remind us to be selfless leaders. Properly practiced, leadership is essentially an other-oriented endeavor. School leadership is meant to facilitate learning by directly influencing the professional work of teachers and staff and by indirectly influencing the learning of students. This is a call for school leaders to make sure they are putting others at the forefront of their motivation, conversations, and day-to-day work (Normore & Brooks, 2016). If school leaders are not working to improve themselves for the express reason of leading others and organizations toward heights they never knew they could reach, what is the point?

REFERENCES

Abinales, P. N., & Amoroso, D. J. (2005). *State and society in the Philippines.* Lanham, MD: Rowman & Littlefield.

Anderson, B. (1988). Cacique democracy and the Philippines: Origins and dreams. *New Left Review, 169,* 3.

Brooks, J. S., & Normore, A. H. (2010). Educational leadership and globalization: Toward a glocal perspective. *Educational Policy, 24*(1), 52–82.

Brooks, J. S., Jean-Marie, G., Normore, A. H., & Hodgins, D. W. (2007). Distributed leadership for social justice: Influence and equity in an urban high school. *Journal of School Leadership 17*(4), 378–408.

Brooks, J. S., & Sutherland, I. E. (2014). Educational leadership in the Philippines: Principals' perspectives on problems and possibilities for change. *Planning & Changing, 45*(3/4), 339–355.

Coates, A. (1968). *Rizal, Philippine nationalist and martyr*. Manila, Philippines: Malaya Books.
Constantino, R. (1970). *Dissent and counter-consciousness*. Manila, Philippines: Malaya Books.
Constantino, R. (1975). *The Philippines: A past revisited (Vol. I)*. Manila, Philippines: Malaya Books.
Counts, G. S. (1925). Education in the Philippines. *The Elementary School Journal, 26*(2), 94–106.
Fox, H. F. (1965). Primary education in the Philippines: 1565–1863. *Philippine Studies, 13*(2), 207–231.
Giroux, H. A. (2004). Cultural studies, public pedagogy, and the responsibility of intellectuals. *Communication and Critical/Cultural Studies, 1*(1), 59–79.
Hau, C. S. (2000). *Necessary fictions: Philippine literature and the nation, 1946–1980*. Manila, Philippines: Ateneo University Press.
Jean-Marie, G., Normore, A. H., & Brooks, J. S. (2009). Leadership for social justice: Preparing 21st century school leaders for a new social order. *Journal of Research on Leadership in Education, 4*(1), 1–31.
Kramer, P. A. (2006). *The blood of government: Race, empire, the United States, and the Philippines*. Chapel Hill, NC: University of North Carolina Press.
Merchant, B. M., & Shoho, A. R. (2006). Bridge people: Civic and educational leaders for social justice. In Catherine Marshall & Maricela Oliva (Eds.), *Leadership for social justice: Making revolutions in education* (pp. 85–109). Boston, MA: Pearson Education.
Normore, A. H. (2004). Ethics and values in leadership preparation programs: Finding the North Star in the dust storm. *University Council for Educational Administration (UCEA), Journal of Values and Ethics in Educational Administration, 2*(2), 1–7.
Normore, A. H., & Brooks, J. S. (Eds.) (2016). *The dark side of leadership: Identifying and overcoming unethical practice in organizations*. Bingley, UK: Emerald Group Publishing Limited.
Palma, R. (1949). *The pride of the Malay race: A biography of Jose Rizal*. New York, NY: Prentice Hall.
Postman, N., & Weingartner, C. (1971). *The soft revolution*. New York, NY: Dell.
Rizal, J. (2006). *Noli me tangere*. (H. Augenbraum, Trans.). New York, NY: Penguin. (Original work published in 1886)
Rizal, J. (2009). *El filibusterismo*. (L. M. Guerrero, Trans.). New York, NY: Longman. (Original work published in 1891)
Rizal, J., Blumentritt, F., & Alzona, E. (1962). *Historical events of the Philippine Islands*. Manila, Philippines: José Rizal National Centennial Commission.
Sandlin, J. A., O'Malley, M. P., & Burdick, J. (2011). Mapping the complexity of public pedagogy scholarship 1894–2010. *Review of Educational Research, 81*(3), 338–375.
Scheurich, J. J., & Skrla, L. (2003). *Leadership for equity and excellence: Creating high achievement classrooms, schools, and districts*. Thousand Oaks, CA: Corwin Press.
Schwartz, K. (1971). Filipino education and Spanish colonialism: Toward an autonomous perspective. *Comparative Education Review, 15*(2), 202–218.

CHAPTER 9

A Life Lived Well
American Indian Educator, Scholar, and Leader Dr. John W. Tippeconnic III (Comanche/Cherokee)

Susan C. Faircloth (Coharie)
UNIVERSITY OF NORTH CAROLINA–WILMINGTON, UNITED STATES

> A good leader is someone who puts others first and doesn't say "I" but rather, "we." ... Leadership, like education, is about people. It's a people business.
>
> —John W. Tippeconnic

FROM STUDENT TO SCHOLAR

Dr. John W. Tippeconnic III, a member of the Comanche Nation, was born in 1943 in Lawton, Oklahoma. After graduating from a boarding school operated by the Bureau of Indian Affairs in New Mexico, he earned a bachelor of science degree in secondary education (math and social studies) from Oklahoma State University in 1966, a master's of education in educational administration from Penn State in 1971, and a PhD in educational administration from Penn State in 1975. Tippeconnic was introduced to education early in life. His father, John, a Native speaker of the Comanche language, was the first Comanche to earn a master's degree. He went on to serve as a principal and teacher on the Navajo Reservation. His mother, Juanita, who was Cherokee, worked as a cook at this same school (Terrill, 2016). Tippeconnic (2000a) "often felt more like a teacher's aide than a student in [his] dad's schools. Education was so important to [his] parents that when [he] graduated from high school the choice was not whether [he] would go to college, but where he would go" (p. 40).

After graduating from Oklahoma State University, Tippeconnic began his career in education as an 8th-grade math teacher in the Albuquerque (New Mexico) Public Schools, where there were no American Indian students in his classes. He later became a teacher in a boarding school on the Navajo Reservation where all of his students were American Indians grounded in the Navajo language and culture. The boarding school environment was familiar to him because both he and his parents had attended boarding schools for elementary and secondary education. As Tippeconnic once said:

> My father stressed education and I think he stressed this because he was a product of the government's educational policy. He too went to the bureau boarding school and the approach then was assimilation into the mainstream as soon as possible. The school reflected this. Anything Indian was downgraded, was not to be done in the school setting. They [administrators] aimed at "De-Indianizing" the students. . . . [My father] had a lot of unpleasant memories of that process. (quoted in Fixico, 2013, p. 64)

As a professor of educational leadership and administration, Tippeconnic worked to prepare future generations of school leaders who understood the role of language and culture in education and who valued the diversity that students and their families bring to schools.

After pursuing his graduate studies, Tippeconnic worked as an assistant to the president and vice president of academic affairs at Navajo Community College (now known as Diné College) before turning his focus to the national level, where from 1990 to 1992 he served as the director of the Office of Indian Education within the U.S. Department of Education and from 1992 to 1995 as the director of the Office of Indian Education Programs in the Bureau of Indian Affairs, U.S. Department of Interior. Upon leaving federal service, he returned to higher education, where he worked as a professor of educational leadership and policy studies at Arizona State University (1995–1996) before joining the faculty of Pennsylvania State University, where he served as professor and director of the American Indian Leadership Program from 1996 to 2010. In 2010, Tippeconnic left Penn State to return to the Southwest, where he served as a professor and director of the American Indian Studies program at Arizona State University from 2010 to 2016, when he retired with the rank of professor emeritus. He currently works as a consultant for an American Indian, female-owned educational evaluation and research company and teaches an American Indian Studies course at the University of California–San Marcos.

LEADING IN A CONTEXT OF CONTRADICTIONS: PAVING THE WAY FOR TRULY SELF-DETERMINED EDUCATION

Throughout his tenure as a leader in the field of Indian education, Tippeconnic witnessed firsthand the challenge of regaining Indian control over the education of this nation's Indigenous children and youth—a challenge complicated by the federal trust responsibility for Indian education and tribes' right to function as sovereign and self-determined nations within a colonial nation-state that has historically worked to assimilate and acculturate its Indigenous peoples. As Tippeconnic (1991) wrote:

> The concept of "education" is a powerful tool in our society. Formal education housed in schools provides the dominant society with the means to exert control over the socialization process of young, developing individuals. In the United States, we proclaim pride in living in a democracy based on the principles of equality, freedom and social justice for all. Yet, we know that these democratic concepts are more relevant for some than for others, especially the poor and powerless. (p. 180)

As he worked to reconcile the tensions between his role as an agent of the federal government during his tenure with the Department of Education and Bureau of Indian Affairs, he remained committed to the pursuit of authentic and real Indian control of education. This was demonstrated in a 2000 publication in which he wrote:

> In its ideal sense, Indian control means Indian people have the power to decide what their youth and adults are to be taught, how they will be taught and what human and fiscal resources will be used to support teaching and learning—without outside forces influencing or dictating the educational program. . . . Indian control of education is essential to individual Indian identity, tribal self-sufficiency and restoration and vitality of Indian languages and cultures. Educating tribal members in language and culture, tribal histories and tribal sovereignty status is essential to our survival as a people. This is a heavy responsibility that schools cannot assume alone—but they play a major role. (Tippeconnic, 2000b, paragraph 14)

Though a staunch proponent of Indian control, Tippeconnic also demonstrated a commitment to consultation and dialogue with all parties. According to him, "We need tribal leadership that talks, promotes, and acts on Indian Education issues constantly and persistently. We also need to garner more support from the general public" (Tippeconnic, 2000b, p. 46). Tippeconnic understood that Indian education occurs within a complex and dynamic environment influenced by the political and philosophical ideologies of multiple players. His job was to understand these players and to find ways to advance Indian education without being trampled by the systems at play.

LESSONS LEARNED FROM A LIFE LIVED WELL

In 1998, my life was forever changed by a brief phone conversation with Dr. Tippeconnic. While I was asking him to serve as a professional reference, he encouraged me to apply for the doctoral program in educational administration at Penn State, where he was then working. He was optimistic that a funding proposal he had submitted to the U.S, Department of Education would be awarded and that funds would soon be available to support my doctoral studies. A few weeks later, I quit my job and moved to Pennsylvania to study under one of the great leaders in American Indian education. What started out as a professor–student relationship eventually grew into a colleague-to-colleague relationship through which Tippeconnic and I would go on to write together and eventually to co-direct the American Indian Leadership Program at Penn State. We worked together for over 10 years, until he called me into his office to announce that he would be leaving Penn State to become the director of American Indian Studies at Arizona State, the place where his academic career had begun nearly 3 decades earlier. I remember that conversation with a mixture of sadness and joy. I knew that he was going home and that he was opening up a door for me to assume increased leadership responsibilities. My heart was simultaneously broken and mended by the man who had become both my mentor and one of my dearest friends. Over the years, I have reflected on the many lessons I have learned from Dr. Tippeconnic. Ten of these lessons are discussed in brief below.

1. The Centrality of Indigenous Knowledges and Ways of Knowing and Doing. Above all, Tippeconnic knew and respected the fact that Indigenous peoples and their tribal communities hold their own cultural knowledges and ways of doing and engaging with the world. He respected this and held it to equal or greater value than the knowledge gained from Western institutions and other formalized ways of learning and doing. This knowledge and understanding of Indigenous peoples guided him in his work with the more than 600 federally and state recognized Indian tribes across the nation, each with its own culture and many with their own language(s).

2. The Ability to Work Across Difference(s). This is demonstrated best by his appointment to national leadership roles under both Republican- and Democratic-led federal governments. In these roles, he enacted lessons he learned growing up as an American Indian male in a segregated and deeply divided nation. As Tippeconnic relayed in Fixico's (2013) *Indian Resilience and Rebuilding: Indigenous Nations in the Modern American West,* growing up as an American Indian was not easy, but he learned to navigate this challenge with deep reflection, poise, grace, and, perhaps greatest of all, empathy for those who treated him unfairly and unequally. As he told Fixico (2013):

> Once I graduated from college and was working as a professional, people did not look at me just for what I could do. Perhaps they looked at me as what I represented as "an Indian." In order to be accepted I had to perform at or beyond the level of others. I had to prove myself. (p. 62)

As unfair as this was, his life experience prepared him to work in both Indigenous and non-Indigenous institutions, as well as to serve in both Republican and Democratic federal governments.

3. The Power of Calm and "Quiet" Leadership. During the years I have known Dr. Tippeconnic, I have only seen him lose his composure once. It was with one of his colleagues. He sat up straight in his chair, raised his voice ever so slightly, said what needed to be said, and returned to his work. We exchanged knowing glances, chuckled about the event later, and that was that. He moved on and continued to do the work he was called to do. I knew he was hurt by the actions of his colleague, but I admired him for his ability and willingness to let the incident go and move forward.

4. The Moral and Ethical Imperative to Balance the Practical with the Theoretical. Tippeconnic's lifework is rooted and grounded in his lived experience as an American Indian man, educator, and scholar. He conducted his own research and worked with others to mold their scholarship, but he never lost sight of what was important—translating research into practice and asking the critical question: "So what?" In essence, his focus was about more than doing research for the sake of research. He was about making a difference in how people approached research, no matter how small that difference might be.

5. The Need to Tell Our Own Stories Through Data. Tippeconnic knew that there was more to the story of Indian education than risk and failure. He saw the potential in each school and community he visited, and he stressed the importance of collecting and using empirical data to illustrate both the accomplishments and needs of Indigenous schools and communities across the nation. He also knew that if we did not tell our own stories, others would tell them in ways that might not be accurate or authentic.

6. The Ability to Maintain Focused and Realistic Optimism in the Face of Continued Assaults Against Indigenous Peoples and Their Languages, Cultures, and Lands. As his writings reflect, Tippeconnic has witnessed more than 70 years of failed educational policies, stemming from over 500 years of assimilationist practices aimed at eradicating Indigenous peoples, yet he knew firsthand how resilient Indigenous peoples are, and he believed strongly that they have the power and ability to overcome these sustained threats to their existence if they work both individually and collectively to effect change. As Tippeconnic (2000) noted, "When it comes to the education of American Indians and Alaska Natives, it seems we *still* need not only an attitudinal change on the part of the general public, but also more efficient and creative approaches by educators" (p. 39). As this quote demonstrates, Tippeconnic knew the challenges that lay before him, but he had an inner confidence and peace that these challenges could be overcome.

7. The Primacy of Family and Relationships. Although firmly committed to his work as an educator and scholar, Tippeconnic maintained strong and meaningful connections not only to his immediate family members but also to the scores of students and colleagues he worked with over the years. The importance of relationships is also reflected in his work to develop and operate Comanche Nation College, a tribally controlled college in his home state of Oklahoma. His example has touched each of us in profound ways and encouraged and motivated us to live a life committed to improving the educational conditions and subsequent life outcomes of American Indian children and youth and their communities. But the greatest lesson he taught was the importance of keeping our relationships at the forefront so that at the end of our lives we would be known as much for the work we did as the good lives we lived.

8. The Need to Recognize and Articulate Our Worth as Scholars, Not Only to Those Around Us, but to Ourselves. When negotiating a job offer at a major academic institution, Tippeconnic felt uncomfortable engaging in verbal negotiations, so he took out a piece of paper and thoughtfully crafted a list of his must-have and negotiable items. For him, it was more comfortable to slide a piece of paper across the table than to verbally tout his accomplishments and make the case for why the university should compensate him accordingly. Over the years, I have used this technique in my own negotiations and have found it to be quite successful. The lesson learned here is that we must know who we are and what we have to offer and that it is okay to be justly compensated; however, we must also do so in ways that sit well with our own Indigenous value of humility. In the end, what we gain from external agencies and entities is far less valuable than the values and beliefs that are ingrained in us from birth and serve to maintain our authenticity and cultural connectedness.

9. The Importance of Acknowledging Those Who Have Gone Before Us and Committing to Mentor and Care for Those Who Will Come After Us. Throughout this life, Tippeconnic has never failed to reference his father, the first Comanche to earn a master's degree, and the scores of other elders who made it possible for him to achieve everything he did. This is one of the things I admire most about him—his respect for elders and his humility regarding his own success and achievements. On the day I earned my doctoral degree, I walked beside Dr. Tippeconnic across the snowy sidewalks of the Penn State campus. I remember feeling an ache in my heart and tears welling up in the corners of my eyes. I thought that if anyone said anything to me, I would burst out crying. Over the years, I've pondered this feeling and asked myself why I was so emotional on a day that should have been one of the happiest of my life. What I've come to understand is that I was feeling the weight and expectations of all those who had gone before me, including the original cohort of fellows in the American Indian Leadership Program. Tippeconnic was among the members of that cohort. In 1970, he "received a telegram from [the] Pennsylvania State University asking if [he] was interested in participating in a new American Indian Leadership Program. . . . [His] life changed—graduate degrees opened up opportunities [he] had not thought possible" (Tippeconnic, 2000a, p. 40).

Without his willingness to leave his home community and enter the unfamiliar environment of a college campus located in rural, remote central Pennsylvania, I would not have been able to walk beside him nearly 30 years later to earn my doctoral degree from Penn State, nor would I have been able to return to Penn State a few years later to work side by side with him as he prepared me to become an Indigenous scholar and leader. I was humbled by the commitment he had made to me as well as the long, hard fight he had engaged in on behalf of scores of other Indigenous peoples from across the nation, and I was afraid that I would not be able to live up to the work that he and his cohort members had accomplished or the expectations they held for me and my fellow graduates. Nearly 20 years later, I still question if I have what it takes to make them proud. When I feel this doubt pervading my thoughts, all I need to do is pick up the phone or send an email to the man I've come to know as "Tipp." He reminds me that I am worthy and that it is time for him to step aside so that others like me can do the work that still needs to be done. For this, I will forever be indebted.

10. *The Wisdom to Know When It Is Time to Step Aside so Others May Lead.* In 2016, Dr. Tippeconnic announced his retirement as the director of the American Indian Studies program at Arizona State. Today, he is recognized as a professor emeritus and continues to serve Indian country (i.e., Indigenous populations) as a consultant, father, and mentor. His dedication and commitment to Indian education will live on in the scores of lives, both Indigenous and non-Indigenous, that he has impacted over the years. This is evidenced by a national study in which Mackey and Warner (2013) identified him as one of the most influential people in Indian education in the United States. As Dr. K. Tsianina Lomawaima recently said, Tippeconnic "exemplifies Native values of intellectual excellence, hard work and care for others" (quoted in Terrill, 2016).

RELEVANCE OF LESSONS LEARNED TO TODAY'S EDUCATIONAL ENVIRONMENT

Today, the majority of the nation's American Indian children and youth attend public schools. With a change in national leadership and a restructuring of the Bureau of Indian Education, it is highly likely that an even greater number will spend at least a portion of their school years in public schools. This makes it increasingly imperative that educational leaders—both Indigenous and non-Indigenous—work together to ensure that the federal government's trust responsibility for Indian education is upheld and that American Indian children and youth are provided with every opportunity available to learn in educational environments that recognize and hold dear the Indigenous knowledges and ways of doing that they and their tribal communities have fought so hard to sustain. Tippeconnic acknowledged the devastating impact of assimilationist educational policies and practices on Indigenous youth and their communities, yet he remained accepting of the ideal of public education and the power and potential of educators to make a positive and lasting impact. He cared about education, not because it was the vehicle by which he earned a living, but because it was the thing that fed his soul, stretched his imagination, and made him smile at the thought of what the future could bring if truly self-determined Indian education was made possible.

REFERENCES

Fixico, D. L. (2013). *Indian resilience and rebuilding: Indigenous nations in the modern American west.* Tucson, AZ: The university of Arizona Press.

Mackey, H. J., & Warner, L. S. (2013). For our children: A study and critical discussion of the Influences on American Indian and Alaska Native education policy. *Journal of Critical Thought and Praxis, 2*(1), 102–121.

Terrill, M. (2016, May 10). Tippeconnic says farewell. Retrieved from asunow.asu.edu/20160510-arizona-impact-john-tippeconnic-retiring

Tippeconnic, J. W., III. (1991). The education of American Indians: Policy, practice and future direction. In D. E. Green & T. V. Tonnesen (Eds.), *American Indians: Social justice and public policy* (pp. 180–207). ERIC Document Reproduction Service No. ED 351 158.

Tippeconnic, J. W., III. (2000a). Reflecting on the past: Some important aspects of Indian education to consider as we look toward the future. *Journal of American Indian Education, 39*(2), 39–48. Retrieved from www.jstor.org.liblink.uncw.edu/stable/pdf/24398430.pdf

Tippeconnic, J. W., III. (2000b). Towards educational self-determination: The challenge for Indian control of Indian schools. *Native Americas, XVII,* 42.

CHAPTER 10

Jimmy Carter
A Portrait of Moral and Ethical Leadership

Michelle D. Young & Bryan A. VanGronigen
THE UNIVERSITY OF VIRGINIA, UNITED STATES

History will remember President Jimmy Carter as a leader with a strong moral compass. Although moral leadership is often overshadowed by more traditional notions of leadership and management, the leadership that counts, in the end, is the kind that puts people before politics, appeals to their values, taps their emotions, and engenders trust. It is a morally based leadership—a form of stewardship (Sergiovanni,1992). In this essay, we will share the lessons that can be gleaned from the legacy of a great moral and ethical leader: President James Earl "Jimmy" Carter.

FROM RURAL GEORGIA FARMER TO NOBEL PEACE PRIZE WINNER

Jimmy Carter, born in 1924, grew up in a rural area of Georgia, attended the U.S. Naval Academy, and served as a naval officer for over 15 years, prior to moving to Plains, Georgia, in 1953 to work in agriculture. The transition from the navy to agriculture was financially difficult for him. Carter and his family lived in public housing in Plains for the first year, making him the only U.S. president to have lived in housing subsidized for the poor.

Carter served in multiple leadership roles, beginning with positions in local government and the Southern Baptist church. Subsequently, he served as a Georgia state senator (1963–1967) and as governor (1971–1975) before being elected the 39th president of the United States in 1976. Carter's leadership legacy did not end with the U.S. presidency, however. In 2002, he was awarded the Nobel Peace Prize for his work with the Carter Center, his base for advancing human rights across the globe. He traveled extensively to conduct peace negotiations, observe elections, and promote disease prevention and affordable housing initiatives in developing nations (The Carter Center, 2016a). In the United States and internationally, he has become a prominent portrait of moral and ethical leadership.

LEADING BY EXAMPLE AS A STATE SENATOR, GOVERNOR, PRESIDENT, AND EX-PRESIDENT

Although Carter's most significant accomplishments occurred after he left public office, his leadership achievements span a much longer period of time. Carter emerged as a public leader during a time of significant racial tension in Georgia. By 1961, Carter had become a prominent member of the community and the Southern Baptist Convention (SBC) as well as chairman of the Sumter County School Board, where he began to speak strongly in favor of school integration. His support for the *Brown v. Board of Education of Topeka* ruling paved the way for integration in his region, but the White Citizens' Council in his area responded by boycotting Carter's peanut warehouse.

Carter continued to support the integration of public schools, as well as expanded funding for public education, while he served as a Georgia state senator. Later, as governor, he pushed reforms through the legislature to provide equal state aid to schools in the wealthy and poor areas of Georgia, set up community centers for mentally handicapped children, and increased educational programming for convicts. Furthermore, he extended his work for integration and equity beyond public schools to the Georgia state government. He expanded the number of Black state employees, judges, and board members. He placed portraits of Martin Luther King Jr. and two other prominent Black Georgians in the state capitol, even as Ku Klux Klan members picketed outside.

As president of the United States, Carter's attention was divided among a serious energy crisis, a period of sharp inflation and recession, and a time of major conflicts around the globe. Although his final year in office was tarnished by the Iran hostage situation, he began his presidency by providing amnesty to all Vietnam War draft evaders, and from there, contributed significantly to world peace through the Camp David Accords and the SALT II nuclear arms reduction treaty. He also initiated the Women, Infants, and Children (WIC) nutrition program. Finally, recognizing the need for the U.S. federal government to play an intentional role in planning for the future of the country's energy and education needs, he established the U.S. Departments of Energy and Education.

Following his service as president, Carter involved himself in a variety of national and international public policy, conflict resolution, human rights, and charitable causes. In 1982, Carter established the Carter Center to advance human rights and alleviate human suffering. A major accomplishment of the Carter Center has been the elimination of more than 99% of cases of Guinea worm disease, a painful infection caused by drinking water contaminated with parasites, from an estimated 3.5 million cases in 1986 to only 22 in 2015 (The Carter Center, 2016b).

The Carter Center also promotes democracy, mediates and prevents conflicts, and monitors the electoral process in support of free and fair elections (The Carter Center, 2016a). The Carter Center has monitored 96 elections in 38 countries since 1989, the most controversial being the 2004 elections in Venezuela. Carter also assisted the U.S. government with many diplomatic negotiations, including a treaty with North Korea, under which North Korea agreed to freeze and dismantle its nuclear program. He assisted with Israeli and Palestinian negotiations, resulting in the Geneva Initiative; held peace summits; and participated in the development of agreements to reduce violence in various regions of Africa.

In 2002, Carter received the Nobel Peace Prize for his work at the Carter Center "to find peaceful solutions to international conflicts, to advance democracy and human rights, and to promote economic and social development" (The Nobel Peace Prize, 2002). In his acceptance speech, he urged the prohibition of the death penalty in the United States and abroad, noting that the United States, along with nations such as Saudi Arabia, China, and Cuba, still carry out the death penalty despite countless cases of wrongful conviction and gross racial and class-based disparities. Carter has acted as a harsh critic of U.S. policies and activities, from the "disgraceful" pardoning of the tax-evading billionaire Marc Rich by President Clinton (Berke, 2001), to waging an unnecessary war in Iraq "based on lies and misinterpretations" (Buncombe, 2004), and to the continued use of torture at Guantanamo Bay.

In 2007, Carter announced his participation in the Elders, a group of 14 independent global leaders that includes Nelson Mandela, who advocate for peace and human rights (The Elders, 2016). The Elders work globally on issues such as the Israeli–Palestinian conflict, sustainable development, and equality for girls and women.

Finally, from a young age, Carter expressed a deep commitment to his faith. A third-generation Southern Baptist, Carter continues to teach Sunday school and serve as a deacon of his church in Plains, Georgia. As in other facets of his life, Carter criticized and worked against the inequities he identified within the Southern Baptist Convention (SBC). In 2000, he severed connections to the SBC because of its opposition to women as pastors and its adoption of a position advocating the submission of wives to their husbands. In April 2006, Carter, former President Bill Clinton, and Mercer University president Bill Underwood initiated the New Baptist Covenant, an inclusive movement that seeks to unite Baptists of all races, cultures, and convention affiliations.

BEING A MORAL AND ETHICAL LEADER: LESSONS FROM JIMMY CARTER

Jimmy Carter has left a significant leadership legacy—a legacy that allows one to explore some of the more abstract facets of being an educational leader, including moral and ethical leadership. Education is "a moral endeavor" (Goodlad, Sodor, & Sirotnik, 1990, p. xii). Every decision a leader makes carries with it "a restructuring of human life: that is why administration at its heart is the resolution of moral dilemmas" (Foster, 1986, p. 33). This understanding informed the new National Educational Leadership Preparation (NELP) standards, which includes a standard focused specifically on professional norms and ethics (University Council for Educational Administration [UCEA], 2016). Whereas many of the standards rightfully target the technical parts of the job, such as developing instructional capacity and fostering parent–community relationships, NELP Standard Two centers on a leader's personal and professional ethics.

Before moving into a discussion of the specific leadership lessons that can be drawn from Carter's legacy, we offer the following orienting thoughts on moral and ethical leadership. Moral and ethical leadership begins from the self. Moral leaders have a clear understanding of their own values and hold themselves accountable to those values. The ethical character of each leader influences his or her ability and willingness to act on moral principles. Moral and ethical leaders ensure that their own belief systems are in line with the values and needs of the organizations they lead. Moral leaders also play an important role in communicating an organization's values. They do this as role models of ethical behavior, as well as through their decisions, which at times may be unpopular or inconvenient. The ethics that leaders exhibit reflect on their organizations, as well as on themselves, making moral and ethical leadership important for protecting an organization's reputation and for establishing a moral and ethical organizational culture. Through their leadership, moral and ethical leaders help their followers understand, share, and act in accordance with personal and professional values, and by doing so, gain the respect of followers, who are then more likely to identify with their leaders and the goals they set.

In this section, we offer four lessons drawn from the legacy of President Jimmy Carter. The lessons focus on (1) being self-aware, (2) always upholding professional ethical standards, (3) understanding leadership as service, and (4) never misusing power.

1. Be Self-Aware. Our first lesson focuses on the importance of leaders' self-understanding of their worldview, their value systems, and how these two things shape their leadership. Self-awareness may not be one of the first things we think of when asked to define leadership, but it is critical. Self-awareness is one of Jimmy Carter's essential strengths as a leader.

In his gubernatorial inaugural speech, Carter (1971) declared "the time for racial discrimination is over. . . . No poor, rural, weak, or black person should ever have to bear the additional burden of being deprived of the opportunity of an education, a job, or simple justice" (pp. 1–2). Carter's witnessing of the horrors of segregation in Georgia while growing up was *the* life experience, he said, that framed his worldview for the decades to come.

Frequently, a single event has the power to leave a permanent mark on what we believe and how we think about and view the world. Segregation forced Carter to actively reflect on his value systems and beliefs, and, more important, *why* he believed what he did.

Carter also understood the role that religion played in his beliefs and actions. He was frank about how important his faith was to him and how it influenced him as a leader. His understanding of the role his faith and his experiences with segregation played in shaping his leadership helped him develop a firm sense of right and wrong and maintain allegiance to his value system throughout his life, even when his views, such as those on segregation, were unpopular.

Leaders should know and be able to articulate *what* they believe and why. Knowing what comprises one's worldview and making the implicit explicit provides followers with a more complete picture of who one is both as a leader and as a human being. When leaders offer little detail about their decisionmaking rationales, for example, followers can feel alienated, which can cause morale to plummet and trust to disintegrate. Yet this approach—being honest with followers about what life experiences have shaped leaders' view the world—can expose leaders' vulnerabilities. Although some may argue against leaders demonstrating any vulnerability, we believe that doing so makes leaders more authentic and *real*, which can help engender trust, inspire motivation, and deepen commitment.

Learning to be self-aware and self-reflective requires concerted effort on the part of individuals, but this can be facilitated through a variety of means. The choice of method should depend on the nature of a leader's self-awareness level. For example, if we have rarely if ever considered what we believe and why and how it informs our leadership, then reading a leadership autobiography could be very useful. If we have a relatively strong understanding of our beliefs but are less connected to how it impacts our work, we may benefit from reflecting on selected readings, journaling, or practicing mindfulness.

2. Always Uphold Professional Ethical Standards. History will remember Jimmy Carter as a man of impeccable integrity. When he was running for president in 1976, he told gathering after gathering that as president, "I will never tell a lie. I'll never make a misleading statement. I'll never betray the confidence that any of you had in me. And I'll never avoid a controversial issue"(quoted in Wead, 2015). Carter has never been charged with impropriety. As a conservative opinion columnist once noted, "One can disagree with his political views but one cannot find anything wrong with his character" (Wead, 2015).

Carter has always lived by a code of ethics in which he put the people he served before himself and his own interests. He modeled this code in his actions and decisionmaking. He believed in the importance of ethical standards, not just for himself, but for all elected leaders. On May 3, 1977, he delivered a message to the U.S. Congress announcing the Ethics in Government Act, a bill that outlined ethical practices for elected leaders, established an Office of Ethics in the Civil Service Commission, incorporated safeguards against conflicts of interest and the abuse of public trust, and strengthened restrictions on postemployment activities of government officials (Carter, 1977). His message did not point fingers. It recognized the ethical practice of many officials, while also seeking to strengthen the ethical codes to which all government officials were held accountable. He stated:

> The vast majority of government officials, of course, have always followed strict ethical standards. I respect their efforts and integrity. . . . The provisions of the Act would strike a careful balance between the rights of these individuals to their privacy and the right of the American people to know that their public officials are free from conflicts of interest. (Carter, 1977)

Like President Carter, educational leaders should be committed to an ethical code. Professional associations in many nations and states have adopted professional codes of ethics for educational leaders, and in the United States, both the Professional Standards for Educational Leaders (PSEL) and the National Educational Leadership Preparation (NELP) standards outline the importance of ethics for educational leaders (NPBEA, 2015; UCEA, 2016). These standards highlight the importance of ethics in one's behaviors, relationships, and decisionmaking (NPBEA, 2015).

Adopting a personal and professional ethical code, like developing self-awareness, should be undertaken in a deliberative manner. Shapiro and Stefkovich (2016) recommend several steps in developing and adopting an ethical code. The first and second steps involve leaders exploring their morals and values and then drafting their own ethical code. The third step involves comparing and contrasting the ethical codes and standards developed for leaders by professional associations and governmental agencies with their own ethical codes. The final step involves finalizing their own ethical code. Doing so should enable leaders to develop a better understanding of themselves and their leadership, to approach the dilemmas they face with more confidence, and to consistently make decisions that align with their own ethical codes.

3. Understand Leadership as Service. A vast literature expounds on the importance of setting goals, planning and organizing work, outlining performance standards, and evaluating subordinates. These leadership activities are important, even essential. However, they often give short shrift to the *why* of leadership. For Jimmy Carter, the moral purpose of leadership was service.

Carter has frequently been described as a servant leader (Pascall, 2000). The term *servant leadership* was first coined by Robert K. Greenleaf in an essay called *The Servant as Leader* (1970). According to Greenleaf, servant leadership emerges from the desire to lead in service to others. To this definition, Sergiovanni (1996) added that servant leadership is also drawn from a deep commitment to values and emerges from moral authority, explaining that people are, by nature, more responsive to moral obligations than decentered self-interest. Finally, servant leadership invests in authentically engaging with one's followers in an effort to understand more fully their beliefs, values, challenges, and hopes.

As a public official, Carter engaged in efforts that can be understood as the enactment of servant leadership. He was hardworking and conscientious. When he was elected to the Georgia governorship, he began to engineer the reversal of the decades-old policies that had preserved segregation in Georgia. He had the power to enact change and evince moral authority for his followers. He used those resources to implement key civil rights initiatives and policy changes.

In his presidential campaign autobiography, *Why Not the Best?*, Carter (1976) articulated his leadership, explaining that leaders must put their best self forward on behalf of their constituents. While on the campaign trail, Carter stayed with supporters rather than in hotels. This provided him with opportunities to talk with average American citizens about their hopes for the nation and to shape the goals of his presidency, including the restoration of integrity to the office of the U.S. presidency.

Since losing his reelection bid in 1980, Jimmy Carter continued to lead and serve. He has spent the past few decades working on projects with the aim of helping people in the United States and abroad. Through the Carter Center and his involvement in humanitarian endeavors such as Habitat for Humanity, Carter has worked in communities across the globe to tackle problems that, if solved, would significantly improve the lives of countless people and to put his deeply held values into practice. Whether through human rights advocacy, health promotion, or other charitable projects, Carter has worked tirelessly to make life better for his fellow human beings.

Educational leaders are charged with many critical responsibilities, but the most important one is to lead their education communities in the service of student learning. This charge should remain at the forefront of every interaction and every decision, and educational leaders should always reflect upon the following question when making a choice: "How will the decision I'm about to make influence the education students are receiving in this community?"

4. Never Misuse Power. Our fourth lesson focuses on a leader's power and influence. Every leadership role connotes positional authority, which comes with powers that influence scores of people. When leaders understand that their leadership is in service to others and should operate from an ethical code, they will also understand the importance of considering the repercussions of their decisions and actions and working to prevent the misuse of power.

When Carter was president, he was more temperate in his use of presidential power than many of his predecessors. Not only was he concerned with returning trust to the Oval Office, but he understood that actions have consequences and, therefore, must be taken with great care. For example, as president, he made the decision to be less hawkish despite the United States still being in the throes of the Cold War. This earned him the ire of many, especially Republicans; they argued that by not taking a harder line against the enemies of the United States, Carter showed weakness to both citizens of the country and others around the world. However, from Carter's perspective, the awesome powers of the U.S. presidency needed to be used judiciously. Carter understood that his actions would affect the long-term safety and stability of the United States, as well as other areas and regions around the world. As a result, his powers had to be used thoughtfully, with full awareness of their multiple potential repercussions.

A similar understanding of his power and influence informed his decision to publicly withdraw from the Southern Baptist Convention (SBC). In a 2009 opinion piece, Carter noted that religious leaders have an option to interpret holy teachings, and that the SBC had chosen to use that power to subjugate women. The result of such decisions, he asserted, is "the pervasive persecution and abuse of women throughout the world" (Carter, 2009). He pointed out that such atrocities are not only violations of the "Universal Declaration of Human Rights but also the teachings of Jesus Christ, the Apostle Paul, Moses and the prophets, Muhammad, and founders of other great religions" (Carter, 2009).

Although the scope of influence of many educational leaders is much smaller than that of a U.S. president, the lessons nevertheless remain the same. First, positional authority grants specific powers to leaders—and these powers can be used or abused. As president, Carter could have taken a more offensive approach to foreign policy, sending thousands of troops to any place he wanted. His value system, though, kept him centered and checked any potential overreach. Second, every choice matters. Every decision a leader makes will have an impact on someone somewhere. If a principal eliminates a fine arts position in order to hire an intervention specialist, students will have less access to fine arts instruction; yet, struggling readers may improve, which could increase their self-confidence and investment in school. Given this potential influence, leaders need to use their power thoughtfully because there are many people who will, ultimately, need to live and work in the environment that a leader's decisions shape.

CONCLUSION

As president, Jimmy Carter promised renewed confidence in the ethics of elected office. When he was elected, the United States was coming out of a period of significant government scandal and corruption. During his presidency, Carter faced significant challenges—the energy crisis, Soviet aggression, Iran, and above all, a deep mistrust of leadership by U.S. citizens. The United States needed a leader who could restore integrity to the office of presidency and to the democratic values of the United States: "He did that" (Wead, 2015).

Importantly, Carter's political career was marked by failure as much as by success. All leaders, however, experience failure at some point in their careers. It is recovery from failure that separates truly great leaders from the rest. For Jimmy Carter, adversity was an opportunity to reflect on and further build his character, it was an opportunity to ensure that his belief system was in line with the values and needs of those he served, and it was an opportunity to lead morally and ethically by example.

President Jimmy Carter offers lessons in leadership not merely because he once wielded political power, but because he consistently led by the power of his example. Without question, Carter's leadership in peacekeeping and humanitarian efforts since he left office have ensured that he will be remembered as one of the most successful ex-presidents in U.S. history (Brinkley, 1996).

REFERENCES

Berke, R. L. (2001, February 23). The Clinton pardons: This time Clintons find their support buckling from weight of new woes. *New York Times*. Retrieved from query.nytimes.com/gst/fullpage.html

Brinkley, D. (1996). The rising stock of Jimmy Carter: The "hands on" legacy of our thirty-ninth President. *Diplomatic History*, 20(4), 505–530. doi:10.1111/j.1467-7709.1996.tb00285.x

Buncombe, A. (2004, March 22). Carter savages Blair and Bush: 'Their war was based on lies.' *Independent*. Retrieved from www.independent.co.uk/news/world/politics/carter-savages-blair-and-bush-their-war-was-based-on-lies-65445.html

Carter, J. (1971). Inaugural address. Retrieved from www.jimmycarterlibrary.gov/assets/documents/inaugural_address_gov.pdf

Carter, J. (1976). *Why not the best?* New York, NY: Bantam Books.

Carter, J. (1977). Ethics in government message to the Congress. Retrieved from www.presidency.ucsb.edu/ws/?pid=7440

Carter, J. (2009, July 15). Losing my religion for equality. *The Age*. Retrieved from web.archive.org/web/20130703023646/www.theage.com.au/opinion/losing-my-religion-for-equality-20090714-dk0v.html

The Carter Center. (2016a). Waging peace through elections. Retrieved from www.cartercenter.org/peace/democracy/observed.html

The Carter Center. (2016b, January 15). Wiping out Guinea worm. Retrieved from www.cartercenter.org/news/features/h/guinea_worm/30-yrs-public-health-leadership.html

The Elders. (2016). Who are the Elders? Retrieved from www.theelders.org/about

Foster, W. (1986). *Paradigms and promises: New approaches to educational administration*. Buffalo, NY: Prometheus Books.

Goodlad, J., Sodor, R., & Sorotnik, K. (1990). *The moral dimensions of teaching*. San Francisco, CA: Jossey-Bass.

Greenleaf, R. K. (1970). *The servant as leader*. Indianapolis, IN: The Robert K. Greenleaf Center.

National Policy Board for Educational Administration (NPBEA). (2015). *Professional standards for educational leaders 2015*. Reston, VA: Author.

The Nobel Peace Prize. (2002). Retrieved from www.nobelprize.org/nobel_prizes/peace/laureates/2002/

Pascall, G. (2000, January 19). Jimmy Carter: America's servant leader. *Seattle Times*. Retrieved from community.seattletimes.nwsource.com/archive/?date=20000119&slug=4000096

Sergiovanni, T. (1992). *Moral leadership*. San Francisco, CA: Jossey-Bass.

Sergiovanni, T. (1996). *Leadership for the schoolhouse*. San Francisco, CA: Jossey-Bass.

Shapiro, J. P., & Stefkovich, J. A. (2016). *Ethical leadership and decision making in education: Applying theoretical perspectives to complex dilemmas*. New York, NY: Routledge.

University Council for Educational Administration (UCEA). (2016). *The draft NELP Standards are available for public comment*. Retrieved from www.ucea.org/initiatives/the-draft-nelp-standards-are-available-for-public-comment/

Wead, D. (2015, August 20). Jimmy Carter: Dignity, humility, integrity. *Newsmax*. Retrieved from www.newsmax.com/DougWead/Carter-press-conference-Democrat-cancer/2015/08/20/id/671052/

Harold Gatensby
Tlingit Peacemaker and Leader

Polly Hyslop
UNIVERSITY OF ALASKA FAIRBANKS, UNITED STATES

Brian Jarrett
CALIFORNIA STATE UNIVERSITY, DOMINGUEZ HILLS, UNITED STATES

> This circle we're trying to do in my community is not just about offenders and victims, not just about crime, but about all of us working together, learning about each other, learning how to help each other, how to grow, heal together.
>
> —Harold Gatensby

Harold Gatensby is an extraordinary leader. He is from Carcross/Tagish First Nation, located in Yukon Territory in Canada. He is a member of the Kookhittaan clan of the Dakha T'lingit Nation. Thirty years ago, Gatensby was instrumental in reviving traditional Peacemaking Circle practices, a method for resolving conflict between tribe members that had been almost completely lost to history. He led a renaissance in Peacemaking and convinced judges, police officers, community members, and fellow Tribal Elders alike to implement traditional Tlingit Peacemaking as an alternative process to standard sentencing practices. Peacemaking Circles proved to be very effective in reducing criminal behavior and the incidence of recidivism within Indigenous communities in the Yukon Territory of Canada. In 2000, Gatensby received an Individual Merit Award for his community justice work, presented by Her Royal Highness Princess Anne of the United Kingdom. This award brings recognition to individuals who have developed innovative approaches to reducing crime in their communities.

After the initial application of Peacemaking Circles in Carcross, Gatensby was also instrumental in starting a Peacemaking Circle in the village of Kake, Alaska, after meeting Tlingit-Haida Mike Jackson, who is both a recognized facilitator, or "keeper," of the Circle and the resident state magistrate of Kake (Hyslop, 2012; Jarrett & Hyslop, 2014). Since that time, Harold Gatensby and his brother Phil have worked to teach Peacemaking principles to both Indigenous and non-Indigenous peoples throughout the world. His Peacemaking work has taken him to Norway and Belgium to assist governments and communities in tackling social conflicts. Most recently, he and his brother have traveled to northern Albania, where they counseled local justice department officials in their efforts to reduce interclan disputes.

In appearance, Harold is a tall and lean man with long black hair that he keeps tied behind his head. If you ever sit with him at his lakeside home, you will enjoy his poignant storytelling, which is laced with dry-witted jokes. You will recognize him immediately as the guy who is gruff in appearance, and the one who is openly challenging students to question self-defeating assumptions and beliefs they hold about themselves and about the society in which they live. He is resolute in promoting self-reflection and self-honesty. In this, he can be brutally honest because he believes Peacemaking is a process that comes to life when everyone tells the truth, even if that leads to personal discomfort (Jarrett & Hyslop, 2013). He also holds himself to this same standard so that circle participants will feel an immediate kinship with him and his teaching. As he puts it, the willingness to tell one another the truth is to recognize the deep human connection that we all share. He often finishes his lectures by reminding people that humans are all 80% or more water and that we all share this reality in common, even if we are not aware of it.

Harold started his journey to peacemaker as a teen in the territorial juvenile detention facilities. Instead of allowing himself to be defeated by this experience, he chose to become a leader and a voice for First Nation peoples. Gatensby's reflections on his personal journey and lessons on leadership are as follows.

Challenge the system with courage, dedication, and perseverance. In introducing his ideas on Peacemaking, Gatensby risked ridicule and rejection. There were members of his community and the courts who did not want to appear to be challenging the sentencing practices of Yukon Territorial courts. When Gatensby heard that a Peacemaking Circle had already taken place in another First Nation community elsewhere, he informed Judge Barry Stuart that he was interested in starting a Circle there in Carcross. At first, though Judge Stuart was interested and even sympathetic, he was reluctant to allow Gatensby to proceed without applying for funding. But Gatensby was so clear and steadfast in his message that he convinced Judge Stuart to begin conducting the circles without delay (Caley, 1998). Through courage, dedication to traditional knowledge, and just plain dogged persistence, Gatensby pushed on to convince all the relevant juridical actors to develop an entire pilot project in Peacemaking Circles. The pilot's implementation proceeded to quickly transform the judicial process and provided a much-needed improvement to standard sentencing practices. The pilot's success required the court, the lawyers, the police, and the supporting institutions to all work in concert to make it happen. And with Gatensby's leadership, they did. In fact, it did not take long after that first event for Peacemaking to become an accepted court-connected practice.

Don't be afraid to speak with conviction. Gatensby's youth was spent in residential schools and correction centers—both of which aimed, in his view, to break his spirit. Consequently, he became an outspoken critic, unapologetic in his condemnation of these institutions. Canada is overflowing with incarcerated First Nation offenders. Gatensby insists that we need to speak plainly in addressing this fact. In 2012, when he spoke at a jointly sponsored gathering of the University of Alaska Fairbanks and Yukon College, he spared no words in his criticisms of the U.S. and Canadian contemporary judicial systems and their apparent indifference to the plight of young Native men. The tension in the room was palpable as he voiced his heartfelt views. He even left some members of the audience squirming with discomfort. Ironically, though, at the end of his talk, both Native and non-Native people alike spoke highly of his evident authenticity, personal conviction, and willingness to share his views. In fact, his talk was a catalyst for later conversations that brought Native and non-Native people together to discuss the urgent need to reduce recidivism among Native offenders (Gatensby, 2012).

Maintain spirit-based and reflective leadership. Gatensby never takes any credit for leadership. Though he paved the way for Territorial Judge Barry Stuart to become a leading authority on Peacemaking, Gatensby remained gracious in not seeking credit for the gift of traditional knowledge that he had bestowed. Instead, he simply thanked his ancestors for guiding him in their teachings. Sometimes he hikes up a nearby mountain to spend time alone and reflect. He says, "The mountains hold the teachings. When the person is ready and has the desire, the teachings will return" (Gatensby, personal communication, May 13, 2015). He sees himself as a mere steward of traditional knowledge and practices. He is quick to state that he did not invent Peacemaking but instead simply helped revive it when the community was ready for it. In all his work, he feels guided, as if by some energy or spirit larger than himself—a spirit that resides in all people, animals, and all aspects of nature, as he puts it. Somewhat comically, while the authors were interviewing Gatensby at his camp, a moose quite casually walked up to the group, on a nearby path, pausing a while and carefully listening, as if to signal its agreement. In his lectures, to help young people see the intrinsic value of civility, law-abiding behavior, and concern for others, Gatensby would often tell them that breaking man's criminal law is different from breaking God's law—the former is a crime against self. With admonitions and mentorship like this, he sought to encourage young people to tap the strength of their own human spirit and draw from it whenever they find themselves feeling alienated or in distress. Gatensby believes that this is particularly important for young people to develop as human beings.

Seek authentic, heartfelt dialogue. Gatensby is, by his own admission, sometimes gruff, impatient, and short-tempered. He is often not politically correct. But when you ask those who know him, they are quick to acknowledge that he has a heart of gold—a heart that stopped for an astounding 12 minutes a few years back when he experienced a massive cardiac arrest and Gatensby actually died on the operating room table. At the scene, the attending physician informed Gatensby's brother Phil, that Harold was "*gone*" and said that Phil should accept it. But Phil refused to do so. Instead, he began yelling at the physician, declaring that Gatensby was not "*gone.*" Phil then turned to Harold's lifeless body, beseeching him to come back. Amazingly, Gatensby's heart began to beat again—a seemingly miraculous event that the two brothers and their physician talk about to this day. From this experience and others, Gatensby has learned to value the importance of sharing one's authentic feelings with significant others. Nowadays, he encourages his students to do the same, even if doing so risks discomfort and contravention of politically correct speech. In this, he reminds us that we can only really solve shared problems when we speak and listen "with the heart."

Put value on place-based education. When Gatensby is not traveling, he and his wife, Colleen, spend time at the Nares Mountain Wilderness Camp, which he founded in 1995. There, he teaches traditional Tlingit Peacemaking to visitors from around the globe. He has worked to bring attention to the overrepresentation of Indigenous persons in Canadian prisons and the injurious legacy of the residential school system that is also very much a part of his own personal experience. He was sent to a Mission School in Carcross when he was 8 years old. He attributes much of the trouble he experienced as a youngster to the time he spent in this residential school (Caley, 1998). He knew what it felt like to be alienated from his own community and endured the humiliation of "having *outsiders* make the decisions the community had to live with" (quoted in Caley, 1994, p. 185). His willingness to publicly reveal the unfortunate legacy of the residential school system contributed to the Canadian government's move to redress these historical injustices.

Gatensby's teaching on site, at his camp location, is a good case study in place-based education. Place-based education immerses students in the local culture and experiences of the people and their land. The strength of place-based education is the creation of knowledge by and for Indigenous peoples, which can benefit those peoples, and, indeed, everyone:

> The depth of Indigenous knowledge rooted in the long inhabitation of a particular place offers lessons that can benefit everyone, from educator to scientist, as we search for a more satisfying and sustainable way to live on this planet. (Barnhardt & Kawagley, 2005, p. 9)

In contrast, in the contemporary university, students often learn concepts that are disconnected from practice. Instructors often teach academic subjects at a purely theoretical level, cut off from the physical environment or historical context in which that knowledge arose. As a deliberate counterposition, place-based education promotes learning in the unique environment and community associated with the knowledge one is learning. Consistent with this tradition, Gatensby's camp, in which he conducts his lessons, is situated on traditional Tlingit land where Tlingit Elders have passed down knowledge and practices from generation to generation from time immemorial. Those Elders did this though storytelling (Archibald, 2008), which is central to Tlingit cultural practice. Through the stories, concepts become rooted in traditional knowledge and practice. In storytelling, the heart and head become connected.

Harold Gatensby has shown us, by his living example, that good leadership is all about promoting and maintaining healthy relationships with others, with the community, and with the society at large. He reminds us that the word *Tlingit* means "human being." For Gatensby, leadership means providing a space in which others are encouraged to experience their authentic *human* being. In the Circle, they have the opportunity, even if only for the duration of the process, to experience a heartfelt connection to community, history, the natural environment, and, above all, to themselves. That is Gatensby's message to his fellow educators.

NOTE

Both authors have engaged in numerous in-depth conversations with Harold Gatensby and his brother, Phillip Gatensby, along with other peacemakers in Carcross, located in Yukon Territory, Canada. Polly Hyslop met Gatensby in 2007 when they worked together on an environmental conservation project in Yukon Territory. Brian Jarrett first met Gatensby in 2012 when Gatensby presented at the University of Alaska, and also worked with him in 2013 during the filming of the documentary *The Origins of Peacemaking Circles*.

REFERENCES

Archibald, J. (2008). *Indigenous storywork: Educating the heart, mind, body and spirit*. Vancouver, British Columbia, Canada: University of British Columbia Press.

Barnhardt, R., & Kawagley, A. O. (2005). Indigenous knowledge systems and Alaska Native ways of knowing. *Anthropology and Education Quarterly, 36*(1), 8–23. Retrieved from www.fws.gov/nativeamerican/pdf/tek-barnhardt-kawagley.pdf

Caley, D. (1998). *The expanding prison: The crisis in crime and punishment and the search for alternatives.* Toronto, Ontario, Canada: House of Anansi Press Limited.

Gatensby, H. (2012, Oct. 16). Canadian restorative justice practitioners discuss "putting justice back into the hands of the people." Lecture at University of Alaska Fairbanks.

Jarrett, B. & Hyslop, P. (Producers). (2013). *The origins of peacemaking circles* [Unreleased documentary]. University of Alaska Fairbanks.

Hyslop, P. (2012). Restorative justice in rural Alaska. *Alaska Journal of Dispute Resolution, Number 1*. Retrieved from ssrn.com/abstract=2602687

Jarrett, B., & Hyslop, P. (2014). Justice for all: An Indigenous community-based approach to restorative justice in Alaska. *Northern Review, 38*(2014), 239–268. Retrieved from ssrn.com/abstract=2572274

CHAPTER 12

Golda Meir
A Leader for National Revival and Social Justice

Izhar Oplatka
TEL AVIV UNIVERSITY, ISRAEL

Golda Meir, the prime minister of Israel in the years 1969–1974, was born in Kiev, Ukraine, in 1898, in times of pogroms against Jews, and migrated with her family to Milwaukee, Wisconsin, when she was 8 years old. In 1917, she graduated from teacher training college and married her first and only husband, Morris Meyerson. Four years later, the young couple immigrated to Palestine and joined Kibbutz Merhavya, though they left it three years later on. At the same time, Meir became a leading figure in the Israel Labor Movement that believed in Zionism and socialism. Unfortunately, her marriage was unsuccessful and she separated from her husband in 1938.

After the establishment of Israel in 1948, Meir was appointed Israel's ambassador to the Soviet Union. A year later, she became the minister of labor. In 1956, she was appointed minister of foreign affairs, and 10 years later, she was in the highest job in her party—the secretary-general of the Labor Party. When the prime minister of Israel, Levi Eshkol, passed away abruptly, Meir was appointed by the party to replace him.

As prime minister, Meir faced the war of attrition along the border with Egypt, confronted Austrian Chancellor Bruno Kreisky over Soviet Jewish emigration to Israel through Vienna, and was forced to manage one of the worst wars in Israeli history—the Yom Kippur War—in 1973, after the armies of Syria and Egypt attacked Israel by surprise and conquered some areas near the borders. Following the war and its concomitant public protest, she resigned in 1974. Four years later, she died at the age of 80.

THE CONTEXT AND ACTIVITIES AS A LEADER

An understanding of the social and national dynamics that characterized Meir's life commences in Kiev, Ukraine, which was part of Russia in those years. In her autobiography, Meir (1976) recalled the "almost pogrom" that her family had experienced: Rumors about anti-Semitic groups of people marching toward the houses of the Jews sent her family to hide in the basement for most of the day. Afterward Meir dreamt of the sounds of hammers and the sight of planks, images that stayed with her for the rest of her life. Meir's memories of this kind, coupled with her strong fear of Cossacks and the Russian police (Davidson, 1976), reflected the reality of Jewish people in Russia and Eastern Europe, leading many of them to immigrate to the United States, and also leading to the foundation of the Zionist movement aimed at establishing a state for the Jewish people in Palestine.

Because of anti-Semitic attacks against Jews during World War I in Europe, Meir became more deeply involved with Zionist activities and worked many hours on street corners in Milwaukee and nearby cities collecting money for the Jewish National Fund—the organization that was buying land in Palestine from Turkish and Arab landowners. Meir quickly became one of the best speakers in this movement and helped convince many American Jews to donate to the Jewish sector in Palestine. Eventually, she saw the party as the center of her life (Avizohar et al., 1994).

After immigrating to Palestine and spending some years in the kibbutz and in Tel Aviv, and raising her two children, Meir was invited to take on a political job—head of the women's association in the Histadrut, an organization of workers in Palestine. This organization constituted part of the political and public structure in the Jewish part of Palestine under the British mandate that preceded the establishment of the state of Israel. From that time on, she was fully committed to the foundation of a homeland for the Jewish people, traveling around the world for many reasons, such as pledging other leaders to save the Jewish people of Germany before World War II broke out and soliciting money from wealthy Jews in the United States for purchasing weapons. In these jobs, she managed to collect a great deal of money, much more than expected, from the Jewish diaspora, but she failed to convince other leaders to help the Jews during World War II. She swore that she would devote her life to the establishment of a Jewish state in Palestine so that her people would not have to beg for help again.

As minister of labor, Meir strove to provide any Jewish immigrant who moved to Israel from poor countries with a proper job and apartment, and she called upon people not to discriminate against the Arab workers who remained on their land and became citizens of Israel after the new nation was formed. She established the Institute of National Insurance, which promised welfare and nutrition to every citizen, and promoted many socialist laws in the Israeli Parliament. With Ben Gurion, the first prime minister of Israel, she resisted voices that called to limit immigration to Israel for economic reasons, and empathically claimed that Israel is the homeland of every Jew, regardless of age and property. As minister of foreign affairs, Meir established many diplomatic relationships with African countries and strengthened the important relationship between Israel and the United States.

Reflecting on the moment when the Labor Party Central Committee elected Meir as its candidate to the premiership of Israel in 1969, Meir said: "I had never planned to be prime minister; I had never planned any position, in fact. . . . I only knew that now I would have to make decisions every day that would affect the lives of millions of people, and I think that is why perhaps I cried" (quoted in Avner, 2010, p. 201). Meir's greatest motivation to assume the office of prime minister was her ideological conviction rather than a drive for power and authority (Steinberg, 2008).

As prime minister, her leadership style was characterized by a policy orientation that oscillated between ideology and pragmatism (Steinberg, 2008). Her ideological commitment made her goal oriented, and she acted in her cabinet as a strong advocate for her beliefs. She discriminated in favor of those who tended to share her ideological beliefs and relied heavily on her own personal advisors and on those members of the cabinet she trusted most. Likewise, she didn't agree to make full peace between Israel and the Arab countries in return for negotiation about the territories Israel occupied in 1967. Her refusal and her blind reliance on the capabilities of the Israeli army were among the major causes of the Yom Kippur War of 1973. Indeed, after this war, her popularity waned. Many blamed her for the war's failures because of her conservative, simplistic views (Goldstein, 2012).

KEY LESSONS FROM MEIR'S BIOGRAPHY FOR EDUCATIONAL LEADERS

Reading biographies of Golda Meir illuminates five lessons that readers can learn from about educational leadership.

1. Have a calling and fulfill it. Golda Meir grew up in a climate of anti-Semitism and political resentment in Russia (Avizohar et al., 1994) and witnessed the horrible consequences of the Holocaust. Although Jews responded in different ways to these onerous conditions, Meir chose the Zionist ideology that aimed to settle Jews in nonpopulated lands in Palestine and to ensure the safety of the state (Steinberg, 2008). Many years after the almost-pogrom she had experienced as a little child (described above), Meir said:

> If there is any logical explanation necessary for the direction which my life has taken, maybe this is it—the desire and the determination to save Jewish children . . . from a similar scene and a similar experience. (Quoted in Davidson, 1976, p. 9)

Meir was proud to be part of the Jewish people that has maintained its distinct identity for over 2,000 years (Avner, 2010), and despite paying a personal price (e.g., divorce, inability to spend time with her children), she said she could not refuse to do what was asked of her (Meir, 1976). When she was feeling frustrated about the refusal of most countries to allow persecuted Jews in Hitler's Germany to enter their territories, Meir said at a newspaper conference:

> There is one ideal I have in my mind . . . that is that my people should not need expressions of sympathy any more. (Quoted in Davidson, 1976, p. 152)

Amazingly, she was never affected by the question of the success of an undertaking. She indicated that if she felt an action was the right thing to do, she was in favor of it, regardless of the possible outcome (Meir, 1976). In fact, she learned the value of pragmatism and looked for efficient responses to immediate problems and for the achievement of well-defined goals (Steinberg, 2008). She tended to be straightforward (Goldstein, 2012). Educational leaders can learn the following lessons from Meir: First, a leader needs a calling to direct his or her efforts and energize followers. This calling is more than a vision, a topic that is discussed at length in the educational literature (e.g., Kurland, Peretz, & Herz-Lazarowitz, 2010); it is like an inner voice that calls the leader to save the souls of the children and provide them with better opportunities in life.

Second, the calling is not learned at school or in leadership development programs; it is something that is shaped in the leader's mind gradually in light of external conditions to which the leader had been exposed for a long time.

Finally, a calling is necessary but insufficient; the leader must also adopt a pragmatic point of view to make the calling come true. The calling is supposed to inspire the leader in his or her managerial actions on the highest level, but without special and clear goals, the calling is unlikely to be implemented.

2. Always search for social justice! Meir grew up in a poor family. She always remembered being hungry in Kiev and the extreme cold in her house when she was a little girl. Her father was a master carpenter and usually found work, but many times he was not paid for it, because Jews could not even claim their basic rights during those years in Russia (Davidson, 1976). The poverty she experienced for a long time seemed to make Meir a fighter for social justice. When she arrived in Milwaukee, she was among the few people who felt obliged to make friendly contact with a local Chinese person whose unfamiliar appearance made people avoid him. As a 4th-grader, Meir couldn't bear the humiliation of poor children in her school whose only "fault" was not having enough money to pay for their own textbooks and were therefore asked to stand up in class and say they were poor loudly in order to be supplied with textbooks from a special school charity. Meir's response to this was to organize a group of girls to go from door to door in their neighborhood and ask for donations (Meir, 1976).

Despite the fact that her experience growing up in America left her with the belief that each individual is responsible for his or her own fate (Avizohar et al., 1994), Meir felt responsible for the absorption of many Jewish immigrants arriving in Israel after its establishment. She refused to slow down immigration and instead organized large infrastructure projects (such as building roads) to provide newcomers with jobs (Davidson, 1976). Several years later, she expressed much concern about social gaps in Israel and their implications for the development of a just society. She strove for a classless society, socialist regulations that promised minimum standards of living for each citizen, and a centralized economic structure that would provide jobs for everyone.

Meir was a leader for social justice, and her pursuit of social justice has several practical implications for educators today:

- Never compromise with social injustice in your school and always fight for social justice, even if you have to pay a personal price for that.
- You cannot search for social justice in one educational arena and avoid it in others. Social justice should be part of your ideology and calling, not something for negotiation.
- Honesty and modesty are preconditions for leadership for social justice. Only when you pay attention to the weakest people in the society and refrain from flaunting your wealth in front of them can you authentically lead your school in pursuit of social justice.

3. Love people and express it! Many events in Meir's life prove that she simply loved human beings and needed other people around her. At the age of 10, when she attended the play *Uncle Tom's Cabin* and saw the scene in which the cruel planter whipped Tom endlessly, she felt her stomach lurching and suddenly she sprang to her feet and screamed: "No! No! Stop it!" (Davidson, 1976, p. 71). As a leader in the Zionist movement before the establishment of Israel, whenever she sent underground fighters out to defend isolated Jewish farms and towns against ever-increasing Arab attacks, she could never fall asleep (Meir, 1976). As minister of labor, she used to visit many factories and sites of infrastructure projects to talk with workers and make decisions based on real and practical problems (Avizohar et al., 1994). She always participated in her officials' and secretaries' family events and suggested that politicians feel more and think less if they want the world to be a better place (Davidson, 1976). Following Meir's example, school leaders should consider ways to display sincere love toward school members and stakeholders in varied forms and think about their well-being.

4. Be determined, not stubborn! Meir was made of stern stuff. As a little girl, whenever she felt she was right, she simply wouldn't obey—not even a direct order (Davidson, 1976). For example, when asking people to donate money for poor students, Meir never accepted refusals and said: "I was not born among counts and royalty either" (quoted in Davidson, 1976, p. 73). Few people found they could refuse after that! Meir's first job in the Kibbutz was to pick almonds, and the quota was a basketful an hour. She knew that the others were watching her and wondering how long the American would hold up before she quit. But she never quit (Meir, 1976). During the Yom Kippur War, the minister of defense informed her of the rapid depletion of the arsenal (tanks, planes, guns). She replied: "Moshe, one way or another I'll get you your weapons. Your job is to bring us victory, mine is to give you the means to do so" (quoted in Avner, 2010, p. 242). Several days afterward, she flew to Washington to talk with President Nixon and his staff and convinced them to send tons of ammunition and all the kinds of weapons Israel needed to win the war.

In old age, however, she tended to see things in shades of black and white and to be stubborn on certain principles that were no longer applicable in the second half of the 20th century (Steinberg, 2008). In the years before the 1973 war, she became very dogmatic, unwilling to question her own beliefs and resisting any attempt to adopt an opposite reality, such as a long ceasefire with Egypt in return for some withdrawal from the Sinai Desert. She never believed that Arab leaders intended to make real peace with Israel and was sure that their intentions were to destroy the state of Israel (Goldstein, 2012). Even after the traumatic 1973 war, Meir, then age 75, was unable to change her work habits and give up control for fear that such actions would undermine her power. Some insights for educators can be taken from this:

- There is a subtle line between determination and stubbornness, and effective leaders should be careful not to be stubborn. Be determined to achieve your calling, but don't forget to alter your course when the circumstances are changing.
- Always seek hard and complex challenges, but never see the challenges as a purpose of their own; challenges are temporary and contingent and should be modified whenever necessary to improve the school.
- Although the late career of a principal might be a time of personal growth and high self-efficacy (Oplatka, 2010), educational leaders at this stage are in danger of mental fixation resulting in negative implications for the school.

5. Give your followers a sense of partnership. Since Meir was a small child she had "the power of putting other people to work," as a friend wrote to her (Davidson, 1976, p. 126), an ability that dominated her leadership style during her political career. She granted her senior staff a great deal of autonomy, trusted them, and supported them (Avizohar et al., 1994). Only rarely was she involved in her ministers' spheres of responsibility, although she was fully aware of what was going on there (Goldstein, 2012). Yet she was always in command, a symbol of strength and authority, providing a degree of discipline in her government (Steinberg, 2008). She advocated her opinions and ideologies, built consensus, and took on the role of the arbitrator whenever necessary. Some practical understandings educators can take from her career are the following:

- A good leader can combine authority (for example, supervision) and partnership (empowerment, autonomy) to create a better work atmosphere in school.
- A sense of partnership motivates followers to go the extra mile and improve the school considerably, while granting the leader the authority to supervise as needed.

SUMMARY

Golda Meir contributed considerably to the establishment of Israel and to its growth during critical and turbulent times. At every point in her life, she was capable of motivating people to follow her ideologies and her beliefs in Zionism, equality, and social justice. School leaders who are driven by a strong educational calling that emphasizes not only individual achievement but also the pursuit of social justice and equality, as scholars have suggested (e.g., Jean-Marie, Normore, & Brooks, 2009), are likely to create a sense of collaboration and fraternity in their schools, resulting in high student achievement and a positive school climate. But in order to achieve that, as Meir's story shows, they have to be determined, goal-oriented, pragmatic, and participative. Likewise, it is not enough to talk about positive school climate; school leaders need to express love and caring toward every school member, work hard, and face new challenges without fear. A determined (not stubborn) principal who tends to display positive emotions toward teachers, students, and parents is more likely to create a safe and constructive school environment that consistently allows better learning opportunities for students. No doubt, as happened to Meir (Goldstein, 2012), school members will love and admire such a school leader, although he or she might pay a personal price for being such a leader, as Meir once indicated (Avner, 2010).

A PERSONAL NOTE

I was only 7 years old when the Yom Kippur War broke out, and my only memory is running with my mother and sister to a shelter in the nearby building. When I grew up, I felt many negative emotions toward the prime minister who refused any compromise and contributed, at least implicitly, to the death of many soldiers. The opportunity to write this chapter about Golda Meir made me alter my attitude toward her leadership, and like Ariel Sharon, another former prime minister of Israel, I have come to think Meir "was a great leader" (quoted in Goldstein, 2012, p. 600). Every school leader can learn a lot from her story!

REFERENCES

Avizohar, M., Gilboa, M., Globerson, A., Giladi, D., Greenber, Y., & Kaufman, I. (1994). *Golda: Growth of a leader (1921–1956)*. Tel Aviv, Israel: Am Oved Publisher.

Avner, Y. (2010). *The prime ministers: An intimate narrative of Israeli leadership*. New York, NY: The Toby Press.

Davidson, M. (1976). *The Golda Meir story*. New York, NY: Charles Scribner's Sons.

Goldstein, Y. (2012). *Golda: A biography*. Jerusalem, Israel: Bialik Publishing.

Jean-Marie, G., Normore, A. H., & Brooks, J. S. (2009). Leadership for social justice: preparing 21st century school leaders for a new social order. *Journal of Research on Leadership Education, 4*(1), 1–31.

Kurland, H., Peretz, H., & Herz-Lazarowitz, R. (2010). Leadership style and organizational learning: The mediate effect of school vision. *Journal of Educational Administration, 48*(1), 7–30.

Meir, G. (1976). *My life*. New York, NY: Dell Books.

Oplatka, I. (2010). Principals in late career: Towards a conceptualization of principals' tasks and experiences in the pre-retirement period. *Educational Administration Quarterly, 46*(5), 776–815.

Steinberg, B. S. (2008). *Women in power: The personalities and leadership styles of Indira Gandhi, Golda Meir, and Margaret Thatcher*. Montreal, Quebec, Canada: MQUP.

CHAPTER 13

Passing the Torch
The Legacy of Fannie Lou Hamer

Gaëtane Jean-Marie
UNIVERSITY OF NORTHERN IOWA, UNITED STATES

At the precipice of America's changing demographics, White supremacy and xenophobic, homophobic, misogynistic, and racist ideologies were emboldened during the 2016 presidential campaign in the United States. These were heightened by then–presidential candidate Donald Trump, who used his campaign platform to incite hate, use vile language, and engage in fear-mongering rhetoric, such as his call for a ban on Muslims entering the United States or his characterization of Mexican immigrants as criminals and rapists, to create a divide between people across lines of race/ethnicity and gender, seeking to invoke a social and racial hierarchy from the past in explicit ways. The tenor of his campaign was divisive, exemplified by his slogan, "make America great again," which harkened back to the era of the civil rights movement—a period in America's history in which people marched and protested against widespread discrimination, inequalities, and racism/sexism (Atwater, 1996). Trump's rise has been accompanied by a rise in anti-Semitism, the emergence of the alt-right movement (short for alternative right and synonymous with White supremacy), and greater prominence for White supremacist figures such as former Ku Klux Klan leader David Duke, who has endorsed and praised Trump on many occasions.

As a politically engaged individual, I followed the 2016 presidential election closely. Surely, I thought, the American people will not stand for such a demagogue and elect Donald Trump to the highest office in our free world. We are better than that, I assured myself. We have progressed as a society. But the outcome of the presidential election stunned many, including myself. I was numbed, speechless, and despondent. My emotions were not because my candidate did not win but because I felt that many of my fellow Americans were closeted supporters of a divisive, bigoted, and racist candidate. As civil rights activist Fannie Lou Hamer once said, "I question America" (as cited in Surgis, 2014). These famous words were spoken 53 years ago at the tumultuous 1964 Democratic National

Convention in Atlantic City. Similarly, the 2016 election outcome became a soul-searching moment for America.

The global community watched as America sank to a low. The day after the presidential election, I wanted to call in sick from work and shut myself away from society to grapple with what had happened. I needed to process. I was angry and disappointed; the emotions piled up. But I couldn't stay home. Life must go on and I readied myself to metaphorically "wear the mask" as Paul Laurence Dunbar said, referring to the double-consciousness (1896) that people of color use to overcome racial injustices. I am grateful for the kind email I received from a Canadian colleague with the subject line "Thinking of you this morning," in which he shared: "Your work, with your students, faculty, teaching colleagues, and beyond, is critical and needs you to continue to strongly advocate and act toward change. Now more than ever." This act of kindness from my colleague and countless others who reached out to me was consoling. They understood my pain.

What was difficult for me was learning that 53% of White, educated women voted for a candidate who bragged about sexually assaulting women and tweeted that women should have expected to be sexually assaulted when males and females were mixed together in the military. I presumed there would be solidarity among women, that we wouldn't condone such behaviors, and that we would vote against Donald Trump. As history portends, many of my White sisters did not deliver on the promise of sisterhood but played a role in electing President Donald Trump. As I reflected on these events surrounding the presidential election, the words of Fannie Lou Hamer rang true again: "I'm sick and tired of being sick and tired" (Barber & Barber, 2016).

Examining the life of Fannie Lou Hamer during this time of hopelessness brought a renewed energy for activism. Through immersing myself in the literature about Hamer, two purposes emerged from my synthesis that signify the value and importance of her voice during these troubling times: First, I drew upon historical social events involving Hamer to examine how she remained vigilant in her fight for social justice and change. At a time in which the explicit vitriol of Trump's America echoes that of the reactionary forces Hamer battled in her lifetime, it is critical to uphold the principles of tolerance, acceptance, inclusiveness, and diversity that many others have fought for in the social justice struggle. While there's been societal advancement there's much more to do that necessitates a call for social activism. Second, I found solace in a historical figure who passed the baton to the next generation of social activists with her ability to see others' pain and stand in solidarity in the face of overwhelming opposition. In reading biographies of Hamer, I saw that the authors (Alston & McClellan, 2011; Atwater, 1996; Brooks, 2014; Rogers, 2005) described her life under Jim Crow oppression and depicted her remarkable journey of resilience and determination as being defined by barrier transcendence, the quest for social justice, and social-political activism. Importantly, they portrayed the "collaborative struggles of others with whom she worked and fought for a different America" (Weatherford, 2015, p. 53).

HISTORICAL OVERVIEW OF FANNIE LOU HAMER

Fannie Lou Hamer was one of the civil rights movement's most inspiring leaders. The power of her ethos and her rhetorical vision in her freedom quest for oppressed people played a significant role in the struggle (Alston & McClellan, 2011; Atwater, 1996; Rogers, 2005). She helped organize and led struggles for suffrage and full employment, and against Jim Crow laws (Atwater, 1996; Mills, 2007). Although Hamer was a prominent figure of the civil rights movement, her life may be characterized as an untold story—at least it was until several scholars (e.g., Bramlett-Solomon, 1991; Hamlet, 1996, Lee, 1999; Mills, 1994; Rubel, 1990) researched her life and became devoted to capturing an inspiring individual who "left an indelible mark on this nation" (Brooks, 2014, p. 6).

A content analysis of five leading national newspapers from 1964 to 1977 showed little recognition of Hamer's achievements until the end of her life (Brooks, 2014; Brooks & Houck, 2011). Early coverage often mentioned her physical attributes, which was a common feature in coverage of women in that era, but there was also some insight into her contributions at the end. More recently, her life has been captured in books for small children such as Carole Boston Weatherford's *Voice of Freedom: Fannie Lou Hamer: Spirit of the Civil Rights Movement*. Weatherford's (2015) illustrated book of Hamer's life emphasizes the activist's perseverance and courage as she let her booming voice be heard.

The Early Years—An Awakening to the Reality of Black Exploitation

Born Fannie Lou Townsend on October 6, 1917, in the small community of Tomnolen, Mississippi, Hamer was the youngest of 20 children in a family of poor sharecroppers (Weatherford, 2015). Her parents were grateful for another healthy child—although they struggled to provide food for their growing family, they recognized that Hamer would eventually be an additional laborer to support her poor family once she was of age to work in the fields. Forced to leave school after 6th grade, she joined the rest of her family in the fields weeding and picking cotton. Although Hamer had a deep desire to be educated and an innate hunger for knowledge, she would never return to school. In spite of this disappointment, she found solace in and strength from the love of her family and through her Christian faith. Not long after she stopped working in the fields, Hamer began to challenge the segregated structure of Ruleville, Mississippi, the city to which her parents had moved when she was 2 years old. Ruleville attracted a large number of sharecroppers who came seeking work and higher wages, leading to the rapid growth of the population. Detailing Hamer's life during that period, Brooks (2014) asserted:

> Living conditions were horrid in which families lived in huts and children's beds consisted of old cotton sacks filled with grass or cornhusks. Working conditions were equally poor; sharecroppers labored in the hot, humid, mosquito-ridden, and snake-infested fields. In fact, sharecroppers were often kept in the landowners' debt through an exploitative credit-based system, against which Blacks had no recourse. (p. 36)

These deplorable living conditions and inequitable relations between Blacks and Whites created hostility and resentment; younger generations like Hamer's demanded equal treatment and were not going to acquiesce to White supremacist ideology.

Like Hamer's family, many sharecroppers' families and communities found strength in their religion (including sermons and Negro spirituals) in small plantation sanctuaries throughout the South. It was in these sacred spaces that Hamer, in her early years, began to develop her rhetorical skills. She had an affinity for the spoken word, perceiving herself as a prophet, and she used religious symbols to craft messages that resonated with disenfranchised people (Brooks & Houck, 2011; Hamlet, 1996; Mills, 2007; Weatherford, 2015). According to Hamlet (1996), "As a rhetor, Hamer exemplified a high level of intelligence in crafting messages that were based on African American culture and Christian principles. . . . She usually ended each message with a song in the tradition of the African American church, thus creating a bond with other African Americans" (p. 566).

In the 1940s, she met her husband, Perry "Pap" Hamer, who worked on the same plantation. For 18 years, they worked together on the plantation until she was fired for trying to vote. It was not until Hamer was 45 years old that she learned that she had the right to vote as an American citizen (Brooks & Houck, 2011). She was born 47 years after the 15th Amendment had given African Americans the right to vote, and 3 years after her birth, the 19th Amendment granted suffrage to American women (Brooks, 2014). These amendments, however, were not well known to poor Black people like Hamer because of the barriers created by oppressive social circumstances.

In the words of Fannie Lou Hamer, "Nobody's free until everybody's free" (quoted in Weatherford, 2015, p. 44). Hamer's raised consciousness stirred her to take up the struggle for civil rights, social equality, and economic improvement for the African American community (Brooks & Houck, 2011). In 1961, she went into a hospital to have a small uterine tumor removed; instead, doctors performed a hysterectomy without her permission or indication of the necessity (Mills, 2007). Three years later, she shared this story with an audience in Washington, DC, in which she indicated that she was one of many Black women in her town who have been a victim of a "Mississippi appendectomy"—an unwanted, unrequested, and unwarranted hysterectomy given to poor and unsuspecting Black women (Mills, 2007). Her own encounters with racism fueled her drive to battle for basic civil rights and human dignity.

The Middle Years—Social Activism and Racial Uplift

A religious person, Hamer was an avid churchgoer. During the civil rights movement, the Black church was a catalyst for social change. There, people could not only seek solace in religion for their sufferings but also strategize for change and organize protests (Mills, 2007). For Hamer, the Black church was a training ground that propelled her to learn about empowerment and citizenship, fighting alongside others in the struggle for civil rights in Mississippi. When young activists spoke at her church in 1962, informing the people about their right to vote, Hamer felt compelled to register herself and help others register as well. In retaliation for her attempt to register to vote, she lost her job and her family was evicted from the plantation. Hamer also faced threats, was jailed, and was severely beaten while traveling home from civil rights activities. For example, in 1963, she and her comrades were jailed and brutally beaten with blackjacks by two inmates at the behest of the police. Additionally, Hamer and her husband faced other forms of harassment from local officials. For instance, they received a $9,000 water bill even though they did not even have running water in their home (Weatherford, 2015). Night visitors riddled her house with bullets, and she suffered other threats and indignities. But despite all these atrocities, she persevered, resolving to spend her life rallying others to continue the fight.

When she joined the Student Nonviolent Coordinating Committee (SNCC), she took on an active role in mobilizing people to march and protest. Her exposure to activism came through meetings she attended at the Regional Council of Negro Leadership, where she listened to speeches by Northern Black elected officials and National Association for the Advancement of Colored People (NAACP) attorney Thurgood Marshall (Hamlet, 1996). It was during this time that she helped found the Mississippi Freedom Democratic Party (MFDP); this organization drew a national spotlight to the plight of African Americans in the South. Despite not having a chance at winning because most African Americans could not vote, she ran for Congress in the 1964 Democratic primary. Through her campaign, MFDP garnered visibility and provided training in how the election process worked (Brooks & Houck, 2011).

Her testimony at the Democratic National Convention in 1964 was televised across the nation (Mills, 2007). She explained why the credentials committee should recognize the integrated MFDP over the state's segregated official party delegation (Mills, 2007). With television cameras rolling, she sat before the committee and delivered an emotional speech telling the world about the struggles of African Americans who were trying to be "first-class citizens" in Mississippi. With courage and dignity, Hamer stated:

> If the Freedom Democratic Party is not seated now, I question America. Is this America? The land of the free and the home of the brave, where we have to sleep with our telephones off the hooks because our lives be threatened daily because we want to live as decent human beings, in America? (quoted in Brooks, 2014, p. 101)

Her comments on national television captured the attention of President Johnson, delegates at the convention, and people around the country, challenging the official all-White Mississippi delegation that excluded African Americans from voting. In an attempt at appeasement, her organization was offered two delegation seats, but they declined. They wanted visibility for MFDP in the Democratic National Convention and wouldn't compromise over the lack of representation of African Americans who had been staunch supporters of the party.

The Later Years—Against Repression and Oppression

Beyond her passion for electoral politics, Hamer wanted to change conditions in her state, and she organized several efforts to improve the living standards for Mississippians. She testified before U.S. Senate committees on poverty and attended the 1969 White House Conference on Hunger to raise awareness about the deplorable economic conditions of her fellow African Americans (Alston & McClellan, 2011). In 1969, with financial contributions from longtime supporter Harry Belafonte (actor and activist) and others, she purchased 40 acres of land for Freedom Farm, a cooperative for African American farmers, which eventually grew to 640 acres (Alston & McClellan, 2011; Hamlet, 1996). Farmers grew crops and vegetables for their families, and in 1971, the first White family asked to move to Freedom Farm (Atwater, 1996). However, because of financial hardships, bad weather, and poor management, the farm went out of business in 1974. During that time, Hamer's health was declining. Still, she continued to provide clothes, food, money, and whatever else she could to people in need. In 1977, at age 59, Hamer died of heart failure as a result of hypertension and was buried in her hometown of Ruleville (Dreier, 2012).

Before her death, this courageous Black woman—like other underrecognized women—played many roles in the civil rights movement. In celebration of the NAACP's 100th anniversary in 2008, the U.S. Postal Service included Fannie Lou Hamer among 12 civil rights pioneers honored with commemorative postage stamps. In 2009, the International Slavery Museum recognized Hamer as a "Black Achiever" and included a portrait of her in its permanent exhibit, next to one of President Obama (Brooks, 2014).

While pursuing graduate studies, I encountered the activism work of Fannie Lou Hamer in my coursework on women's studies for a postbaccalaureate certificate. Years later, as an affiliate faculty member, I created a course called Black Women and Leadership in the African and African American Studies Department. I needed to share what I had learned about Fannie Lou Hamer with my undergraduate students in the hope of inspiring them about social activism. Perhaps selfishly, I didn't want my students to encounter Hamer's work after their undergraduate studies were over, but sooner, so they could experience the profound courage, zeal, and commitment to social equality Hamer embodied. My students' engagement with the readings and texts about Hamer increased their knowledge about the contributions of people of color historically. For some of my students, this was their first time encountering and engaging with texts about the positive contributions of Black women during the civil rights movement.

DISCUSSION: LESSONS LEARNED FROM THE LIFE OF FANNIE LOU HAMER

Barrier Transcendence. *Barrier transcendence* addresses the ways in which personal attributes, individual behavior, and environmental features may interact within an individual on what can be described as a plane of experience (Santamaría & Santamaría, 2016, p. 79). These factors may increase one's enjoyment and engagement in purposeful activity, enhancing one's ability to recognize and act upon opportunities to enact change, advancement, and movement to the next plane (Santamaría & Santamaría, 2016). Hamer's early life experiences in the cotton fields stirred in her a desire for positive change, and she began to employ various approaches to challenge the status quo to transform societal conditions for African Americans. Through her involvement in the church and attending organizing meetings alongside others, she helped develop a critical mass to challenge "institutional conditions for the greater good" (Santamaría & Santamaría, 2016, p. 80). Lending her oratorical voice, she became a central figure of the civil rights movement in Mississippi. Nonetheless, she remains an anomaly in history books, though concerted efforts are seeking to bring greater attention to Hamer's contributions (Brooks, 2014).

To illuminate the biography of Fannie Lou Hamer is to contribute to the collective effort to make visible the contributions of women in the civil rights movement. Historical texts have not adequately recognized many African American women's contributions to social movements, reducing them to just one or two icons. African American women such as Nannie

Helen Burroughs, Mary McLeod Bethune, Anna Julia Cooper, Septima Clark, Fanny Jackson Coppin, and others were an integral part of social movements to eradicate racism, sexism, and classism in society. They played roles as educators, public speakers, community activists, and civil and women's rights advocates (Jean-Marie & Dancy, 2014; Tillman, 2004). There is a need to amplify the contribution of African American women in social movements, past and present, elevating the discourse on the central roles that they continue to play. The relevance of sharing such history is connected to future generations of women of color who will continue the struggle by taking the baton previous generations have passed to them.

For example, the Women's March on January 21, 2017, to protest the election of President Trump, a day after he was sworn in, was organized by women of color—a handful impacting millions. Such women serve as a reminder that leaders come from everywhere and in every form. Reports from the national news estimated that more than 5 million worldwide and more than a million in Washington, DC, came out that day to make their voices heard. People from different backgrounds came together to stand firm against what President Trump and his new administration stand for and sent a message that the president does not have a mandate to divide the American people. The people will not remain idle and let the administration implement policies to disfranchise the most vulnerable people in American society. Although it is too early to discern if the movement will continue, there are glimmers of hope that individuals will contribute their talents and time to stand against injustice. What's at stake is the progress that has been made in American society to eradicate the injustices that were part of the laws and social practices in earlier times. But the struggle continues in this modern era, especially with a president who has created a platform for spewing hatred and elevating right-wing groups who are boldly advocating for White dominance and overtly promoting divisions along racial lines. In reflecting upon the life of Hamer, who actively fought against social injustices, it is evident that she possessed incredible courage and conviction; she was a strategist and dominant force in ensuring the movement's effectiveness. Today, in moments of despair and exhaustion, the powerful leadership Hamer demonstrated serves as a reminder to press forward in the struggle for social justice. Hamer's life story embodies the lesson of barrier transcendence in that her plight and those of others in society inspired her to purposefully and with conviction fight for social change. Capturing her life story serves as inspiration to enlist others in the call for modern social activism against right-wing fringe elements that have flourished nationwide since the election of President Trump.

The Quest for Social Justice. The history of African Americans in the United States entails social, intellectual, political, economic, and physical resistance to the oppressive conditions and exploitation that permeated their lives (Aptheker, 1971; Marable, 2000; Sitkoff, 1993). Consequently, tied to that history is the quest for social justice echoed in the 1955 speech of Martin Luther King Jr. in Birmingham, in which he called upon the Black community to persist in their resistance against injustices until a better world emerges (Sitkoff, 1993). It is in this vein that Hamer consciously thought about what she was doing: "she was aware, she had a mission, she was self-conscious and knew that hers was a voice that needed to be used" (Alston & McClellan, 2011, p. 63).

Galvanizing the country with her stirring words and her remarkable courage, Hamer became a symbol of the struggle for racial and social justice. From her childhood in a Mississippi sharecropping family ("doggone, dirt-poor doing-without"), through her initial involvement in voting rights (volunteering to register), and on to dangerous antisegregation efforts with the SNCC (arrested and beaten after approaching a White-only lunch counter) and her run for political office, she brought a national spotlight to the disenfranchisement of Blacks in the South. Hamer's heroic activism for social justice can bring hopefulness in the wake of the turmoil America is facing since the election of President Donald Trump. Hamer's life story provides sustenance for engaged activism during a time in our society that necessitates social-political activism like that of the civil rights movement.

Social-Political Activism. Grassroots leadership is often born out of deep convictions that propel people to act. The emergence of Hamer as a leader in the civil rights movement arose from her deep convictions about equal rights for all. Despite her limited education, Hamer's convictions drove her to take up the struggle. She leaves a legacy for the generation that follows her to continue the fight. The struggle for full realization of racial equality for people of color continues; we must not rest on our laurels. The election of President Barack Obama in 2008 and 2012 did not usher in a postracial America. In fact, the 2016 presidential election seemed to turn back the clock, a reminder that the fight for social and racial justice continues. The legacy of these injustices is deeply entrenched in our American society, and there's a danger that complacency may set in if well-intentioned and educated people do not collectively mobilize. It is not enough to speak against injustice; it is critically necessary to act. It matters when we act—when we are proactive rather than reactive. The 2016 president election serves as a lesson to those individuals who were against presidential candidate Trump but failed to vote and to those who did not take seriously his racially divisive and misogynist behaviors and voted for him but have now come to realize that he is not fit to lead for many reasons (i.e., lack of competence, lack of moral authority, and inability to unite the country, to name a few). In this historical moment, proactive social-political activism is critical for standing against the forces that exist today to disenfranchise the poor, people of color, and immigrants and to marginalize people based on religious beliefs.

Millions of people throughout the United States and the world must be compelled to pay attention. Just as Hamer was persistent in her struggle, we have to be vigilant to defeat oppression and social inequity today.

CONCLUSION

Hamer was deeply rooted in social and political activism in the quest for equality and justice for Blacks and all people. She leaves a legacy of protest that serves as the catalyst for social change. The election of President Trump created a renewed sense of urgency, with mass demonstrations taking place in many cities throughout the United States. Hundreds of thousands of people are gathering and marching to demand high-quality health care, equal protection under the law, religious freedom, funding for education, equal access, and more. Although the protests themselves are relevant, they must also be tied to actions if they are to be effective. Participation in voting, which starts with voter registration, is paramount to our demonstration for social justice. Hamer passed the torch to future generations to take up the struggle for the full realization of racial equality and the right to self-determination for all oppressed people.

REFERENCES

Alston, J. A., & McClellan, P. A. (2011). *Herstories: Leading with the lessons of the lives of Black women activists*. New York, NY: Peter Lang.

Aptheker, H. (1971). *Afro American history: The modern era*. New York, NY: Carol Publishing Group.

Atwater, D. F. (1996). Editorial: The voices of African American women in the civil rights movement. *Journal of Black Studies, 26*(5), 539–542.

Barber, R., & Barber, S. (2016, October 6). 'Sick and tired of being sick and tired': Making the connection between disenfranchisement and disease. *Facing South: A Voice for a Changing South*. Retrieved from www.facingsouth.org/2016/10/sick-and-tired-being-sick-and-tired-making-connection-between-disenfranchisement-and-disease

Bramlett-Solomon, S. (1991). Civil rights vanguard in the Deep South: Newspaper portrayal of Fannie Lou Hamer, 1964–1977. *Journalism & Mass Communication Quarterly, 68* (3), 515–521.

Brooks, M. P. (2014). *A voice that could stir an army: Fannie Lou Hamer and the rhetoric of the Black freedom movement*. Jackson, MS: University Press of Mississippi.

Brooks, M. P., & Houck, D. W. (Eds.). (2011). *The speeches of Fannie Lou Hamer: To tell it like it is*. Jackson, MS: University Press of Mississippi.

Dreier, P. (2012). The 100 greatest Americans of the 20th century: A social justice hall of fame. New York, NY: Nation Books.

Dunbar, P. L. (1896). We wear the mask. *Lyrics of lowly life*. Ann Arbor: University of Michigan.
Hamlet, J. D. (1996). Fannie Lou Hamer: The unquenchable spirit of the civil rights movement. *Journal of Black Studies, 26* (5), 560–576.
Jean-Marie, G., & Dancy, T. E. (2014). Pedagogy of the discipline: How Black studies can influence educational leadership. In A. H. Normore, & J. S. Brooks (Eds.), *Educational leadership for ethics and social justice: Views from the social sciences* (pp. 43–61). Charlotte, NC: Information Age.
Lee, C. K. (1999). *For freedom's sake: The life of Fannie Lou Hamer*. Urbana: University of Illinois Press.
Marable, M. (2000). *Dispatches from the ebony tower: Intellectuals confront the African American experience*. New York, NY: Columbia University Press.
Mills, K. (2007). *This little light of mine: The life of Fannie Lou Hamer* (Paperback ed.). Lexington: University Press of Kentucky.
Rogers, E. (2005). Afritics from margin to center: Theorizing the politics of African American women as political leaders. *Journal of Black Studies, 35* (6), 701–714.
Rubel, D. (1990). *Fannie Lou Hamer: From sharecropping to politics*. Englewood Cliffs, NJ: Silver Burdett Press.
Santamaría , L. J., & Santamaría, A. P. (2016). *Culturally responsive leadership in higher education: Promoting equity, access, and improvement*. New York, NY: Routledge.
Sitkoff, H. (1993). *The struggle for Black equality: 1954–1992*. New York, NY: Hill and Wang.
Surgis, S. (2014, August 21). 'I question America': Remembering Fannie Lou Hamer's challenge to white supremacy. *Facing South: A Voice for Changing the South*. Retrieved from www.facingsouth.org/2014/08/i-question-america-remembering-fannie-lou-hamers-c.html
Tillman, L. (2004). Chapter 4: African American principals and the legacy of Brown. *Review of Research in Education, 28*, 101–146.
Weatherford, C. B. (2015). *Voice of freedom: Fannie Lou Hamer: Spirit of the civil rights movement*. Somerville, MA: Candlewick Press.

CHAPTER 14

Incrementalism Beats Flamboyance
Ethel M. Smith

Catherine M. Marshall & Becca Merrill
UNIVERSITY OF NORTH CAROLINA AT CHAPEL HILL

The continuing struggle for a world that values women's contributions and respects women's rights has had within-struggle debates over the best strategies, best leaders, best coalitions, and highest priority of goals. In the pre– and post–Civil War debates in the United States, questions included whether abolition of slavery, prohibition of alcohol, or eliminating the barriers to women owning property and voting should take precedence. By the early 1900s, debates included whether women's suffrage or an equal rights amendment should be the focus. Embedded in this debate were additional divides: In demanding equal rights, were women giving up unique, valuable roles and status? Would an equal rights amendment only benefit White, educated, middle-class women? Should we ally with men, with people of color, with other organizations such as trade unions? Should we work through state, federal, or constitutional policy and politics? What sort of strategies and leadership should be employed? How radical should we be (Becker, 1981)? Twenty-first-century feminists have added self-critiques, including those of feminist critical policy analysts. These analysts doubt the adequacy of any struggle that depends upon governments and institutions that (1) were structured essentially for the benefit of White males and capitalists (Ferguson, 1984; Fraser, 1989; MacKinnon, 1989; Marshall, 1997); (2) stressed the continued Whiteness of the feminist movement (Hill-Collins, 1990); (3) stressed the need to focus on women's capacities for caring, nurturance, and collaboration, to the exclusion of other, nonstereotypical abilities; and (4) focused on how women's perspectives can contribute to peace, caring for the environment, and so on, prescribing the "appropriate" areas of influence for women.

Activists' strategies, through recent history, have ranged from working the system through letters, petitions, monitoring and reporting politicians' actions, joining or forming coalitions, and writing blogs and other media, to demonstrations, sit-ins, special symbols, slogans, clothing, boycotts, and a range of acts of violence (Shaw, 1996). However, educational leaders are already working within the system.

That is why our chapter centers on an activist leader of the early 1920s and 1930s era. No, we're not talking about Susan B. Anthony, Elizabeth Cady Stanton, or Alice Paul, who might have been at least footnotes in your history texts. Ethel M. Smith was never the flamboyant, charismatic rabble-rouser; like today's educational leaders, she worked within the system, but, when necessary, she also worked the system. Today, too, careful strategies are used by social justice leaders holding positions within the system (Marshall & Ward, 2004).

PART I: BIOGRAPHY

With the influences of her working-class and traditional background, Ethel M. Smith devoted her life to labor reform and women's rights (Butler, 2002; Smith, 1948). Having seen her father's ethics and hard work, she acted on the belief that hard work and ability are rewarded. She garnered the skills needed to work in the U.S. Census Bureau as a stenographer and then as a clerk in the Bureau of Fisheries (Smith, 1948), and, in the same bureau, she gained research and analytical training as secretary to the chief of scientific inquiry.

Her trust in the merit system turned out to be unfounded. After 12 years of civil service, Smith (1948) was repeatedly passed over for promotions and paid less than her male predecessors. In 1912, she confronted her supervisor and heard a disillusioning rationale about how the men who are being promoted have families to support. This comment inspired her to become secretary for the congressional committee of the National American Women Suffrage Association (NAWSA). Smith (1948) wrote, "What now seemed to me most worth while was to work for betterment of the conditions of human life, and closest to me of all were the problems of the women who work for their living" (p. 74).

PART II: POLITICAL ACTIVITIES

Joining, Coordinating, Initiating, Framing, and Educating

Though continuing her work on suffrage, Smith became active in the labor movement. Beginning in 1918, she served as national legislative secretary for the Women's Trade Union League (WTUL) (Who's Who—League Officers, 1926), later serving on that organization's executive board. Smith supported the WTUL's labor platform, which included an 8-hour workday, a 5-day and 44-hour workweek, and equal pay for equal work (Who's Who—National League Officers, 1926). From within her local office's workers' union, she helped organize the National Federation of Federal Employees (NFFE), as well as a Washington, DC, chapter of the WTUL (Smith, 1948).

Smith's ideas of effective political activity aligned with the WTUL's traditional style of working within the political system to create change. Smith harnessed the printed word to educate the public and lobbied congressional leaders through personal interaction and policy briefs.

Rights of Women in the Workforce

With the United States' entry into World War I in 1917, Smith became an established advocate for women's protections and rights in the workplace, as women took jobs in industry in the absence of thousands of drafted men. She urged NAWSA to parlay the increased presence of women in the workforce into a strengthened and organized force for suffrage and women's rights (Butler, 2002).

Smith's talents as writer and publicist shone between 1918 and 1920, while she served as secretary of the WTUL's legislative committee. She spearheaded a successful campaign aimed at placing the agenda of the WTUL in the public eye, especially through newspapers, including the *Washington Post* and *New York Times* (Butler, 2002).

Smith's tool was the written word. She called attention to the inequitable pay suffered by women in federal employment (Butler, 2002). Her literary spotlighting of the discrepancies in pay and responsibilities between men and women in specific federal jobs influenced an appropriations bill to equalize pay between the sexes in the Bureau of Engraving and Printing in the House of Representatives. The bill led to a raise for some women federal employees, although the full appropriation for equal pay was not realized (Butler, 2002).

Smith saw the need for a foothold to create more equitable conditions for women wage earners through protective legislation but also a legal rationale to regulate the terms of the labor contract. In 1918, when the District of Columbia passed the Keating-Trammell Act, a minimum-wage act for women and minors, Smith was selected for the minimum wage board, which had the legal authority to investigate industry pay and conditions in industries affected by the Keating-Trammell Act (Smith, 1948). This was catalytic, but business leaders challenged women-specific legislation vigorously (Butler, 2002), and in 1923, the Supreme Court overturned the minimum-wage act as unconstitutional (Smith, 1924b).

Positioning Women Workers Within the Women's Suffrage Movement

During the debate for the passage of the 19th Amendment to the Constitution, giving women the right to vote, Smith remained active through her membership in NAWSA. However, she distanced NAWSA from the more aggressive National Woman's Party (NWP), led by Alice Paul (Smith, 1924a). Ultimately, both NAWSA and the NWP were credited with the passage of the amendment (Butler, 2002).

For equal rights in federal employment, Smith organized and directed the publicity bureau for the NFFE, starting in 1920. This became the venue for her writing in the organization's official magazine, *The Federal Employee*. In addition, she managed publicity relations with the 215 chapters of the NFFE and organized local and national publicity campaigns (Butler, 2002).

Smith took the WTUL policy position that piecemeal legislation was necessary to address specific injustices for women wage earners (Federal Amendment, 1922). She believed that women's disempowered position in industry and society necessitated protective legislation for them. She believed, in alignment with the WTUL, that passage of the Equal Rights Amendment (ERA) promulgated by the National Woman's Party would decimate contemporary protective legislation and prevent further protections for wage-earning women (Butler, 2002). Smith viewed the ERA as granting theoretical equality, but not realized equality for women (Smith, 1929). Writing for the WTUL's *Life and Labor Bulletin*, Smith (1926) averred, "It is too much to believe that any one formula could bring about equality for men and women . . . or that it could be accomplished by any one stroke." Thus, after the passage of the 19th Amendment, Smith continued to be an activist for women's labor rights through women-specific legislation. Smith successfully thwarted the ERA by reaching out to union affiliates such as the American Federation of Labor (AFL), printing articles in the union bulletin (Smith, 1924a, 1926), and lobbying congressional leaders against the measure. She was also part of a delegation of women representatives who visited President Coolidge in the White House to persuade him against the amendment (Smith, 1924a).

Smith's push for women-specific legislation marks a break from her earlier work in the NFFE, where she advocated for sex-neutral policies in federal employment. For example, regarding the reclassification of civil service exams, Smith stated that sex should not be taken into account at all. She argued that women could prove that they could compete with men through their competency on entrance exams (Butler, 2002). Her line of reasoning did not follow to women in private industry, where Smith advocated for women-specific legislation.

Her work did not stop with passage of the 19th Amendment or her efficacious efforts against the ERA. Smith organized grassroots efforts and worked to build a policy issue network for women's rights among organizations with similar goals. Almost solely because of Smith's advocating, the WTUL joined the Women's Joint Congressional Committee (WJCC), a parent organization that networked women's organizations across the nation and lobbied Congress on women's issues (Butler, 2002). Smith was a part of the subcommittee of the WJCC and the representative of the WTUL who successfully lobbied Congress to create the Women's Bureau in 1920.

Ethel Smith and the Women's Bureau

The Women's Bureau was a federal organization dedicated to studying and making policy recommendations for gainfully employed women. However, Congress appropriated a significantly lower sum to the Women's Bureau than it provided for comparable federal bureaus headed by men. Smith, along with the WTUL and WJCC, immediately and again successfully lobbied Congress to increase appropriations through vehemently citing equal pay for equal work and the highly skilled qualifications necessary for positions within the Women's Bureau (Butler, 2002; Secretary Legislative Department, 1923).

When the Women's Bureau researched civil service exams and found that women were barred from taking over 60% of exams, Smith worked closely with the bureau's director, campaigning to open exams to everyone, regardless of sex (Butler, 2002). The Civil Service Commission, in response to a report filed by the Women's Bureau, acquiesced to the recommendation. However, Smith and the Women's Bureau's victory was greatly attenuated when the commission upheld the right for federal hiring managers to specify whether a man or woman was *preferred* for a position, regardless of exam performance (Butler, 2002).

Next, in 1923, Smith joined the efforts of federal labor organizations and government boards to pass the Civil Service Reclassification Act. The act would commission a board to describe the duties of each federal position and create a salary schedule for said positions, allowing clear comparisons between position and compensation (Butler, 2002). The same basic system of federal employment and pay exists today.

Also in 1923, Smith expanded her concern with women's issues to also encompass children's labor. She railed against the U.S. Supreme Court for invalidating a federal child labor law for the second time. Her solution was not to disempower the justices on the court, but rather to empower Congress to protect U.S. children (Smith, 1923).

The Same, Yet Different

After a decade dedicated to the labor movement, Smith reentered the federal civil service for the Unemployment Census of 1930, then a position in the Information Service of the Bureau of Home Economics in the U.S. Department of Agriculture. She later transferred to the Federal Social Security Board, created to administer the newly minted Social Security Act. By the time she retired in 1944, Smith had the well-earned pleasure of fair work in a materially different federal employment. Her compensation was in the "upper brackets of Civil Service salaries" (Smith, 1948, p. 76), an equality that had been denied to her and other women in earlier times. The issues she fought for are contemporary realities that are part of millions of women's and men's working lives.

It was not one well-crafted speech or the deft use of media that made Ethel M. Smith successful; she was never catapulted to fame for committing a radical act. Her political hallmarks were steadiness, collaboration, and education as she incrementally created and contributed to solutions. Smith was sought after by organizations and branches of the federal government because she was sharp, highly skilled, and a consensus builder. Her repeated paths to success follow this pattern: She articulated a vision, persuaded and garnered support through reasoning and education, and, after any setback, went about crafting the next solution.

PART III: LESSONS LEARNED FROM ETHEL M. SMITH'S LEADERSHIP

Of course, historical, social, economic, and political challenges are part of the context. Smith's challenges included debates among activists over how best to improve women's status within an embedded patriarchy, at a time when activism for workers' rights and mere mentions of race and gender issues led to marginalization. These conditions have not disappeared, and because few educational leaders today have in-depth knowledge of women leaders for social justice, this analysis should serve as a springboard for identifying a broader range of leadership models such as those in Marshall and Gerstl-Pepin's text (2004).

As a model of social justice leadership, Ethel M. Smith was a relatively quiet, unflamboyant activist who plodded along the path toward a better society. However, society continues to be an oblivious beneficiary of her unsung work. As we learn more about connections between economic and physical well-being (Wehby, Dave, & Kaester, 2016), the importance of Smith's contributions becomes more evident. We can glean the following lessons for education leaders for the 21st century.

Have a Philosophical Stance. Smith stayed the course, holding firm in her stance that specific workplace protections for women were essential for inclusive social justice. Thus, she asserted her sense that equal opportunity has to begin in organizations. Though she encountered significant pushback from middle-class women's rights activists, Smith staunchly defended her stance. She would tell us: Be prepared to encounter pushback from numerous areas. Stay the course and be ready and able to defend your vision and policies.

Incremental Progress Is More Important Than Fame. Knowing the power of White males who made the rules and handed down judgments affecting women, Smith strived for incremental gains that would minimize backlash. Thus, headline-grabbing confrontations, Smith felt, were not effective. She parlayed her credibility and competence in positions in the federal workplace to command women's rights and labor audiences. She treated defeats as temporary. She would tell us: Rather than call attention to yourself, call attention to the irrevocable logic of your cause. You might not win a place in history, but you will leave one less target (yourself) for your opponents.

Educational leaders who are of color or women are expected to be exceptionally competent, unassertive, and non-self-promoting. For these groups, to be flamboyant and commanding of credit and attention is to invite backlash. Giving away credit is "soft power" and co-opts those who would otherwise stymie social justice action. The ability to have "power with" rather than "power over" persuades others to open their eyes to previously unseen inequities and to join in willingly.

Educate, build consensus, and set actionable goals. Smith's strengths were writing arguments and rationales that spoke to a wide range of women. She used her organizational skills to educate others and to create a wide network of people who respected her leadership. Her careful wording crafted the right message and built consensus. Smith used her position and the logic respected by federal bureaucracy, establishing analytic and legal rationales for action as a bedrock foundation for making a difference. Smith would tell us: To lead, you must create a platform from which you will be seen leading. Build consensus through careful educational messaging and by conveying a strong rationale for your vision.

Be the Outsider-Within. Use your position as a competent and respectable organization member, but stay keenly attuned to the voices of those whose needs and voices are often deemed unworthy of attention. By recounting Ethel Smith's stances and strategies, we can see the power of being an "outsider-within." The principal or central office administrator is, by definition, an insider in the profession and within the district's organization. Positioned as an insider, a social justice–minded professional can promote equity and offer support to marginalized populations.

Social justice activists in education recognize that their own institutions continue discriminatory practices, worsened now by market-based neoliberalism. Institutional controls, privatization, choice, and accountability can damage the prospects of already marginalized students. In education hierarchies, the political power driving these initiatives makes social justice values and actions even more risky for social justice leaders. Risky, too, is any "outing" of the biases against those marginalized by their race, class, gender, or sexual orientation. Further, affiliation with unacceptable values, organizations, or causes can lead to dismissal.

For today's leaders, taking social justice action means upsetting the very power arrangements that gave them promotion to their jobs! Thus, taking action for social justice means a delicate crafting of strategy. They must maintain their position with an aura of competence and rationality to maneuver among the many risks associated with the pursuit of social justice ideals.

You Don't Have to Make a Splash to Make a Difference. Leaders may position themselves in particular ways and then undertake covert action. Like Ethel Smith, they try to avoid direct confrontation that would create backlash, given that they might threaten others' sacred cow (popular programs, powerful colleagues, or community leaders).

A widely used strategy among activist educators studied by Marshall and Anderson (2009) is "keeping it on the down-low" by promoting social justice in ways that are silent, secret, and covert.

Thus, as we glean lessons from Ethel Smith, we apply them to a new context—the 21st century—and to social justice advocacy leaders in education. These leaders must chip away, accept modest gains, and find low-key, quiet, unobtrusive avenues for progress. They must use, even stretch, existing equity rhetoric and policies where other practitioners may have conveniently avoided paying attention to them. Smith's example of incremental but sustainable gains and delicate advocacy yielded more effective progress for social justice leaders than the efforts of some other, more famous characters in history texts.

REFERENCES

Becker, S. D. (1981). *The origins of the equal rights amendment: American feminism between the wars*. Westport, CT: Greenwood Press.

Butler, A. E. (2002). *Two paths to equality: Alice Paul and Ethel M. Smith in the ERA debate, 1921–1929*. Albany: The State University of New York Press.

Federal amendment. (1922, August). *Life and Labor Bulletin 1*(1). Retrieved from hdl.handle.net/2027/coo.31924069101123

Ferguson, K. E. (1984). *The feminist case against bureaucracy*. Philadelphia, PA: Temple University Press.

Fraser, N. (1989). *Unruly practice: Power, discourse and gender in contemporary social theory*. Minneapolis, MN: University of Minnesota Press.

Hill-Collins, P. H. (1990). *Black feminist thought: Knowledge, consciousness, and the politics of empowerment*. New York, NY: Routledge

MacKinnon, C. A. (1989). *Toward a feminist theory of the state*. Cambridge, MA: Harvard University Press.

Marshall, C. (1997). Dismantling and reconstructing policy analysis. In I. Goodson (Ed.), *Feminist critical policy analysis: A perspective from primary and secondary schooling* (pp. 1–42). Washington, DC: The Falmer Press.

Marshall, C., & Anderson, A. (2009). Is it possible to be an activist educator? In C. Marshall & A. Anderson (Eds.), *Activist educators: Breaking past limits* (pp. 1–32). New York, NY: Routledge.

Marshall, C., & Gerstl-Pepin, C. (2004). *Re-framing educational politics for social justice*. Boston, MA: Pearson.

Marshall, C., & Ward, M. (2004). "Yes, but. . .": Education leaders discuss social justice. *Journal of School Leadership, 14*, 530–563.

Secretary Legislative Department. (1923, January). Our legislative activities in Washington. *Life and Labor Bulletin 1*(5). Retrieved from hdl.handle.net/2027/coo.31924069101123

Shaw, R. (1996). *The activist's handbook*. Berkeley, CA: University of California Press.

Smith, E. M. (1923, December). To empower Congress to protect the children. *Life and Labor Bulletin 2*(16). Retrieved from hdl.handle.net/2027/coo.31924069101123

Smith, E. M. (1924a). Labor's position against the Woman's Party amendment. *Life and Labor Bulletin 2*(18). Retrieved from hdl.handle.net/2027/coo.31924069101123

Smith, E. M. (1924b). Labor's position against the Woman's Party amendment. *Life and Labor Bulletin 2*(20). Retrieved from hdl.handle.net/2027/coo.31924069101123

Smith, E. M. (1926, March). Equal rights—Internationally. *Life and Labor Bulletin 4*(40). Retrieved from hdl.handle.net/2027/coo.31924069101123

Smith, E. M. (1929). *Toward equal rights for men and women*. Retrieved from www.worldcat.org/title/toward-equal-rights-for-men-and-women/oclc/1828406

Smith, E. M. (1948). An informal history of Virginia-Kentucky Pattersons in Illinois; their forbears and their kin including the Lewises of Llangollen. Retrieved from www.worldcat.org/title/informal-history-of-virginia-kentucky-pattesons-in-illinois-their-forbears-and-their-kin-including-the-lewises-of-llangollen/oclc/5421505

Wehby, G., Dave, D., & Kaester, R. (2016). Effects of the minimum wage on infant health (Working Paper No. 22373). Retrieved from National Bureau of Economic Research website: www.nber.org/papers/w22373

Who's who—National League officers. (1926, October). *Life and Labor Bulletin 4*(45). Retrieved from hdl.handle.net/2027/coo.31924069101123

CHAPTER 15

Ella Flagg Young
Individuality, Freedom for the Teacher, and Freedom for the Pupil

Jackie M. Blount
THE OHIO STATE UNIVERSITY

Ella Flagg Young became Chicago's superintendent of schools in 1909. During her 6 years in this role, no other woman in the country, if not the world, held a higher position of public service. She was born in Buffalo, New York, in 1845; moved with her family at an early age to Chicago; entered teaching at the age of 17 after 2 years in a teacher preparation program; became a teacher of teachers and then one of the first few women in the country to assume the principalship of a large school; was promoted to assistant superintendent, again, one of the first women nationwide to do so; earned a professorship of education at the University of Chicago; and, finally, ascended to the superintendency. At the national level, newly enfranchised women teachers overwhelmingly elected her in 1910 to be the first woman president of the National Education Association (NEA), wresting exclusive control from an entrenched educational power elite. To suffragists and their supporters everywhere, Young had become a potent symbol of the public good that women might accomplish if they were granted the opportunity (Blount, in press-b; McManis, 1916; Smith, 1979).

Far less well known, though, is that Young also possessed a razor-sharp intellect fed by a lifetime of voracious reading—inextricably linked with a commitment to meaningful action. She collaborated intensively with numerous educators, activists, artists, and other intellectuals of her time. Young earned her doctoral degree as Dewey's first student at the University of Chicago. She then became a professor, serving alongside him. Dewey readily credited Young with deeply influencing his work, helping him better understand not only schools—assistance he needed, given his limited experience—but also how democracy and education connected at the most fundamental levels, including the necessity for the overwhelming majority of school workers—women—to have full democratic rights and privileges. Young inspired Dewey to begin thinking about connections between education and democracy. He penned his first such work, "Democracy in Education" (1903), in response to her book *Isolation in the School* (1900) (Blount, in press-a), eventually publishing his fully developed thought in *Democracy and Education* (1916).

CONTEXT AND ACTIVITIES AS A LEADER

A reporter interviewed Ella Flagg Young, rumored in 1891 to be a candidate for superintendent of Chicago schools. What were her hobbies? Young replied, "Individuality. Freedom for the teacher and freedom for the pupil" ("Howland's Possible Successor," 1891). This odd response deflected the reporter's effort to learn anything personal about the notoriously private Young. It also succinctly conveyed her central focus over the half-century she had spent teaching in and leading Chicago's schools. At a time when most of the nation's leading lights in education pushed relentlessly to consolidate control of schools and prepare standardized curricula to be delivered with impeccable efficiency by a rapidly growing contingent of women teachers, Young's statement provided a perfect counterpoint. Almost 2 decades later, when Young became superintendent, she and the teachers and students of the Chicago schools proved not only that it was possible for a large system to empower its members without devolving into chaos, but that the collective and individual quality of work could increase and morale could soar.

Surprisingly, Young did not always care for schools. After attending for only a few months, the 13-year-old Ella Flagg quit school, bored with the monotonous, rote pedagogical approaches of the time. Years later, she countered this early experience by developing original approaches for teaching students and teachers alike, emphasizing respect for individuality and valuing the freedom of all. She learned her craft—in her own way—by teaching in some of the most challenging classrooms in the city, much like those where she had grown up, and creatively addressing the complex needs she encountered. She was an idiosyncratic thinker who, in turn, insisted on cultivating and respecting the unique qualities of each student and teacher.

Ella Flagg Young's life history illuminates a larger story about the teaching profession's shift from being men's to women's work. More notably, though, it captures a critical turning point in education history when women sought not only to teach, but also to become leaders of the schools and systems that they already dominated numerically—just as they were campaigning for suffrage and other expanded rights. However, as women streamed into the classroom, teaching became ever-more-demeaning work, stripped of intellectual and creative fulfilment—while simultaneously and conversely, school administration was configured as work specifically for men, granting them enlarged powers (Blount, 1998; Tyack & Hansot, 1982). Young resisted this trend in countless ways throughout her lifetime. She strongly contended that women should become school leaders in significant numbers and, even more important, that the work of teaching itself should be far more empowering.

Her influence was important. Amazingly, women school workers succeeded to an impressive degree in taking charge of Chicago's schools during Young's life; however, a fierce backlash movement eventually undercut many of these gains. Politicians campaigned to hire men with "[r]ed blood, hard muscle, virile speech, [and] manly manners" to run schools, with enlarged salaries and significantly increased powers (Churchill, 1916, p. 940). They simultaneously sought to cut teachers' salaries, centralize and standardize curricula (removing creative and intellectual control from teachers), and increase other control mechanisms (evaluation schemes, dress codes and other gender/sexuality-normed strictures, and so on). They also sought to "remove the schools from politics," which amounted to shifting important school-related decisions away from popular vote and toward appointed experts who made unilateral decisions—just when women were winning suffrage state by state, then nationally. Many of the backlash strategies instituted to limit women's powers at that time still remain in school employment today (Blount, 1998; Smith, 1979).

KEY LESSONS

Several key lessons unite Young's long career as an educator, leader, and scholar.

Community, Empowerment, and Gender. Young understood that as schools became larger and more systematized—and as the proportion of women teachers increased—teachers' intellectual and creative freedoms generally were being curtailed. She recognized that, "While system and routine are absolutely necessary, they should not be allowed to smother the personality of teacher or child" ("Howland's Possible Successor," 1891, p. 1). Instead, she consistently and adamantly argued that there should be much greater freedom afforded to both teachers and students, and furthermore, that individuality should be cultivated and appreciated. This ran counter to the prevailing view among the educational elite of the time, the almost exclusively male "educational trust" of the NEA, as well as among school officials in growing numbers of school districts around the country. Young worried that schools were devolving into a default tendency toward "isolation," where structures and functions fractured into ever-smaller compartments that kept people from communicating, cooperating, thinking freely, or feeling empowered (Young, 1900).

Young noted that this growing trend toward isolation and teacher disempowerment had gendered roots. In an electrifying speech she delivered to an overflowing audience of thousands of the city's educators, Young (1899) compared the plight of teachers, disempowered by a new class of administrators determined to exert minute control, to that of a bored housewife: "Teachers have been forced to resemble too closely the housewife who goes about from room to room, making sure that no speck of dust rests therein,—the housewife who deceives herself into thinking that she would enjoy a brush with the world outside, or things in art, literature, and science if she only had time after attending to the important, the essential things in this world—the specks of dust" (p. 411).

Individuality and Freedom in Concert. Young maintained that teaching and educational work generally were vastly complex endeavors that required flexible intelligence and openness. As principal, Young encouraged teachers in her school to create their own unique instructional strategies and content. She fostered conditions in which teachers together formed a mutually supportive, empowering community, celebrating the pedagogical creations of members and jumping in to help one another troubleshoot lessons when invited to do so. In Young's school, teachers were powerful. They originated and executed their ideas. They helped one another. Together, they made decisions—with Young—about matters important to the school: curriculum, pedagogy, personnel matters, and student programming. In this way, the gifts of each teacher were maximized and brought fully to bear rather than filtered out or stopped by some administrative bottleneck, with demoralizing, disempowering consequences. Young led her school much as a gifted conductor brings an ensemble of talented musicians into synchrony: by transparently and skillfully clearing the way for each to speak expressively— separately and together—in infinite interlocking combinations and for the mutual benefit of all.

Thought and Action Together. Young consistently maintained that thought and action must happen together. Practice must be driven by intelligent and creative thought. Conversely, thought or theory must be grounded by and integrally connected with practice. She combined theory and practice seemingly effortlessly, a gift derived from long and determined conscious effort.

Young's voice was a powerful one, raised in opposition to the most stultifying effects of systematized schooling and the de-skilling of teaching. Though she spoke directly to the experiences of women, her words resonated deeply with women and men alike who sought to make schools central to the cultivation of a democratic citizenry. She inspired intensive political and professional organizing among school workers, women's groups, and citizens everywhere who were concerned about giving all human beings their due. She made raging enemies among powerful, well-heeled figures who sought instead to treat teachers as servile and who also aggressively conspired to silence her.[1]

CONTEMPORARY RELEVANCE

Isolation, Disempowerment, and Gender. In many respects, schools in the early 21st century have changed from those of 100 years ago in that services provided have expanded dramatically, digital technologies are deployed extensively, teachers have unionized in most states, and many employment and student protections have been instituted. Nonetheless, teaching arguably continues to be work that has been stripped of many of its creative, empowering possibilities, especially with the advent of extensive student testing; prescribed, if not mandated, curricula and pedagogies; and long hours and heavy work responsibilities, combined with relatively low wages for work requiring a college degree—all while the ratios of women and men teachers as well as of superintendents are essentially the same now as they were a century ago (Blount, 2005; Tallerico & Blount, 2004).

Educators throughout the profession and their allies may find it helpful to understand that teaching does not have to be configured with these limitations. Young herself broke down social barriers in schools by asking teachers for their ideas—and then actively supporting teachers in executing them. She actively encouraged development of projects arising organically from among teachers, finding funds, supplies, community support, and facilities as needed, for example. She refused credit directed toward her, but instead readily celebrated achievements initiated by teachers—and, in turn, students. Teachers and students invariably produced outstanding work because they chose to—and they enjoyed it. School leaders might ask themselves how they can release some of their own positional control and instead support the organic development of teachers' professional growth and decisionmaking.

Individuality and Freedom in Concert. As Young consistently maintained, teachers must be free to bring their intellectual and creative talents to their work. They, in turn, can then cultivate those talents in their students as well as among one another. Conditions for teachers will necessarily be perpetuated for their students, so both must be respected and granted latitude as well as careful support. Young managed to foster a climate that supported freedom and individuality in the schools and organizations she led.

---

1. This subject requires extensive elaboration and will be described fully in Blount, *Freedom for the Teacher* (in progress).

She expected discussions in which everyone contributed ideas freely and interacted fruitfully—free of squelching influences. She actively encouraged fresh thought. As a former student and colleague explained, "'What new ideas have you today in this work?' was a common question of hers, and the person called upon for such help felt that she was really a part of the creative force of the school" (McManis, 1916, pp. 61–62). Though this approach may sound quite simple and not necessarily like the basis of an overarching approach to educational leadership, it is, in fact, the crucial core of mutual respect, collaboration, and empowerment toward collective ends. These simple ways of interacting, writ large, produce a network of individuals sharing the load (reducing administrative and other bottlenecks while distributing responsibility more equitably) and working in concert toward shared ends, all while asserting their individuality (or unique gifts).

Thought and Action Together. Young argued strenuously that educators needed to continuously read thought-provoking works and engage in stimulating discussions as they sought to refine their professional practice. From the very start of her career, she devoted several nights a week to systematic reading and study in support of her work, including history, philosophy, literature, and educational theory/research. As principal, she invited teachers to her home on a regular basis to discuss books they had chosen, a practice that teachers enjoyed so much, they were inspired to create new individual and collective innovations. Those teachers then cultivated the same desire to link thought and action together as they worked with their students—and then often subsequently moved into school leadership positions. Young maintained that bridging the gap between theory and practice is a result of disciplined cultivation rather than something left to chance. She insisted on this cultivation in herself—and the people who worked with her eagerly aspired to it as well.

Clearly, these three sets of lessons overlap and are tightly interconnected. Each strategy strengthens the intellectual engagement, curiosity, creativity, social trust, and shared decisionmaking abilities of teachers, students, and leaders alike. Everyone is better able to share in the collective responsibility of educating students well, distributing power more evenly while minimizing the dysfunctional bottlenecks so characteristic of strict hierarchies. Individuals feel a greater sense of purpose largely because they have legitimately helped originate collective courses of action. They also enjoy the freedom to bring their full creativity and intellectual power to their classrooms, confident in knowing that unique approaches are celebrated. Ella Flagg Young and those who modeled their work on hers demonstrated that such leadership not only was possible, but that it actually improved the lives of teachers and students in schools.

REFERENCES

Blount, J. M. (1998). *Destined to rule the schools: Women and the superintendency, 1873–1995*. Albany: The State University of New York Press.

Blount, J. M. (2005). *Fit to teach: Same-sex desire, gender, and school work in the twentieth century*. Albany: The State University of New York Press.

Blount, J. M. (in press-a). Ella Flagg Young and the gender politics of *Democracy and education. Journal of the Gilded Age and Progressive Era*.

Blount, J. M. (in press-b). *Freedom for the teacher: The life and thought of Ella Flagg Young*.

Churchill, T. W. (1916). The superintendent as the layman sees him. *Addresses and Proceedings of the NEA, 1916*. Washington, DC: NEA.

Dewey, J. (1903, December). Democracy in education. *The Elementary School Teacher, 4*(4), 193–204.

Dewey, J. (1916). *Democracy and education*. New York, NY: Macmillan.

Howland's possible successor. (1891, August 27). *The Chicago Daily Tribune*, p. 1.

McManis, J. (1916). *Ella Flagg Young and a half-century of the Chicago Public Schools*. Chicago, IL: McClurg.

Smith, J. K. (1979). *Ella Flagg Young: Portrait of a leader*. Ames, IA: Educational Studies Press.

Tallerico, M., & Blount, J. M. (2004, December). Women and the superintendency: Insights from theory and history. *Educational Administration Quarterly, 40*(5), 633–662.

Tyack, D., & Hansot, E. (1982). *Managers of virtue: Public school leadership in America*. New York, NY: Basic Books.

Young, E. F. (1899, June 1). The educational outlook. *The Intelligence*, 410–412.

Young, E. F. (1900). *Isolation in the school*. Chicago, IL: University of Chicago Press.

CHAPTER 16

Aung San Suu Kyi
A Leadership Journey Toward
Peace and Democracy

Whitney McIntyre Miller & Margaret Grogan
CHAPMAN UNIVERSITY, UNITED STATES

Aung San Suu Kyi was born in Rangoon, Burma (sometimes considered Myanmar) on June 19, 1945.[1] Despite being the daughter of Burmese liberation leader Aung San, Suu Kyi did not find her role in Burmese politics until after she returned home from studying and living abroad. Coming home in 1988 to care for her dying mother (Keane, 2010), Suu Kyi realized that she had a powerful role to play in fighting the military junta, which had come to power in 1962 (Nobel Media, 2014). In 1988, she created the National League for Democracy (NLD), and became the party's secretary general (Caraus, 2014; Nobel Media, 2014). Her role with the NLD and her call for a democratic, ethnically harmonious society drew attention to her and resulted in her being detained by house arrest beginning in 1989 (Keane, 2010; Nobel Media, 2014). Although her party won the national election in 1990, the military generals refused to allow an assembly to convene and kept Suu Kyi under house arrest for nearly 15 of the next 21 years (Nobel Media, 2014; Pederson, 2015). On November 13, 2010, Suu Kyi was released from house arrest, and 5 years later, when the NLD once again won the national elections, Suu Kyi became the state counsellor of the Burmese government (Biography.com, 2016; CIA, n.d.; Nobel Media, 2014). Having married a British national and had two children with him, Aung San Suu Kyi is constitutionally not eligible to serve in the role of president (Biography.com, 2016; Popham, 2016).

FROM HOUSE ARREST TO STATE COUNSELLOR

Aung San Suu Kyi had two distinct periods of her life that we will discuss in terms of her leadership context and activities. The first was prior to and

---

1. In her writing, Aung San Suu Kyi refers to her country as Burma instead of Myanmar, so this paper will do the same.

during her time under house arrest; the second is the present, when Suu Kyi is free from house arrest and is serving in the political role of state counsellor.

During the first period, Suu Kyi began to explore the history and culture of the Burmese people in her doctoral studies abroad, and she felt a growing connection to her father and country. The more she connected to her country, the more compelled she felt to speak out about the authoritative regime that had come into power (Caraus, 2014). Upon returning home and forming the NLD, Suu Kyi began to speak out further against the government, which led to her first house arrest in 1989 (Keane, 2010). Suu Kyi refused the push to leave the country, and instead demanded the establishment of a civil government and freedom for political prisoners (Biography.com, 2016; Keane, 2010). During this time, she was often held in isolation and was unable to see her husband and children (BBC, 2015; Popham, 2016). Despite her party winning a majority of seats in a 1990 election, the military junta refused to allow a transition in power and Suu Kyi remained under house arrest until 1995 (Biography.com, 2016; Keane, 2010).

Suu Kyi continued to fight for democracy in Burma, even declaring representatives from the winning party the rightful government. She was once again put under house arrest in 2000 when she tried to travel despite restrictions (Biography.com, 2016; Keane, 2010). Released for just a year between 2002 and 2003 (Keane, 2010), Suu Kyi remained under house arrest until 2010. During this time, she experienced continued harassment by the military regime, the disbanding of her party as a result of new election rules, and being convicted of a crime for the perceived violation of her house arrest (Biography.com, 2016; Keane, 2010; Popham, 2016). During this time, Suu Kyi continued to resist the forces of the government, speak out in favor of democracy, and wage a political fight for her country's freedom.

Suu Kyi was released from house arrest and permitted to visit with one of her sons for the first time in 10 years; her husband had died in 1999. Her release came less than a week after Burma's first elections, which prevented her from running for office (BBC, 2015; Pederson, 2015; Popham, 2016). As the newly elected government began to form, Suu Kyi and the NLD began to engage in politics once again, re-registering as a political party at the very end of 2010 (Pederson, 2015). When the next elections were held in 2012, the NLD won 43 of the 44 seats for which they ran (Pederson, 2015). Suu Kyi won one of those seats, and became the leader of the opposition movement; the party became cautiously optimistic about the future of the country (BBC, 2015; Biography.com, 2016; Popham, 2016).

Despite the advance of democracy in the country, the pace of democratization was quite slow, a fact that frustrated Suu Kyi. Leading up to November 2015, there had still been little reform, and the parliament failed to overturn the constitutional rule that had banned her from running for president. In November of that same year, however, the country held its first openly contested election and the NLD won two-thirds of the available seats, making them the majority party in parliament. Although the election was seen as free and fair, hundreds of thousands of people were denied the right to vote, including most notably the minority Muslim Rohingya group (BBC, 2015; Popham, 2016).

Following the landslide victory, the NLD chose a new president for the country in March 2016. Because Suu Kyi was constitutionally barred from holding this position, Htin Kyaw, Suu Kyi's longtime advisor, was selected instead (Biography.com, 2016; CIA, n.d.). In order to allow Suu Kyi a more prominent role in the government, a state counselor position was created for her (Popham, 2016). As state counselor, she indicated her intention to "rule 'above the president'" (Biography.com, 2016, para. 15) until the constitution could be changed. At the time of this writing, she continues to serve in this role.

Suu Kyi is internationally recognized for her work toward democracy in Burma. She was awarded the Rafto Prize in 1990, the Nobel Peace Prize in 1991, the International Simón Bolívar Prize in 1992, the Jawaharlal Prize in 1993, and the U.S. Congressional Gold Medal in 2007 (Biography.com, 2016).

A STORY OF IDENTITY, TRANSITION, POWER, AND PEACE

Aung San Suu Kyi's life is a fascinating portrait of identity, transition, power, and peace. In this section, we discuss the four leadership lessons that can be gleaned from her story. These lessons are about the role of identity in courageous leadership, transitions from informal to formal leadership roles, the gendered nature of heroic leadership, and the complexities of leading for peace.

Role of Identity in Courageous Leadership

The story of Suu Kyi teaches us that leaders draw strength and courage from identity in order to overcome serious challenges and maintain purpose. Identity is not always an easy thing to uncover and understand, as it is quite often layered. In Suu Kyi's case, her identity is a combination of her strong sense of being Burmese and her father's daughter, her education abroad, her role as a wife and a mother, and her passion for democracy. In the various phases of her life, she drew strength from all of these identities, and utilized them to understand better the complex contexts in which she was operating. Understanding our various identities, and being deep-rooted in those understandings, can help position us to work within constraints of our leadership contexts. In many ways, Suu Kyi's connection to identity is the strength that provided her with a moral grounding and a purpose from which to work.

It is this sense of purpose, or the notion that one *can't not* do something (Scharmer, 2009), that makes her a transformational leader (Burns, 2003); she is grounded in her identity, and utilizes its strength and power to raise everyone up, to bring an entire country into democracy.

Transitions from Informal to Formal Leadership Roles

Another important lesson is that the transition from an informal leadership role to a formal one both limits and enhances power. Prior to the NLD's victory in the 2012 elections, Suu Kyi's leadership role was one of informal authority (Heifetz, 2016). Although she did not have a formal role in the government, she was able to lead through her identity and moral standing. All through her time under house arrest, she was seen as a social leader who drew on hope and stood for democratic rights and freedoms (Caraus, 2014). Once she moved into a formal political appointment, even if it was not an elected position because of constitutional constraints, her role and ability to exercise leadership naturally transitioned. She evolved into a leader with positional power who had to make difficult decisions and deals, work with others, and strategize about the direction of power and influence in her country. This, however, limits some of the freedoms she had enjoyed as a moral, informal authority and may force her to make connections with groups seen as existing across a political divide.

This type of change in leadership role is experienced not only by those in leadership, but also by their supporters, who may feel that their expectations are no longer being met in the new context. When transitions to formal leadership roles occur, we must also learn to shift our expectations, realizing that those in formal leadership roles do not have the capacity to solve our problems for us, as much as we might wish they could (Heifetz, 2016). Instead, these leaders serve to facilitate the work that a whole country must do together to address current and future challenges. This is particularly hard to digest when a leader, such as Aung San Suu Kyi, has already won the Nobel Peace Prize. Finding ways for all those involved in the transition to reconcile the change from principled action to practical politics, which is not necessarily devoid of morals or principles, is essential for moving forward.

In shedding the mantle of dissident and accepting the political office of state counsellor, Aung San Suu Kyi became no longer just a symbol of freedom and humanitarian rights for Burma. She finds herself in the midst of difficult negotiations and compromises as she navigates the unstable path toward realizing her goal of bringing justice and democracy to Burma. As a result, Suu Kyi has faced severe criticism for her refusal to take sides in the negotiations over the rights of the Rohingya, the country's Muslim minority group. However, she has taken up her role as a formal leader, and in so doing has done nothing that political figures like Nelson Mandela or Barack

Obama would not have done to inch forward with the larger work of governing a fragile, unreliable coalition of diverse ethnic groups.

As a cautionary note, we acknowledge that a postcolonial reading of Suu Kyi suggests that her gender, culture, race, class, and education intersect in powerful ways to differentiate her from the Western notion of leader as politician (Nair, 2004). Suu Kyi is portrayed by both the Burmese and the Western media as a "feminized and exoticized figure of resistance" (Nair, 2004, p. 275). How this will play out as she enacts the formal role of leader remains to be seen.

Gendered Nature of Heroic Leadership

Heroic leadership is gendered—women "heroes" face criticism that men do not. Suu Kyi is seen as a hero to many in Burma. She has held up the mantle of democracy through some very challenging times and situations that many of us would not be able or willing to endure. Although traditionally, especially in Western societies, we tend to think of heroic leaders as male, we are not without heroic female examples, such as Joan of Arc and Mother Teresa. Being female does have its privileges. In some cases, being female might limit the potential of violence acted against you. It might also give you more space or leeway to enact leadership. The challenges a female hero faces, however, are often greater than the positive aspects. Heroic female leaders face greater criticism about their principles and goals, the means by which they achieve these goals, and their single-mindedness. Would men be as criticized for their firm political stance or for putting politics and country over family? Would a male be chastised for taking a position above the president even though there is no constitutional option for her to serve as president (see Popham, 2016)? Finally, we must understand from where this criticism is coming: Do we see it more from the West or from other Asian countries? Has this emerged as Suu Kyi has transitioned from what some see as being close to a martyr to being a strong political figure? Would our opinions on this transformation be the same if Suu Kyi were male?

Leadership for Peace Is Complex and Messy

In her roles both as a political prisoner and as a politician, Suu Kyi can be viewed as a leader for peace; the fact that she received the 1991 Nobel Peace Prize augments this argument. Leadership for peace is complicated and complex, and involves both challenging existing forms of aggression and working to build new, more peaceful structures and systems (McIntyre Miller, 2016). These tasks are further challenged by Suu Kyi's role shift from being an informal to a formal authority. Peace leadership, as defined by McIntyre Miller and Green (2015), requires a person to work on inner peace, which can be seen in Suu Kyi's commitment to meditation and

Buddhist teachings. It also requires advanced peace and leadership knowledge and education, which we see in Suu Kyi's formal education and her studies of nonviolence tradition. It requires building coalitions and relationships with people from all sides of an issue. This may seem like a tall order in Suu Kyi's case, when these groups seem to stand in opposition to her former principles and opinions, leading to claims of hypocrisy and of getting one's hands dirty. Leadership from a position of power, however, often leads to deal-making and uncomfortable alliances. Finally, it includes connecting to a larger system and environment, which, for Suu Kyi, means connection with other Asian countries and the Western world. It involves bringing the case for peace beyond the immediate context, to the various parties that influence and surround it. In order to engage in peace leadership, one must be willing to do work in all of these areas, despite how doing so might challenge norms, expectations, and preexisting relationships. Peace leadership helps pave the path toward peaceful goals, even if that path is not always straight or direct.

LESSONS FROM A STATE COUNSELOR'S POLITICAL DILEMMAS

Suu Kyi's narrative is instructive for principals and superintendents who lead from a moral core. Educational leaders fighting for equity and justice in their schools will find inspiration in her unrelenting opposition to a brutal regime that denied human rights to its people. Indeed, there have been many modern-day freedom fighters in U.S. schools, such as Jaime Escalante, Geoffrey Canada, Erin Gruwell, and Michelle Rhee. Suu Kyi demonstrates what it means to forge alliances with a powerful opposition once in a formal leadership position. Suu Kyi's example provides us with insight into the value of perseverance, cultural relevance, political deal-making, and courage. The world stage on which her drama has played out illuminates the ugly underside of political activism, which has relevance for every leader who wants justice for his or her students. The four lessons in her story can shed light on the context of educational leadership.

Role of identity in courageous leadership. Research confirms that educational leaders are often motivated by the desire to give back to their own communities or to fight against discriminating educational policies and practices that have shaped their own lived experiences (Grogan & Shakeshaft, 2011). Like Suu Kyi, leaders who strive for more equity and justice in their schools bring perspectives that are deeply rooted in a strong sense of identity. However, as we see in Suu Kyi's example, a public identity evolves over time and does not necessarily remain under the leader's control—especially after the transition from an informal leadership role to a formal one. One of the major implications for educational leaders lies in how Suu Kyi grappled with (and is still grappling with) this tension. She demonstrates the courage to disappoint some of her local and global supporters as she continues to negotiate and form coalitions with her former enemies. Instead of acquiescing to international pressure to rehabilitate the Rohingya, for instance, she is mindful of the Burmese laws that prevent a quick solution.

Transitions from informal to formal leadership roles. School and district leaders do not often see themselves as politicians but, like Suu Kyi, many come to realize the political nature of their work. In her early days, she did not want a leadership position. She felt driven to accomplish her father's work for the good of Burma (Aung, 2010). Recently, she acknowledged, "I've been a politician all along" (Connor, 2016, para. 10). And although educational leaders have no connections to party politics as Suu Kyi does, the realities of all formal leadership involve making unpopular decisions and living with trade-offs. The work of implementing educational reforms and bringing about deep change in organizations is rooted in Burns's (2003) notion of transformational leadership and Shields's (2011) concept of transformative leadership. Suu Kyi's example reinforces the moral dimension to this leadership. A clear vision of better serving students and families who have not benefited from traditional educational policies motivates many to go into school leadership. Suu Kyi's story is a powerful example of how challenging it can be for leaders to remain steadfast while negotiating the turbulent waters of opposition.

Gendered nature of heroic leadership. The lesson of gendered heroic leadership resonates on many levels with women in school and district leadership. Shakeshaft, Brown, Irby, Grogan, and Ballenger(2007) confirm the gendered context in which all women principals and superintendents operate, but the extra dimension of gendered heroism embedded in Suu Kyi's leadership raises interesting questions for women in educational leadership. Women of color have been known to take on superintendencies in some of the most difficult urban districts in the United States (Brunner & Grogan, 2007). Their tenure is sometimes short because of the extremely fractured political context of the work. Suu Kyi's story shows that women who are fighting for justice can be placed on a pedestal under terms not of their own making. In the eyes of her followers, Suu Kyi's capacity to lead was magnified by her gender and her commitments to her people. Are principals and superintendents who identify with the marginalized communities they seek to lead rendered even more vulnerable because they are elevated to the status of hero by those who have high hopes for their success? How does this expectation constrain their actions and possibly set them up for failure? Women heroes are not given the same freedoms that male heroes are. Women leaders' private lives are scrutinized far more critically (Grogan, 1996).

Leadership for peace is complex and messy. Suu Kyi provides us with an excellent example of peace leadership (McIntyre Miller & Green, 2015) enacted on a world stage. We can learn a great deal from the scope of Suu Kyi's challenges and the messiness that has been her life story over the past 30 years. Educational leaders may work on a much smaller scale, but many of the same challenges to integrate diverse needs are present nonetheless. So, too, are the wins and losses that ebb and flow as educational policies change. Leaders learn that policy implementation is often far from intent. Suu Kyi's NLD party actually won the election in 1999, but the government refused to honor the public's wishes. Undeterred, Suu Kyi and her followers kept up their resistance, but they did not resort to violence. They relied instead on acts of public disobedience and continued to work collectively to achieve a democracy; this work continues today.

REFERENCES

Aung, S. S. (2010). *Freedom from fear: And other writings*. New York, NY: Penguin Books.
BBC. (2015, November 13). Profile: Aung San Suu Kyi. *BBC*. Retrieved from www.bbc.com/news/world-asia-pacific-11685977
Biography.com. (2016, April 8). Aung San Suu Ky. *Biography.com*. Retrieved from www.biography.com/people/aung-san-suu-kyi-9192617
Brunner, C. C., & Grogan, M. (2007). *Women leading school systems: Uncommon roads to fulfillment*. Lanham, MD: Rowman & Littlefield Education.
Burns, J. M. (2003). *Transforming leadership: A new pursuit of happiness*. New York, NY: Grove Press.
Caraus, T. (2014). Aung San Suu Kyi and cosmopolitanism as the "Revolution of Spirit." In T. Caraus & C. A. Parvu (Eds.), *Cosmopolitanism and the legacy of dissident* (pp. 87–110). New York, NY: Routledge.
Central Intelligence Agency. (n.d.). *World factbook: Burma*. Retrieved from www.cia.gov/library/publications/the-world-factbook/geos/bm.html
Connor, L. (2016, May). Aung San Suu Kyi and the cult of personality. *The diplomat*. Retrieved from thediplomat.com/2016/05/aung-san-suu-kyi-and-the-cult-of-personality/?allpages=yes&print=yes
Grogan, M. (1996). *Voices of women aspiring to the superintendency*. Albany: The State University of New York Press.
Grogan, M., & Shakeshaft, C. (2011). *Women and educational leadership*. San Francisco, CA: Wiley and Sons.
Heifetz, R. (2016, November 4). *Adaptive leadership*. Keynote address, International Leadership Association, Atlanta, GA.
Keane, F. (2010). Introduction. In S. S. K. Aung, *Letters from Burma*. New York, NY: Penguin Books.
McIntyre Miller, W. (2016). Toward a scholarship of peace leadership. *International Journal of Public Leadership, 12*(3), 216–226.

McIntyre Miller, W., & Green, Z. (2015). An integral perspective of peace leadership. *Integral Leadership Review, 15*(2). Retrieved from integralleadershipreview.com/12903-47-an-integral-perspective-of-peace-leadership/

Nair, S. (2004). Human rights and postcoloniality: Representing Burma. In G. Chowdhry & S. Nair (Eds.), *Power postcolonialism and international relations* (pp. 254–284). New York, NY: Routledge.

Nobel Media. (2014). Aung San Suu Kyi—facts. Retrieved from www.nobelprize.org/nobel_prizes/peace/laureates/1991/kyi-facts.html

Pederson, R. (2015). *The Burma spring: Aung San Suu Kyi and the struggle for the soul of a nation.* New York, NY: Pegasus Books.

Popham, P. (2016). *The lady and the generals: Aung San Suu Kyi and Burma's struggle for freedom.* London, England: Rider.

Scharmer, C. O. (2009). *Theory U: Leading from the future as it emerges.* San Francisco, CA: Berrett-Koehler.

Shakeshaft, C., Brown, G., Irby, B., Grogan, M., & Ballenger, J. (2007). Increasing gender equity in educational leadership. In S. Klein, B. Richardson, D. A. Grayson, L. H. Fox, C. Kramarae, D. Pollard, & C. A. Dwyer (Eds.), *Handbook for achieving gender equity through education* (2nd ed., pp. 103–130). Florence, KY: Lawrence Erlbaum Associates.

Shields, C. (Ed.). (2011). *Transformative leadership: A reader.* New York, NY: Peter Lang.

CHAPTER 17

Understanding Real "Black Girl Magic"
Anna Julia Cooper as a Thought Leader

Gloria Ladson-Billings
UNIVERSITY OF WISCONSIN–MADISON

> It is not the intelligent woman v. the ignorant woman; nor the white woman v. the black, the brown, and the red, it is not even the cause of woman v. man. Nay, 'tis woman's strongest vindication for speaking that the world needs to hear her voice.
>
> —Anna Julia Cooper, *A Voice from the South*, 1892

My initial inclination for this chapter was to write about W. E. B. Du Bois, for Du Bois has been an intellectual hero of mine for many years. I first learned of him from my 5th-grade teacher, Mrs. Ethel Benn at Belmont Elementary School in West Philadelphia, where I sat in a classroom—indeed, an entire school—filled with Black children. Every year, I introduce Du Bois to a new group of graduate students (some international) who never knew of his immense corpus, including his classic, *The Souls of Black Folk* (Du Bois, 1903). I argue that the intellectual history of the United States is incomplete without a discussion of Du Bois. He was an extraordinary scholar and, among his notable accomplishments, he was the first African American to earn a PhD from Harvard University. He could rightly be considered the precursor to the critical theorists, having spent part of his graduate years in Germany at the University of Berlin, beginning in 1892, years before Marcuse, Adorno, and other critical scholars began their work. However, as important as Du Bois is as a thinker, scholar, and activist, I settled on an even lesser known education leader in the person of Anna Julia Cooper.[1]

Anna Julia Haywood Cooper (1858–1964) was born in slavery but became one of the most prominent African American scholars in U.S. history.

---

1. The summary of Anna Julia Cooper's life is derived from Giles (2006) and Martin-Felton (2000).

Cooper was an author, public speaker, and educator who was the fourth African American to earn a PhD. She earned that advanced degree from the University of Paris–Sorbonne in 1925. Soon after slavery's end, Cooper entered the St. Augustine Normal School and Collegiate Institute in her hometown of Raleigh, North Carolina. St. Augustine was an Episcopal-run school opened for newly freed slaves. Anna Julia Haywood distinguished herself as a student and fought against the school's gendered policy of only allowing young women to pursue the "ladies' course." She demonstrated superior ability in both the humanities and sciences. Upon completion of her coursework, she became a tutor and later an instructor at St. Augustine. One of the young men she tutored, George A.C. Cooper, would later become her husband for two years until his death.

Seemingly because of her husband's early death, Cooper was able to continue her education in order to provide for herself. She earned a bachelor's degree from Oberlin College, where she once again insisted on pursuing the "course for men." Later, she earned a master's degree in mathematics from Oberlin in 1887. Cooper became a teacher and later principal at the M Street High School in Washington, DC, and in 1892, she published her only book, *A Voice from the South: By a Woman from the South*. This book and her numerous speeches on civil rights and women's rights are thought to be some of the early foundations of Black feminist thought.

Cooper delivered a paper entitled "The Intellectual Progress of the Colored Women of the United States Since the Emancipation Proclamation" at the World's Congress of Representative Women in 1893 in Chicago. She also delivered a paper on "The Negro Problem in America" at the first Pan-African Conference in London in 1900, where W. E. B. DuBois also played a leading role. By the time Cooper was in her 50s, she attempted to earn her doctorate at Columbia University. However, her decision to adopt her late half-brother's five children forced her to stop her studies in 1915. Undeterred, Cooper transferred her Columbia credits to the University of Paris–Sorbonne and eventually earned her doctorate in 1925. Her dissertation was titled *The Attitude of France on the Question of Slavery Between 1789 and 1848*. She earned this degree at the age of 65.

WHY ANNA JULIA COOPER MATTERS

Anna Julia Cooper was a leader who fought the twin evils of racism and sexism that were so prominent in the late 19th and early 20th centuries. Those aspects of Cooper's life make her an important scholar-model for me as an African American woman scholar. It is particularly important to talk about Cooper in this moment because of the ongoing challenge of combatting inequity. I think of her in the same ways I think of teacher-turned-journalist Ida B. Wells, civil rights leader Ella Baker, and current-day critical race legal scholar Kimberlé Crenshaw. What all of these women (and many others) have in common is the way they made it clear that race, gender, and class all matter and that this focus on "intersectionality" is necessary if we are to understand how our identities help us deal with the realities of students and families in our schools and communities.

Today, popular culture has a "trending topic" something called "Black Girl Magic." Specifically, this refers to the way that Black women and girls have made incredible strides in the society despite the way structural odds are stacked against them. People said to have "Black Girl Magic" include Michelle Obama, Beyoncé and her sister Solange, Serena and Venus Williams, Kerry Washington, Viola Davis, and Taraji P. Henson. But "Black Girl Magic" also applies to ordinary, everyday people like Grace Hardison, a 100-year-old Black woman the state of North Carolina tried to take off the voter rolls because of a glitch in her address that resulted in a voting notice being returned as "undeliverable" (Berman, 2016). Hardison wrote to President Obama to let him know of her plight and the subsequent negative publicity resulted in the state being forced to reverse its decision. Hardison demonstrated "Black Girl Magic."

Another example of everyday "Black Girl Magic" can be found in the work of Alicia Garza, Patrisse Cullors, and Opal Tometi, the three Black women who developed the Black Lives Matter movement. The underlying concept of "Black Girl Magic" asserts that despite the way Blackness and women are demeaned, Black women continue to be in the forefront of the fight for equity and justice. "Black Girl Magic" has a long tradition in African American communities, and Anna Julia Cooper fits proudly into that tradition.

I have focused on Anna Julia Cooper because few African American educators have had their stories told. Michele Foster (1997) conducted a literature search and learned that there were fewer than half a dozen first-person narratives by African American teachers written in over a century. We know so little about the experiences of African American educators, yet they have been one of the most stabilizing forces in the Black community. My own career has been greatly shaped by Black women educators. I began my schooling in a large, urban, segregated elementary school. Almost all of the approximately 800 students in my school were Black, with the exception of the children from one very poor White family. The other White families in my neighborhood sent their children to Catholic schools. Although there were White teachers in my schools, it was the Black teachers who made the real difference in my perception of myself as a student who was capable of achieving more than what was expected of someone with my background.

When I think of Anna Julia Cooper, I envision my 5th-grade teacher, Ethel Benn. Mrs. Benn was unapologetically proud to be a Black woman. She was elderly (but in truth, she was probably younger than I am right now) and she dressed like a "church mother." She wore flowery dresses with what looked to be cotton stockings and orthopedic-looking shoes. As a 9-year-old, I was not looking forward to having her as a teacher and I begged my mother to transfer me to a younger teacher's classroom. My mother, in her wisdom, refused. "You haven't even given her a chance," my mother replied.

In my year with Mrs. Benn, I learned more than I imagined I could. She was in charge of the school chorus and all the students in her class were required to be in the chorus, whether we could sing or not. Being in the chorus meant that we would travel all around the city and sing in front of audiences beyond our school community. Mrs. Benn was also especially knowledgeable about the history of Black Americans. She would subversively teach us about the significant contributions of African Americans because she knew that the curriculum failed to include them. Mrs. Benn started me on my lifelong journey to learn about W. E. B. Du Bois. When she initially told us about Du Bois, I assumed she was making it up. No one in my neighborhood would believe that a Black person had graduated from Harvard. Mrs. Benn turned out to be one of the most significant figures in my education life. Because of her, I sought to learn more about Black women in education.

Anna Julia Cooper is one of the women I discovered. According to Grant, Brown, and Brown (2016), "All facets of Cooper's life (activist, educator, author, optimist, 'womanist', intellectual) intersected to produce a powerful crusader against race, gender, and class oppression" (p. 29). Cooper's "integrated" life became a template for the kind of career I sought to have. Instead of focusing on "work-life" balance, I have strived to see how the various pieces could work together in an integrated, synergistic life. Some of the lessons I learned from Anna Julia Cooper include the following.

1. Good teaching requires one to bring her whole self into the classroom. Students want to know who their teachers are and something about their life experiences. It requires a delicate balance between developing empathy and being an exhibitionist. Students are interested in the struggles of their teachers that reveal something of their humanity, but they do not want to hear teachers brag about what they did and/or what they have.

2. Intersectionality is crucial for Black women. Before the recent 2016 presidential election, I would have made this claim for all women. But, recognizing that far too many White women prize their racial identity above all else, I am reluctant to suggest agreement across racial lines. I do know that Black women are forced to operate in the nexus between race and gender. Cooper understood that, and though she never broke her solidarity with Black people, she realized that being a Black woman added another dimension to the fight for equality and justice. Today, much of the heat and light around the activism of Black Lives Matter tends to focus on the murder of Black men, but Black women have paid this ultimate price as well. Something about their gender continues to render them less worthy in discussions of equity and civil rights.

3. *Black women as emblems of democracy.* For many years I taught U.S. history to middle-grade students. The typical approach to this school subject is chronological, starting with "The Age of Exploration" and moving into the "Colonial Period," the "American Revolution," and the "Constitutional Convention." However, I have often said that if I had a chance to design a U.S. history curriculum, I would force students to begin with the video clip of Fannie Lou Hamer stating her case to be seated at the 1964 Democratic National Convention, and I would pose the question: "Does democracy work for this woman?" Indeed, if it does, there is a high probability that what the Framers came up with is a "living" document that is elastic and expansive enough to attend to the rights of a citizen who is Black, female, and poor. Anna Julia Cooper epitomized the democratic principles by demonstrating that her identity categories did not keep her from pursuing "a more perfect union."

4. *Unapologetic advocacy for Black children.* Anna Julia Cooper made no apologies for focusing her work on the betterment of Black children. A number of times in my career, I have been asked why I focus on Black children/youth. Never have any of my colleagues been asked why they focus on White students. As I read Anna Julia Cooper, I understood that being an unapologetic and unashamed advocate for Black students was the only way to "normalize" their experience and advocate for resources that would allow them to realize their educational potential.

5. *Self-determination.* According to May (2007), Anna Julia Cooper pushed for the right of all human beings to "participate in creating and defining new paradigms of knowing and being that draw upon race and gender-specific particularities of lived experience, of cultural memory and of complex legacies of resistance" (p. 41). Today, Black academics still fight for the right to name themselves and their research agendas.

CODA

Anna Julia Cooper's work is prescient as we consider the state of Black education in the United States (and throughout the world). The challenges beyond education include housing, employment, health, mass incarceration, and political disenfranchisement. Cooper speaks to the totality of these concerns because, fundamentally, she speaks to democracy and the responsibility of those in power in a democratic system to ensure the "peace and domestic tranquility" of its citizenry. When we consider that Cooper's life spanned more than a century (she died at the age of 105), we know that she was witness to everything from the end of chattel slavery to the excitement of the modern civil rights movement. Throughout her life and career, she stayed the course in the fight for equality and justice. She raised the voice of the Black woman because she had seen it marginalized, not just by the White power structure, but also by Black men. She authored perhaps the first Black feminist work in her book, *A Voice from the South* (1892), and she provided an important perspective for the infant civil rights and women's movements.

Cooper is a paragon of "Black intellectual thought" (Grant, Brown, & Brown, 2016). More educators need to read and study her work to develop a fuller picture of the impact and import of thinkers outside of the mainstream canon. She belongs in the same conversation with Horace Mann, Booker T. Washington, and John Dewey. And although many Americans do not know her, all those who hold U.S. passports possess a document with her words listed in it: "The cause of freedom is not the cause of a race or a sect, a party or a class—it is the cause of humankind, the very birthright of humanity." Thank you, Anna Julia Cooper—you are the embodiment of "Black Girl Magic"!

REFERENCES

Berman, A. (2016, October 27). North Carolina Republicans tried to disenfranchise a 100-year-old African American woman. *The Nation*. Retrieved from www.thenation.com/article/north-carolina-republicans-tried-to-disenfranchise-a-100-year-old-african-american-woman/)

Cooper, A. J. (1892). *A voice from the south*. Xenia, OH: The Aldine Printing House.

Du Bois, W. E. B. (1903). *The souls of Black folk*. Chicago, IL: A. C. McClurg & Co.

Foster, M. (1997). *Black teachers on teaching*. New York, NY: W. W. Norton & Co., Inc.

Giles, M. S. (2006). Special focus: Dr. Anna Julia Cooper 1858–1964: Teacher, scholar and timeless womanist. *The Journal of Negro Education, 75*, 621–634.

Grant, C. A., Brown, K. D., & Brown, A. L. (2016). *Black intellectual thought in education: The missing traditions of Anna Julia Cooper, Carter G. Woodson, and Alain LeRoy Locke*. New York, NY: Routledge.

Martin-Felton, Z. (2000). *A woman of courage: The story of Anna Julia Cooper*. Washington, DC: Education Department, Anacostia Museum of the Smithsonian Institution.

May, V. M. (2007). *Anna Julia Cooper, visionary Black feminist: A critical introduction*. New York, NY: Routledge.

About the Contributors

William Ayers is formerly distinguished professor of education and senior university scholar at the University of Illinois at Chicago. He writes about social justice and democracy, and teaching as an essentially intellectual, ethical, and political enterprise. His books include *A Kind and Just Parent*, *To Teach*, *Teaching Toward Freedom*, *Demand the Impossible!*, and two memoirs, *Fugitive Days* and *Public Enemy*.

Jackie M. Blount is professor of educational studies at the Ohio State University. Her books include *Fit to Teach: Same-Sex Desire and Gender in School Work in the Twentieth Century* (2005) and *Destined to Rule the Schools: Women and the Superintendency, 1873–1995* (1998). Her work has also been published in journals such as the *Review of Educational Research*, *Educational Administration Quarterly*, and *Harvard Educational Review*. Currently, she serves as president of the History of Education Society (U.S.) and is writing a biography of Ella Flagg Young.

Jeffrey S. Brooks is professor of educational leadership in the Faculty of Education at Monash University in Melbourne, Australia. His research focuses on educational leadership for social justice. He has edited or co-edited 10 books and is the author of *Black School, White School: Racism and Educational (Mis)leadership*, *The Dark Side of School Reform: Teaching in the Space Between Reality and Utopia*, and *Foundations of Educational Leadership: Developing Excellent and Equitable Schools* (co-authored with Anthony H. Normore).

Melanie C. Brooks is a senior lecturer in educational policy in the Faculty of Education at Monash University. She is a J. William Fulbright Senior Scholar grant recipient to the Philippines and has conducted research in the Philippines, Thailand, Indonesia, the United States, and Egypt. Her areas of expertise include Islamic education, religious extremism, multicultural education, and school leadership and policy.

Lisa Catherine Ehrich is an adjunct associate professor in the Faculty of Education at Queensland University of Technology, Australia. Her research interests include school leadership and mentoring for professionals. In 2016, with Fenwick W. English, she wrote *Leading Beautifully: Educational Leadership as Connoisseurship*, published by Routledge.

Fenwick W. English is the R. Wendell Eaves Senior Distinguished Professor of Educational Leadership in the School of Education at the University of North Carolina at Chapel Hill. He is the past president of the University Council for Educational Administration (UCEA) and the National Council of Professors of Educational Administration (NCPEA). In 2013, he was named a Living Legend of the field by NCPEA.

Dr. Susan C. Faircloth (an enrolled member of the Coharie Tribe of North Carolina) is a professor in the Educational Leadership Department at the University of North Carolina–Wilmington. Her research interests include Indigenous education, the education of culturally and linguistically diverse students with special educational needs, and the moral and ethical dimensions of school leadership. She has published widely in journals such as *Educational Administration Quarterly*, *Harvard Educational Review*, *The Journal of Special Education Leadership*, *International Studies in Educational Administration*, *Values and Ethics in Educational Administration*, *Tribal College Journal of American Indian Higher Education*, *Rural Special Education Quarterly*, and *Journal of Disability Policy Studies*.

Margaret Grogan is dean of the Donna Ford Attallah College of Educational Studies, Chapman University, California. She has authored, coauthored, or edited six books, including *Women and Educational Leadership* (with Charol Shakeshaft, 2011). She is the specialty chief editor for the leadership in education section of the journal *Frontiers in Education*.

Haiyan Qian is associate professor of the Department of Education Policy and Leadership at the Education University of Hong Kong. Her research focuses on school leadership and education change in the Chinese context. Her recent work in the area has appeared in *Educational Management Administration & Leadership*, *International Journal of Educational Development*, and *Asia Pacific Journal of Teacher Education*.

John M. Heffron is professor of educational history and culture and director of the MA program in educational leadership and societal change at Soka University of America in Aliso Viejo, California. His research is situated at the intersection of cultural and intellectual history, social and economic development, and the transnational sources of schooling. His most recent books include *The Evolution of Development Thinking: Governance, Economics, Assistance, and Security*, coauthored with William Ascher et al.; *Cultural Change and Persistence: New Perspectives on Development*; and *Leadership for Development: What Globalization Demands of Leaders Fighting for Change*, with Dennis A. Rondinelli.

Polly Hyslop is of Upper Tanana Dineh and Scottish ancestry. She was born at a fish camp located near the village of Northway in the interior of Alaska. She grew up in Tanana, located near the Yukon River. Her interests include

Indigenous leadership in rural Alaska and peacemaking. She serves on the Peacemaking Advisory Initiative for the Native American Rights Fund. She teaches in the Indigenous Studies Program/Center for Cross-Cultural Studies at the University of Alaska Fairbanks. She and Dr. Brian Jarrett coauthored the article "Justice for All: An Indigenous Community-Based Approach to Restorative Justice in Alaska."

Petar Jandrić is professor in digital learning and program director of BSc (Informatics) at the University of Applied Sciences in Zagreb (Croatia) and visiting associate professor at the University of Zagreb (Croatia). His research interests are focused on the intersections between critical pedagogy and digital cultures. His personal website is petarjandric.com.

Brian Jarrett is director of the Program on Negotiation, Conflict Resolution, and Peacebuilding at California State University, Dominguez Hills. He is a lawyer and professional mediator and arbitrator in both the United States and Canada. He also holds a PhD in sociology. His interests include mediation, arbitration dispute systems design (DSD), restorative practices, and therapeutic jurisprudence (TJ). In recent years, he has originated work in integral mediation, which promotes interdisciplinary practices in mediation. His practice ranges from work with local communities to international organizations. In both his written work and classroom teaching, Jarrett works to bridge theory and practice in the field of dispute resolution.

Gaëtane Jean-Marie is dean of the College of Education and Richard O. Jacobson Endowed Chair of Leadership in Education at the University of Northern Iowa. Her research focuses on educational equity and social justice in K–12 schools, women and leadership in the P–20 system, and leadership development and preparation in a global context. Her publications include books, book chapters, and academic articles in peer-reviewed journals.

Gloria Ladson-Billings is the Kellner Family Distinguished Chair in Urban Education at the University of Wisconsin–Madison.

Catherine A. Lugg is a professor of education at the Graduate School of Education, Rutgers University. Her research focuses on political ideology, social movements, and the politics of education. Her latest book is *U.S. Public Schools and the Politics of Queer Erasure* (Palgrave).

Catherine M. Marshall is the R. Wendell Eaves Distinguished Professor of Educational Leadership and Policy at the University of North Carolina. Her books include *Designing Qualitative Research* (Sage), *Reframing Educational Politics for Social Justice* (Allyn & Bacon), *Feminist Critical Policy Analysis* (Falmer), *Leadership for Social Justice* (Allyn & Bacon), and *Activist Educator* (Routledge). The Politics of Education Association and the University Council for Educational Administration have both given her Lifetime Achievement Awards.

About the Contributors

Becca Merrill is a doctoral student in the Policy, Leadership, and School Improvement program of the School of Education at the University of North Carolina at Chapel Hill. She is currently writing her dissertation proposal, which is a meta-analysis of teacher working conditions. Her areas of interest include teacher retention, the achievement gap, and education policy.

Peter McLaren is Distinguished Professor in Critical Studies and codirector of the Paulo Freire Democratic Project at the Donna Ford Attallah College of Educational Studies, Chapman University, professor emeritus of urban education at the University of California–Los Angeles, professor emeritus of educational leadership at Miami University of Ohio, and honorary director of the Center for Critical Studies in Education at Northeast Normal University in China, where he also holds the position of chair professor.

Whitney McIntyre Miller is an assistant professor of leadership studies in the Donna Ford Attallah College of Educational Studies at Chapman University in Orange, California. She centers her research around peace leadership and issues of community development and leadership, with a particular focus on postconflict societies. She is currently the co-convener of the Peace Leadership Affinity Group of the International Leadership Association.

Sonia Nieto is professor emerita of language, literacy, and culture at the University of Massachusetts–Amherst. She has devoted her professional life to issues of equity, diversity, and social justice. She is the author of 11 books, including the highly acclaimed *Affirming Diversity: The Sociopolitical Context of Multicultural Education*, now in its 7th edition (5th–7th with Patty Bode). The recipient of numerous awards for her scholarship and advocacy, including eight honorary doctorates, she was elected a member of the National Academy of Education in 2015.

Anthony H. Normore (Tony) holds a PhD from the University of Toronto. He is professor of educational leadership and department chair of graduate education at California State University, Dominguez Hills. He has been a visiting professor of ethics and leadership at Seoul National University, a visiting professor in the Department of Criminal Justice Studies at University of Guelph/Humber, and a graduate professor of law, ethics, and leadership for the Summer Leadership Academy at Teachers College, Columbia University. His 30-plus years of professional education experiences have taken him throughout North America, South Central Asia, Eastern Asia, the United Kingdom, continental Europe, and the South Pacific. Tony's research focuses on urban leadership growth and development in the context of ethics and social justice. He is the author or coauthor of several books, including *What the Social Sciences Tell Us About Leadership for Social Justice and Ethics* (2014, Information Age Publishing), *Moral Compass for Law Enforcement Professional* (2014, International Academy of Public Safety), and *Collective Efficacy: An Interdisciplinary Approach to International Leadership Development* (2013, Emerald Group Publishing), and numerous scholarly articles and book chapters. Dr. Normore was recently appointed as chief leadership and ethics officer and the chairman of the Criminal Justice Commission on Credible Leadership Development with the International Academy of Public Safety.

Izhar Oplatka is a professor of educational administration and leadership at the School of Education, Tel Aviv University, Israel, and the head of the Department of Educational Policy and Administration. His research focuses on the lives and career of school teachers and principals, emotions and educational leadership, and the foundations of educational administration as a field of study. His most recent books include *Higher Education Consumer Choice* (2015, with Jane Hemsley-Brown, Palgrave); *The Legacy of Educational Administration: A Historical Analysis of an Academic Field* (2010, Peter Lang Publishing); and *Organizational Citizenship Behavior in Schools* (2015, Routledge, with Anit Somech).

Atiya S. Strothers is first and foremost a servant and social justice advocate who is very passionate about education, religion, and civic engagement. She received her PhD in education from Rutgers University and is a current postdoctoral fellow for academic diversity at the University of Pennsylvania under the direction of Dr. Marybeth Gasman. Prior to her doctoral work, she earned a BS in business administration from the University of Pittsburgh and an MEd from Rutgers University. Dr. Strothers uses history to address the social, political, and institutional influences on educational equity and access. Specifically, her research agenda focuses on leadership, faculty diversity, graduate education, and mentorship.

Bryan A. VanGronigen is a PhD student in education administration and supervision in the Curry School of Education at the University of Virginia. His research focuses on organizational resilience and change management in PK–12 schools and districts, PK–12 school leadership teams, and educational leaders' judgment and decisionmaking processes. His work has been published in *Educational Policy* and by the Center on School Turnaround at WestEd.

Allan Walker is the Joseph Lau Chair Professor of International Educational Leadership and dean of the Faculty of Education and Human Development at the Education University of Hong Kong. His research focuses on culture and school leadership in East and Southeast Asia. His most recent book is *Deciphering School Leadership in China: Conceptualisation, Context and Complexities* (coauthored with Qian Haiyan).

Michelle D. Young, PhD, is the executive director of the University Council for Educational Administration (UCEA) and a professor of educational leadership at the University of Virginia. Young's scholarship focuses on how university programs, educational policies, and school leaders can support equitable and high-quality experiences for all students and adults who learn and work in schools. Her recent publications include *Mentoring Educational Leadership Doctoral Students: Using Methodological Diversification to Examine Gender and Identity Intersections*, *The Handbook of Research on the Education of School Leaders* (2nd ed.), and *How Are Standards Used? By Whom? And to What End?*

Index

19th amendment, 117–118
1964 Democratic National Convention, 104–105
2016 U.S. presidential campaign, 104, 105
2017 Women's March, 111

Abinales, P. N., 65
About the book, 1–4
Absence from school curriculum, 110
Abuse of power, 86–87
Abyssinian Baptist Church, 58, 60
Accessible ideas, 68
Accountability, viii
Acculturation. *See* Assimilation goal
Achua, C. F., 36
Actionable goals, 121
Active value creation, 27
Activism strategies, 115–116
"Adventures of a Schoolmaster" (Rizal), 66
Adversity, 88
African American. *See* Black American
Agency, vii, viii–ix, x, 18–19
Agency for Business and Career Development (ABCD), 8
Albuquerque Public Schools, 72–73
Alinsky, S., 51, 52, 53–54, 49–55
Alston, J. A., 105, 106, 109, 112
Alt-right movement, 104, 111
Alzona, E., 64
American Educational Studies Association Critics' Choice, 39
American Indian, 72–79, 90–94
American Indian leaders. *See* Gatensby, Harold; Tippeconnic III, John W.

American Indian Leadership Program, 73, 75, 78
American Indian Studies, Arizona State University, 75
Amoroso, D. J., 65
Anderson, A., 122
Anderson, B., 65
Anderson, R. S., 23
Anjum, B., 36–37
Anti-Semitism, 97, 98, 104
Antonia Pantoja (Jimenez), 11
Aptheker, H., 111–112
Archibald, J., 94
Arizona State University, 73, 75
Arrest, 17, 23, 35, 64, 131, 132
Artistic expression, 64, 65, 68, 70
Asante, M. K., 59
ASPIRA/ASPIRA Association, 8, 9–10
ASPIRA Consent Decree, 8
ASPIRA v. New York City Board of Education, 8
Assimilation goal, 73, 74, 76
Assumptions about leaders, xi
Ateneo de Municipal Manila, 64
Attitude change in general public, 76
Attitude of France on the Question of Slavery Between 1789 and 1848 (Cooper), 141
Attunement, 121
Atwater, D. F., 104, 105, 106, 109
Aung, S. S., 137
Aung San, 131
Authenticity, 18–20, 92, 93
Authority, viii, 66, 86, 87, 102
Avizohar, M., 97, 98, 100, 101–102
Avner, Y., 98, 101, 102
Avolio, B. J., 18

153

Back of the Yards, 51
Back of Yards Neighborhood Council, 49
Baker, Ella, 141–142
Balance of traditional and progressive approaches, 35, 37
Ball, S. J., 37
Ballenger, J., 137
Barber, R., 105
Barber, S., 105
Barnhardt, R., 94
Barrier transcendence, 110
BBC, 132, 133
Becker, S. D., 115
Begley, P. T., 20, 36
Belafonte, Harry, 109
Belonging, sense of, 9–10, 17
Benn, Ethel, 142–143
Bergére, M. C., 33, 34, 35
Berke, R. L., 82
Berman, A., 142
Bethel, D. M., 23, 25, 26, 27, 28
Bildung, 40
Bilingual education, 8
Biography.com, 131, 133
Black, D., 46
Black American. *See also* Civil Rights Movement (U.S.); Race; Racial segregation; Racism
 educators, 57–63, 124–129, 141–143
 portrayal in education, 110, 143
 youth advocacy, 144
Black American leaders. *See* Cooper, Anna Julia; Hamer, Fannie Lou; Proctor, Samuel DeWitt
Black feminism, 141, 145
"Black Girl Magic," 142
Black Lives Matter movement, 142
Blacks. *See* Black American
Blending of traditional and progressive approaches, 35, 37
Blount, J. M., 3, 124, 125, 126, 128
Blourock, B., 10
Blumentritt, F., 64
Boarding schools. *See* American Indian: Indian education
Boff, L., 41, 44
Bond, A., 57, 58
Book overview, 117–118
Boston University, 57

Bramlett-Solomon, S., 106
Brinkley, D., 88
Brooks, J. S., 65, 69, 70, 102
Brooks, M. P., 105, 106, 107, 108, 109, 110
Brown, E., 36
Brown, A. L., 143, 145
Brown, G., 137
Brown, K. D., 143, 145
Brown v. Board of Education of Topeka, 81
Brunner, C. C., 137
Bryant, D., 37
Buddhism, 23, 135–136
Buncombe, A., 82
Burdick, J., 68
Bureau of Indian Affairs, 72, 73, 74
Burma (Myanmar), 131–138
Burns, J. M., 134, 137
Butler, A. E., 116, 117, 118–119

Caley, D., 91, 93
California State University School of Social Work, 9
Calling, 99, 102
Calmness. *See* Quiet leadership
Camp David Accords, 81
Capacity building, 51–52
Capital (Marx), 42
Capitalism, 44, 45
Capital punishment, 82
Caraus, T., 131, 132, 134
Carcoss/Tagish First Nation, 90
Carter, James Earl. *See* Carter, Jimmy
Carter, Jimmy, 80–88
Carter Center, The, 80, 81–82
Center for Critical Studies in Education (Northeast Normal University, China), 39
Central Intelligence Agency (CIA), 133
Cesar, D., 15–16
Challenges. *See* Adversity
Challenging, 51
Challenging the system, 51, 91–92
Chapman University, 39
Chapters overview, 3–4
Chartist movement, 46
Chen, S. Y., 36
Chicago Public Schools, 124
Chicago Teachers Union, xi

Child labor law, 119
China, 32–37
Chua, C. S. K., 33
Church allies, 50, 51, 57, 58, 60–62, 108
Churchill, T. W., 126
Church leadership, 61
Civil arrest, 17, 23, 64, 108. *See also* House arrest
Civil rights, xii, 86, 104–105, 108, 109–110, 141, 145
Civil rights movement (U.S.), xii, 50, 58, 59, 106, 110–111, 112
Civil Service Commission, 119
Civil service exams, 119
Civil Service Reclassification, 119
Class-based disparities, 82
Class division, 42
Classless society, 47, 100
Classroom without walls, 24–25
Coalition building, 136–137
Coates, A., 66
Codes of ethics, 85
Cognition versus evaluation, 26–27
Collaboration, 9, 11, 101–102, 120, 129
Collective action, 46–47, 52
Collective responsibility, 129
College of Medicine for Chinese, 32
Colonialism, 14, 15, 64, 65–66, 67
Columbia University, 6, 9, 141
Comanche Nation, 72
Comanche Nation College, 77
Commitment, 36, 78, 98, 100–101, 116, 136
Communication competencies, 35, 36–37, 51, 97, 107, 108–109, 117, 126
Communist Manifesto (Marx), 44
Community, viii, 8–10, 9–10, 24–28, 29, 62–63, 127
Community activism
 civil rights, 112–113
 and conflict resolution, 90
 and education, xi–xii
 for social justice, 5, 6, 7, 49, 50, 53
 and sustainable development, 14, 15, 17–20
 women's rights, 118–119, 121
Community Studies as the Integrating Focus of Instruction (Makiguchi), 24

Compromise, 54, 103, 134
Confidence, ix, 20, 34
Confidence in people/humanity, 19–20
Conflict, 52, 54–55, 82
Conflict resolution, 90–91
Confrontational action, 49, 50, 52, 53, 59, 91, 92, 108
Confrontation avoidance, 120, 121, 122
Congress of Industrial Organizations (CIO), 50
Connor, L., 137
Consensus building, 102, 120, 121
Constantino, R., 64, 67
Constitutional constraints, 134, 137
Context for interpretations of the Gospel, 40–41
Control, 125–126
Conviction. *See* Commitment
Cooper, Anna Julia, 140–145
Cooper, George A. C., 141
Cooperative living, 25–26
Core values, 28, 29, 36
Cosmopolitanism, 32, 33
Counts, G. S., 65
Courage, 65, 91–92, 106, 109, 111, 133, 136–137
Crenshaw, Kimerlé, 141–142
Cries from the Corridor (McLaren), 39
Crime reduction, 90
Criminology study, 49
Critical consciousness, 43, 47
Critical education, 39–40
Critical reflection, 47
Criticism of leaders. *See* Public criticism of leaders
Critic of justice system, 92
Crow, G., 29
Crowson, R. L., 55
Crozer Theological Seminary, 57
Cullors, Patrisse, 142
Cultural immersion, 93–94
Cultural openness, 32–33, 36
Cultural suppression, 66
Cultural traditions, 11, 33, 35–37, 65, 66, 75, 90–94, 142

Dancy, T. E., 111
Danish Voluntary Fund for Developing Countries, 17

Data, 76
Dave, D., 120
Davidson, M., 97, 98, 99, 100–101
Day, C., 20, 36, 88
Deal making, 136, 137
Death penalty, 82
De Cure, G., 33–34, 35, 37
Dedication. *See* Commitment
Democracy, 25–26, 32, 82, 124, 131–138, 145
"Democracy in Education" (Dewey), 125
Democratic National Convention, 108–109
Democratic Party, xi, 75
Democratic principles, 144
Democratic processes, 52, 53, 55
Denunciation of money, 41–42
Desertification, 16
Despondency, 105
Determination. *See* Commitment
Dewey, John, 124–125
Dialogue, vii, ix, x, 10, 30, 93
Dilthey, W., 29
Diné College (Navajo Community College), 73
Diplomacy, 82, 97, 136
Directness, 99
Disabilities, 81
Discourse. *See* Dialogue
Discrimination. *See* Disabilities; Racial segregation; Racism; Sexism
Divisiveness, 105, 111
Donmoyer, R., 29
Douglass, F., 54
Douglass, Frederick, 54
Dry bones story, 61
Dreier, P., 109
Du Bois, W. E. B., 140, 143
Dunbar, P. L., 105

Eacott, S., 19
Eagley, A. H., 18
Eastman Kodak Company, 51
Economies, 34, 81, 82
Education
 advocacy, 82–83
 American Indian, 73–74, 75, 76, 78, 79, 93
 and communication, 121
 community role in, 24–26, 62–63
 and democracy, 25–26
 and empowerment, 18
 and happiness, 28
 as journey, vii–viii
 leadership, 19–20, 73
 public, 61, 81
 reform, 24, 54–55
 value/importance of, 17, 57, 72, 73, 106
Efficiency, viii
Ehrich, L. C., 53
Eilam, G., 18
Eisenhower, Dwight D., 59
Elders, The, 82
Elected official, 80, 81
Election observer, 80, 82
El Filibusterismo (Rizal), 64, 67, 69
El Solidaridad, 64
Employment, 17, 100, 106
Empowerment of informal leaders, 55
Energy crisis, 81
Engels, F., 44
Engels, Friedrich, 46, 47
English, F. W., 19, 29, 53
Envirocare Limited, 16
Environmental movement. *See* Green Belt Movement
Equality
 educational, 29, 81
 gender, 118, 119
 social, 34, 45, 60, 102, 112–113
 between teacher and administration, 27
 between teacher and student, vii
Equal Rights Amendment (ERA), 115, 118
ERA (Equal Rights Amendment). *See* Equal Rights Amendment (ERA)
Eschaton, 44
Ethics, 80, 83, 85, 88
Ethics in Government Act, 85
Evaluation versus cognition, 26–27
Execution, 64
Exile, 35
Expectations for a leader, xi, 134, 137
Exploitation of labor, 44

Facten sammler (fact gatherers), 26
Fact gatherers *(facten sammler)*, 26
Failure, 35, 36, 98

Faith, 9, 36, 53, 76–77
Family, 27–28, 61, 63, 77, 106
"Federal Amendment", 118
Federal Employee, The, 118
Federal employment, 119–120
Federal Social Security Board, 119
Feminism, 115
Ferguson, K. E., 115
Feuerbach, Ludwig, 46
First Nations. *See* American Indian
Fitzpatrick, J. P., 7
Fixico, D. L., 73, 75
Foreign affairs (Israeli), 96
Foreign influence, 33. *See also* Western influence
Foster, M., 142
Foster, W., 29, 83
"Found order," 28
Fraser, N., 115
Freedom Farm, 109
Freire, Paulo, 40, 41, 43
Fullan, M., 19, 36
Furman, G., 20

Gangs, 9–10, 49
Gardner, W. L., 18
Garrison, J. W., 26
Garza, Alicia, 142
Gatensby, Harold, 90–94
Gatensby, Phil, 91, 93
Gebert, A., 23, 24, 25
Gender, x, 82, 125–127, 128, 135, 137, 141
Geographic mobility, 33
Geography of Human Life, A (Makiguchi), 24, 26
George, B., 18
Georgia, 80–84, 86
German communism, 47
Gerstl-Pepin, C., 120
Getting out of the way, 27
Giladi, D., 97, 98, 100, 101–102
Gilboa, M., 97, 98, 100, 101–102
Giles, M. S., 140n1
Giroux, H. A., 68
Global conflict, 81, 82
Global perspective, 26, 30, 34, 46, 86, 91
Global reach, 91, 93, 97
Globerson, A., 97, 98, 100, 101–102

Goldstein, Y., 98, 101, 102, 103
Goodlad, J., 83
Gorsevski, E. W., 17
Gospel, 40–41, 46
Gospel of a Poor Sinner (Miranda), 47
Goulah, J., 23, 24, 25, 26
Graduation School for Community Development, 9
Grant, C. A., 143, 145
Grassroots activism. *See* Community activism
Green, Z., 135, 138
Green Belt Movement, 14, 15, 16, 17–18
Greenber, Y., 97, 98, 100, 101–102
Greenleaf, R. K., 85–86
Greensboro sit-ins, 59
Grogan, M., 29, 136, 137
Gu, Q., 36
Gutierrez, G., 43

Habitat for Humanity, 86
Halberstam, J., xi
Hamer, Fannie Lou
 background, 106–110
 lessons, 110–113
 as source of inspiration for author, 104, 105–106
Hamer, Perry (Pap), 107
Hamlet, J. D., 106, 107, 108, 109
Hansot, E., 125
Happiness goal of education, 28
Harassment, 35, 132
Hardison, Grace, 142
Hard revolutions and soft revolutions, 69
Hardworking, 116
Harney, Julian, 46
Harris, A., 36
Harvard University, 140, 143
Hau, C. S., 67
Hayanga, A., 17, 18
Haywood, Anna Julia. *See* Cooper, Anna Julia
Health promotion, 80, 81, 86
Hegel, Georg Wilhelm Friedrich, 46
Heifetz, R., 134
Heng, T. S. S., 34
Heroic leadership and gender, 135, 137
Herz-Lazarowitz, R., 99

Hickman, L. A., 26
Hierarchy notion, vii
Hill-Collins, P. H., 115
Hispanic Young Adult Association (HYAA), 7
Histadrut, 97
Historically Black colleges and universities (HBCU), 58, 59
Hodgins, D., 69
Honesty, 17, 91, 100, 143
Hong Kong, 33
Honolulu, 32, 33
Hope, 44, 66, 76
Hopkins, D., 36
Horton, M., 53
Horwitt, S. D., 49, 50, 51, 54
Houck, D. W., 106, 107, 108
House, R. J., 36
House arrest, 131, 132
Howland's Possible Successor, 125, 126
Hoyt, E. P., 23
Htin Kyaw, 133
Hughes, Velma, 57
Hughes, Zecharia, 57
Human complexity, xi
Human connection, 91
Humanitarian work, 86
Human rights, 80, 82, 86, 107
Human spirit, 43
Humility, 77
Hunter College, 6
Hurwitz, E., Jr., 55
Hyslop, P., 91
Hysterectomy, 108

Ibarra, Crisostomo, 65, 67
Iconic leaders, 1
Idea for the book, 1–2
Identity, x, 6, 9–10, 133, 136–137
Idolotry of money, 41–42
Ikeda, D., 25, 26
Imber, M., 29
Immigrants, 6–7, 45
Immigration policy, 97, 100
Improvisation, 55
Incremental progress, 119, 120
Indebtedness to elders, 78
Indian Resilience and Rebuilding (Fixico), 75

Indians (American). *See* American Indian
Indigenous peoples (American). *See* American Indian
Individual agency, xii
Individual involvement, 61
Individuality, 125, 127, 128–129
Individual wisdom, xii
Industrial Areas Foundation, 50
Inequality, 66, 69
Infant rights, 145
Informal leaders, 55
Inherited benefits and deficits, 63
Injustice, 45
Inner peace, 135–136
Inspiration, 1, 6, 7–8, 36, 65, 105, 111, 136
Institute of National Insurance, 97
Institutional violence, 66
Institution building, 6–7
Intellectual stimulation, 129
Intergroup animosity, 49
International conflict. *See* Global conflict
International diplomacy, 82, 97
International perspective. *See* Global perspective
International reach. *See* Global reach
International recognition, 39–40
International Slavery Museum, 110
International support, 17
Interpretation, 40–41
Intersectionality, 143–144
Irby, B., 137
Isolation, 128
Isolation in School (Young), 125
Israel, 96–102
Israel Labor Movement, 96

Jackson, Mike, 90–91
Jandrić, P., 48
Japan, 23–30, 35
Jarrett, B., 91
Javidan, M., 36
Jean-Marie, G., 69, 102, 111
Jensen, B., 37
Jesus Christ, 40–43, 45, 46, 87
Jewish National Fund, 97
Jewish State. *See* Israel; Zionism

Jim Crow laws, 106
Jimenez, Lillian, 10, 11
Jobs, 100, 106
Joffee, M., 24
Johansson, O., 20
Johnson, Lyndon, xii, 109
Joseph P. Kennedy Jr. Foundation, 15
Judicial reform, 91–92
Justice, passion for, 11, 60

Kaester, R., 120
Kake, Alaska, 90–91
Kaufman, I., 97, 98, 100, 101–102
Kawagley, A. O., 94
Keane, F., 131, 132
Keating-Trammell Act, 117
Kennedy, John F., Jr., 15, 59
Kenya, 14–15
Kiev, Ukraine, 96
King, Martin Luther, Jr., 59, 112
Kingdom of God, 45
Kirkscey, R., 17
Klopp, J. M., 17
Knowledge, 29–30
Kobayashi, V. N., 23
Kramer, P. A., 65
Ku Klux Klan, 59
Kumar, R., 36–37
Kuomintang (KMT), 32
Kurland, H., 99

Labor Party, 96
Labor Party Central Committee, 98
Labor rights, 50, 96, 97, 107, 115, 116–117
Language aptitude, 33, 34, 35, 39
Language of science versus language of theology, 40
Lee, C. K., 106
Leithwood, K., 36
Lèse-majesté, 23
Lewis, John L., 50
Lewis, Karen, xi
Liberation theology, 40
Life and Labor Bulletin, 118
Life in Schools (McLaren), 39
Limitations of office, 134, 137
Lingard, B., 37
Listening, x, 9, 51, 92

Littrell, J., 29
Livelihood *(minsheng zhuyi)*, 32, 34
Living conditions, 107, 109
Lloyd, C. A., 36
Local alliances, 53
Local context, importance of, 37
Logic, 121, 122
Love, 100, 102
Lussier, R. N., 36

Maathai, Wangari, 14–20
Macfarlane, Helen, 45–46
Mackey, H. J., 78
MacKinnon, C. A., 115
Makiguchi, Tsunesaburo, 23–30
Marable, M., 111–112
Marshall, C., 115, 116, 120, 122
Martin-Felton, Z., 140n1
Martyrdom, 67
Marx, Karl, 40, 41–47
Mau Mau Uprising, 15
May, V. M., 144
McClellan, P. A., 105, 106, 109, 112
McIntyre Miller, W., 135, 138
McLaren, Peter, 39–48
McManis, J., 124, 129
Medium of communication, 68
Meir, Golda, 96–102
Mentoring, 10, 62, 75, 77, 92–93
Merchant, B. M., 69
Meyerson, Morris, 96
Miami University of Ohio, 39
Militarized society, 23
Miller, M., 49, 50, 51–52, 53, 54
Mills, K., 106, 107–108
Milwaukee, Wisconsin, 96
"Mind and body unity," 28
Minsheng zhuyi (livelihood), 32
Minzhu zhuyi (nationalism), 32
Miranda, J. P., 41, 42, 46, 47
Mississippi, 106–107
"Mississippi appendectomy," 108
Mississippi Freedom Democratic Party, 108
Mistrust in leadership, 88
Misuse of power, 86–87
Mobil Oil, 17
Modern values, 33, 34, 35
Mohamed, A., 18

Moi, Daniel arap, 17
Money as god, 42
Montgomery Bus Boycott, 58
Moos, L., 20
Moral grounding
  Carter as exemplar, 80, 82–83, 85–86
  Maathai as exemplar, 20
  Proctor as exemplar, 60, 61, 62
  Suu Kyi as exemplar, 133, 134, 136, 137
Morris, V. C., 55
Moral authority, 66, 86–87
Munzer, Thomas, 47
Mutual interdependence, 27, 30, 34
Myanmar (Burma), 131–138

Nair, S., 135
Nares Mountain Wilderness Camp, 93–94
National American Women Suffrage Association (NAWSA), 116, 117–118
National Council of Women in Kenya, 15
National Educational Leadership Preparation standards, 83, 85
National Education Association (NEA), 124
National Federation of Federal Employees (NFFE), 117, 118
Nationalism, 23, 27, 32
National League for Democracy (NLD; Burma), 131
National Policy Board for Education Administration, 85
National Women's Party, 118
National Youth Academy, 61–62
Native American. *See* American Indian
Navajo Community College (Diné College), 73
Navajo Reservation, 73
Negotiation, 77, 80, 82, 98, 134, 137
New Baptist Covenant, 82
Newborn teaching, ix
New York City, 6–8
Nichiren, 23
Nieto, S., 7
Nobel Committee, 14–15
Nobel Media, 131
Nobel Peace Prize, 14, 80, 82, 135

Noli Me Tangere (Rizal), 64, 65–66, 69
Nonviolence tradition, 136
Non-voting, 112
Norfolk Navy Yard, 57
Normore, A. H., 69, 70, 102
North Carolina A&T University, 57, 59
Nuclear arms reduction, 81, 82

Obama, Barack, 112
Oberlin College, 141
Ochs, K., 37
Ofcansky, T. P., 14
Office of Economic Opportunity, 60
Office of Indian Education, 73
Oklahoma, 77
Oklahoma State University, 72
O'Malley, M. P., 68
Openness, 33
Oplatka, I., 101
Oppression, 65–66, 67, 69
Opthalmology, 64
Optimism, 76
Origins of Peacemaking Circles, The, 94
Otieno, A. O., 16
Outsider-within, 121

Pace, E., 59, 60
Pace of democratization, 132–133
Palestine, 96, 97, 98
Palma, R., 64
Pantoja, Antonia, 5–12
Parent responsibility, 27–28
Participatory democracy, 17–18
Partnership. *See* Collaboration
Pascall, G., 85
Passion, 9, 18–19, 34, 36, 133
Patrikeeff, F., 33–34, 35, 37
Paul, Alice, 118
Paulo Freire Democratic Project, 39
Pay for women, 117–118
Peace Corps in Africa, 59–60
Peace goal, 27, 30, 80, 135–136, 138
Peacemaking Circles, 90–94
Pedagogy of Insurrection (McLaren), 40
Pederson, R., 131, 132
Pennsylvania State University, 72, 73, 75
Perazzo, J., 50, 51
Peretz, H., 99

Perry, W., 5, 11
Perry, W. (Mina), 10–11
Perseverance, xi, 12, 91–92, 106, 108, 136
Persistence. *See* Perseverance
Personal character, 28
Personal fulfillment, 28
Personality integration, 25
Philippines, 64–68
Phillips, D., 37
Philosophical stance, 120
Place-based education, 93–94
Pogroms, 96, 98
Political alliances, 136
Political context, 41
Pond Street Baptist Church, 57
Popham, P., 131, 132, 133, 135
Porter-Gehrie, C., 55
Positional authority, 86–87
Positive outlook, 19–20
Postman, N., 69
Poverty
  among American Indians, 74
  among Black Americans, 61, 101, 106–107, 113, 142
  in Israel, 80, 83, 97, 99, 101
  in Kenya, 14, 15, 18.19
  perspectives of Jesus and Marx, 40, 42–43, 45
  and Puerto Ricans, 6, 7
  in rural Georgia, 80, 83
Power, vii–viii, 53–54, 66, 68, 86–87, 122, 128, 129
Practice and theory, 127–128
Pragmatism, 55, 99, 100
Presbey, G. M., 18
Presidential Medal of Freedom, 6
Pride, 6, 9, 65, 68, 74
Private consulting, 73
Proctor, Herbert, 57
Proctor, Samuel DeWitt, 57–63
Proctor, S. D., 57, 58, 59, 60, 61, 63
PRODUCIR, 9
Professional ethics, 84–85
Professional growth, 128
Professionalization of school leaders, 27
Professional Standards for Educational Leaders, 85
Pronouns, x
Property ownership, 115

Prophetic perspective, 41
Protagonistic agency, 47
Protasio Rizal Mercado y Alonso Realonda, José. *See* Rizal, José
Psychological consistence, 28, 29
Public criticism of leaders, 121, 134
Public identity, 136–137
Public intellectualism, 68, 69–70
Public office, 81, 96
Public policy, 81
Public recognition, 106
Puerto Rican Association for Community Affairs (PRACA), 7
Puerto Rican Development Project, 8
Puerto Rican Forum, 7–8
Puerto Rican–Hispanic Leadership Forum, 7–8
Puerto Rican immigration to United States, 6–7
Puerto Rican Institute for Political Participation (PRIPP), 8
Puerto Rican Research and Resources Center, 9
Puerto Rico, 5–12
Purpose, 28, 29, 36, 133–134
Puyi, 34

Qian, H. Y., 36, 37
Qing Dynasty, 32, 33, 34
Queer Art of Failure, The (Halberstam), xi
Questioning injustice, xi, 52
Quiet leadership, 59, 76, 120, 122

Race, 54, 58, 81, 82, 93, 112, 113, 143
Racial segregation, 59, 83–84, 86, 106–107, 108–109, 112
Racism, 69, 82, 83–84, 93, 104, 107, 108–109, 141–142
Rafto Prize, 133
Raleigh, North Carolina, 141
Readiness to act, 68, 70
Reason, 121, 122
Recidivism reduction, 90, 92
Reforestation. *See* Green Belt Movement
Relationships, 9, 18–20, 26, 51, 77, 136
Religiosity, 57, 58, 60–62, 80, 82, 84, 106, 107, 108

Religious philosophy, 40–47. *See also* Buddhism
Republican Party, xi, 75
Republic of China (ROC), 32–37
Research, 7–8, 29–30, 60, 76, 116, 129
Research into Methods and Content of Geography Instruction (Makiguchi), 24
Residential schools. *See* Education: American Indian
Resiliency, 35, 36, 76
Resistance, xi, 67, 112–113, 132
Respect, x, 9–11, 21, 29, 49, 51, 75, 125, 128–129
Responsibility, 78, 87, 98, 100
Restore China Society (Xingshong hui), 35
Reveille for Radicals (Alinsky), 52
Revolution, 67, 69
Ridicule, 53–54
Rights for persons with disabilities, 81
Rizal, José, 64–68
Rizvi, F., 37
Robinson, M. J., 36
Rochester campaign, 51, 54
Rogers, E., 105, 106
Rohingya, 133, 134
Role models, 6
Role of language and culture in education, 73
Roosevelt, Franklin, xii
Rowe, K. J., 36
Rubel, D., 106
Rules for Radicals (Alinsky), 51, 52
Rutgers University, 58, 60

SALT II, 81
Sammons, P., 36
Sandlin, J. A., 68
Sanmin zhuyi, 32
Santamaría, A. P., 110
Santamaría, L. J., 110
Santo Tomas University, 64
Sapporo Normal School, 24
Save the Land Harambee. *See* Green Belt Movement
Scharmer, C.O., 134
Scheurich, J. J., 29, 69

Scholarship, 10, 39–40, 76, 77, 140–141
School leaders, viii–ix, 126
Schutz, A., 49, 51
Science-based practice, 70
Scientific understanding, 41
"Scratch line," 63
Seal, M., 52
Secretary Legislative Department, 119
Segregation. *See* Racial segregation
Self-awareness, 83, 91
Self-determination, 74, 144
Self-efficacy, 16, 52
Self-empowerment, 52
Self-honesty, 91
Selflessness, 70
Self-reflection, 25, 84, 88, 91, 92
Self-respect, 33, 52
Self-sacrifice, 78
Self-worth, 77
Sellar, S., 37
Sensitivity, 36
Sentencing practices, 90, 91–92
Sergiovanni, T., 80, 86
Servant as Leader, The (Greenleaf), 85–86
Servant leadership, 85–86
Service, 11, 58, 60, 85–86
Sexism, 104, 105, 141–142
Shakeshaft, C., 136, 137
Shamir, B., 18
Shapiro, J. P., 20, 85
Sharecroppers, 106–107
Shared leadership, 10
Shaw, R., 115
Shields, C., 137
Shoho, A. R., 69
Shriver, Sargent, 59–60
Sinha, A., 36–37
Sitkoff, H., 111–112
Skrla, L., 69
Slavery, 140–141, 145
Smith, E. M., 116, 117, 118, 119, 120
Smith, Ethel M., 116–122
Smith, J. K., 124, 126
Sobrino, J., 44, 45, 46
Social and economic problems, 14
Social commentary, 65–66
Social context, 41

Social development, 82
Socialism, 45, 46, 97
Social Security Act, 119
Social welfare reform, 49–50
Sodor, R., 83
Soft revolutions and hard revolutions, 69
Soka, 23
Soka education, 24–25
Solace, 105
Song, 107
Sorotnik, K., 83
Souls of Black Folk, The (Du Bois), 140
Southern Baptist church, 80, 82
Southern Baptist Convention, 81, 87
Spain, 64, 65
Spirit-based leadership, 92
Spirituality, 93, 135–136. *See also* Religiosity
Standards of conduct, 27
Starratt, R. J., 19, 36
St. Augustine Normal School and Collegiate Institute, 141
St. Cecilia Intermediate Primary, 15
Steadiness, 120
Stefkovich, J. A., 20, 85
Steinberg, B. S., 98, 99, 101, 102
Stewardship of cultural knowledge, 91–92
Storytelling, 60, 66–67, 76, 91, 94
Strauss, David, 46
Structure of the book, 2
Stuart, Barry, 91, 92
Stubbornness, 101
Student Nonviolent Coordinating Committee, 108
Student/school control mechanisms, 125–126
Suffrage. *See* Voting rights
Sumter County School Board, 81
Sun Mei, 32
Sun Yat-sen, 32–37
Surgis, S., 104
Suspicion of foreign influence, 33
Sustainable development, 16
Sutherland, I. E., 65
Suu Kyi, Aung San, 131–138
Sympathetic interaction, 25–26, 29

System of Value-Creating Pedagogy (Makiguchi), 24

Taiwan (Republic of China), 32
Takeuchi, Y., 24
Tallerico, M., 128
Tan, C., 33
Tate, Bessie, 57
Teacher, vii–viii, ix, 126, 128
Teaching profession, 61, 72–73, 96, 124, 125–126
Temporary Woodlawn Organization (TWO), 51
Terrill, M., 72
"The Intellectual Progress of the Colored Women of the United States Since the Emancipation Proclamation" (Cooper), 141
"The Negro Problem in America" (Cooper), 141
Thinking through, 51
Thought and action, 129–130
Three Principles of the People, 32
Tillman, L., 111
Ting-Toomey, S., 36–37
Tippeconnic III, John W., 72–79
Toda, Josei, 23
Tolerance, 36
Tometi, Opal, 142
Toronto, 39
Townsend, Fannie Lou. *See* Hamer, Fannie Lou
Trade-offs. *See* Deal making
Training, 51–52
Transitions from informal to formal leadership roles, 134
Tree-planting campaign. *See* Green Belt Movement
Trump, Donald, xi, 104, 111, 113
Trust, 128
Truth, 26, 46
Truth–value distinction, 26
Tyack, D., 125

Uncertainty, 55
Uncle Tom's Cabin (Stowe), 100
Understanding of the issues, 53
Unemployment Census, 119
Unexamined values, x–xi

Uniqueness of each situation, 52
United Nations Conference on Desertification, 16
United Nations Conference on Human Settlements, 16
United Nations Environment Program, 16
United Nations Fund for Women, 17
Unity (community), 49
Unity (psychological), 28, 29, 30
Universalism, 35
Universal tropes, x–xi
University College of Nairobi, 15
University Council for Educational Administration, 83, 85
University of California, Los Angeles, 39
University of California, San Marcos, 73
University of Chicago, 49, 124
University of Paris–Sorbonne, 141
U.S. Department of Education, 74, 75
U.S. foreign policy, 87, 88
U.S. Naval Academy, 80
U.S. Supreme Court, 8

Value-creating education, 26
Value creation, 23, 26, 30
Value production, 44
Value–truth distinction, 26
Vietnam War draft evaders, 81
Violence, 67, 82, 108
Virginia State University, 57
Virginia Union University, 57
Visible critique, 68
Vision, 35, 36, 99, 112, 120
Voice from the South, A (Cooper), 141, 145
Voice of Freedom (Weatherford), 106
Von Hoffman, N., 50, 51, 52, 53
Voting rights, 106, 107, 108, 109, 112, 113, 115, 117–118, 133

Wages for women, 117–118
Walker, A., 36, 37
Wang, G. W., 32, 34, 35, 36
"Wangari Maathai – Nobel Lecture", 17
Ward, M., 116
Warner, L. S., 78
Washington, DC, 9

Wead, D., 84, 88
Weatherford, C. B., 106, 107, 108
Wehby, G., 120
Weingartner, C., 69
Weitling, Wilhelm, 47
Wells, Ida B., 141–142
Western influence, 33, 35, 75
Western values, 135
White House Conference on Hunger, 109
White Supremacy, 104, 111
Who's Who—National League Officers, 116
Why Not the Best? (Carter), 86
Wisdom, vii, viii, ix, x, 78
Women, Infants, and Children (WIC) nutrition program, 81
Women's Bureau, 119
Women's Joint Congressional Committee (WJCC), 118–119
Women-specific legislation versus sex-neutral policy, 118
Women's rights, 15, 17, 87, 105, 115–122, 141, 145
Women's roles, 115
Women's studies, 110
Women's suffrage, 105, 115, 117–118
Women's Trade Union League (WTUL), 116, 119
Work conditions, 107
Work ethic, 101
Working-class background, 116
Working-class rights, 46
Working with the system versus rejection of system, 69
World's Congress of Representative Women, 141

Xenophobia, 104

Yom Kippur War, 96, 98
Young, Ella Flagg, 124–129
Youth, 8, 9–10, 61, 73–74, 77, 92–93, 144
Yuan Shikai, 34
Yukon Territory, Canada, 90

Zionism, 97, 98, 100, 102